I0445933

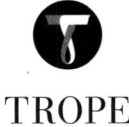

TROPE

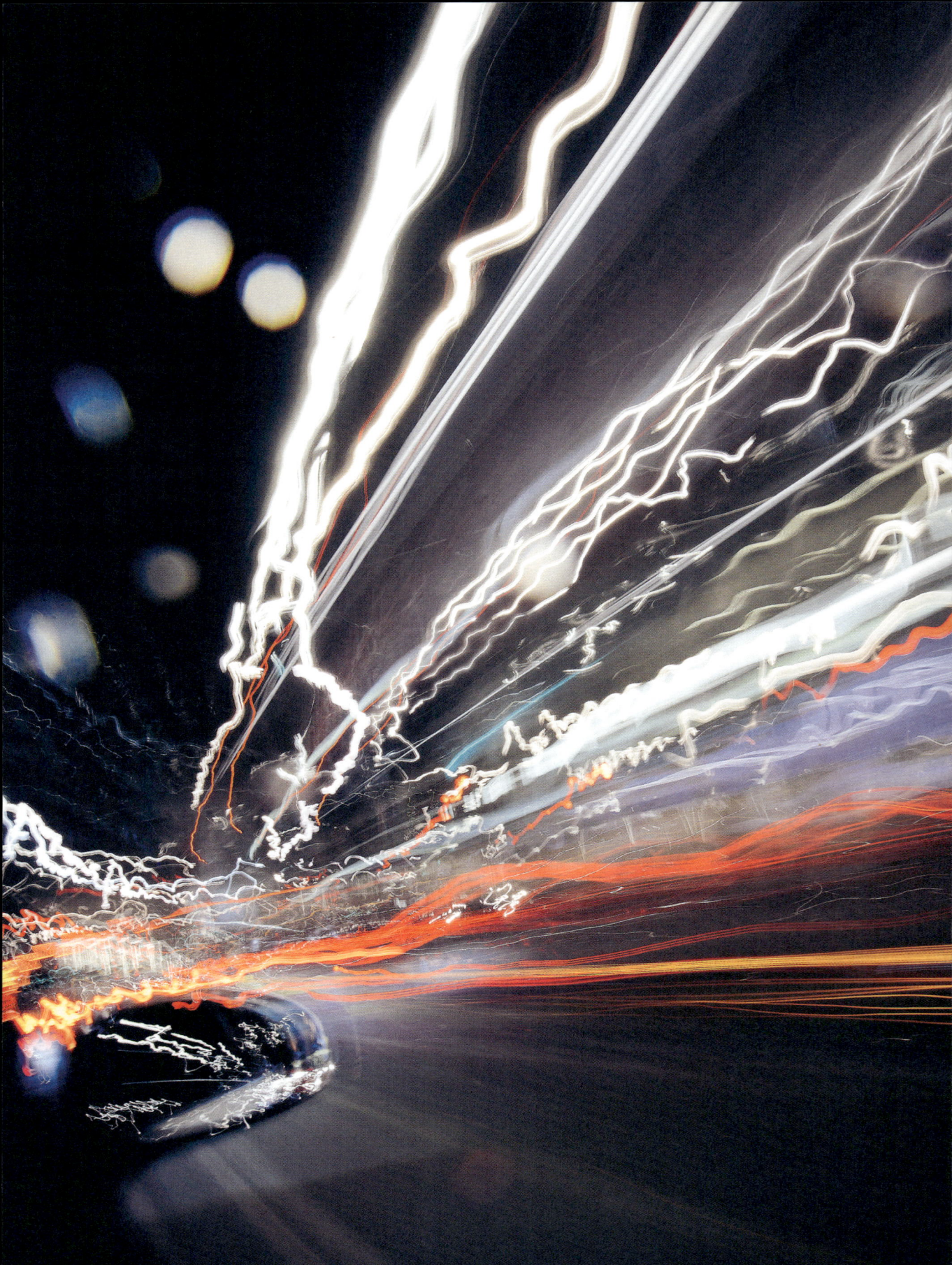

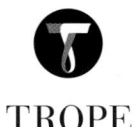

TROPE

OPE ODUEYUNGBO
Parallel Lines

TROPE EDITION

VOLUME II

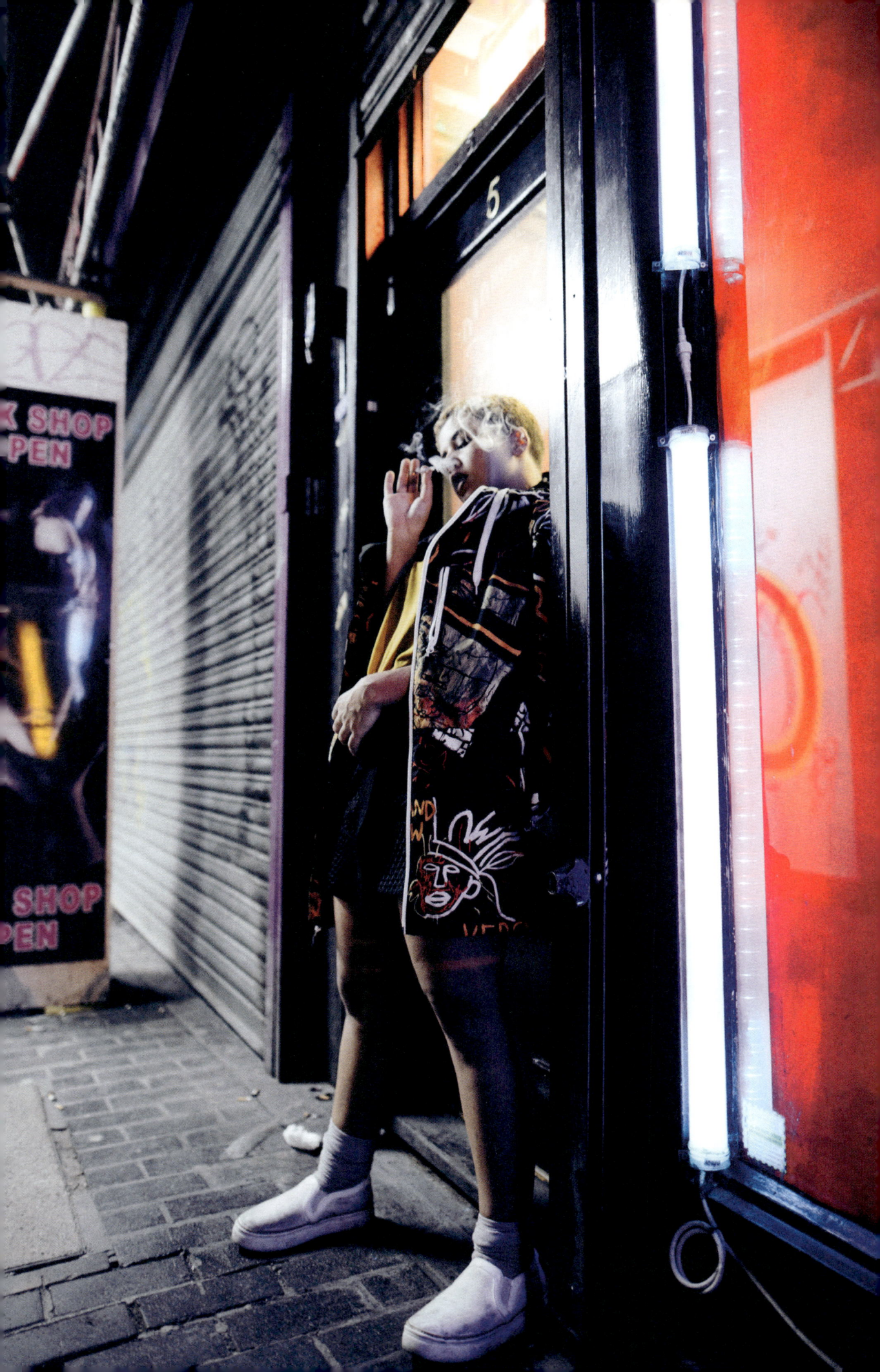

INTRODUCTION

Welcome to *Parallel Lines*, the second volume of the Trope Editions Emerging Photographers Series, featuring the work of photographer and social influencer Ope Odueyungbo, a Londoner from New Cross.

When you meet Ope for the first time, you may notice that he is a man of few words. What you may not see right away, however, are the extroverted and introverted sides to his commercial and personal work — a study in contrast. His images are striking in their precision, light and perspective, with the grit and edge of a South Londoner. The models he photographs have a very similar vibe: urban and very architectural. In fact, his work is strongly influenced by his early graphic design studies.

In sharp contrast to his commercial work, his personal images have a reportage sensibility and honesty, capturing the warmth of his subjects and surroundings. His personal photographic journey has taken him around the world, including to Nigeria, where his parents are from and still home to his grandmother and extended family. It is this juxtaposition in Ope's body of work that really caught our attention.

For many professional photographers in today's image-conscious social media world, we rarely see an artist move between their commercial and personal worlds with such ease and fluidity. Perhaps surprising for someone as reserved and quiet as Ope, he connects with his subjects in a way that seems to bring out their best.

Ope's mindfulness and awareness are not only reflected in his images, but in his words. His thoughtful captions and outlook on life are evidenced throughout his social media postings. To quote Ope in his own words, '*The path of life is never without trials and tribulations. Through this comes the openness to receive greatness.*'

We created this new contemporary book series to introduce young and emerging artists from around the world to a wider audience. Enjoy seeing the world through Ope's eyes and feel the 'good vibes' flowing through his work.

Sam Landers
Editor

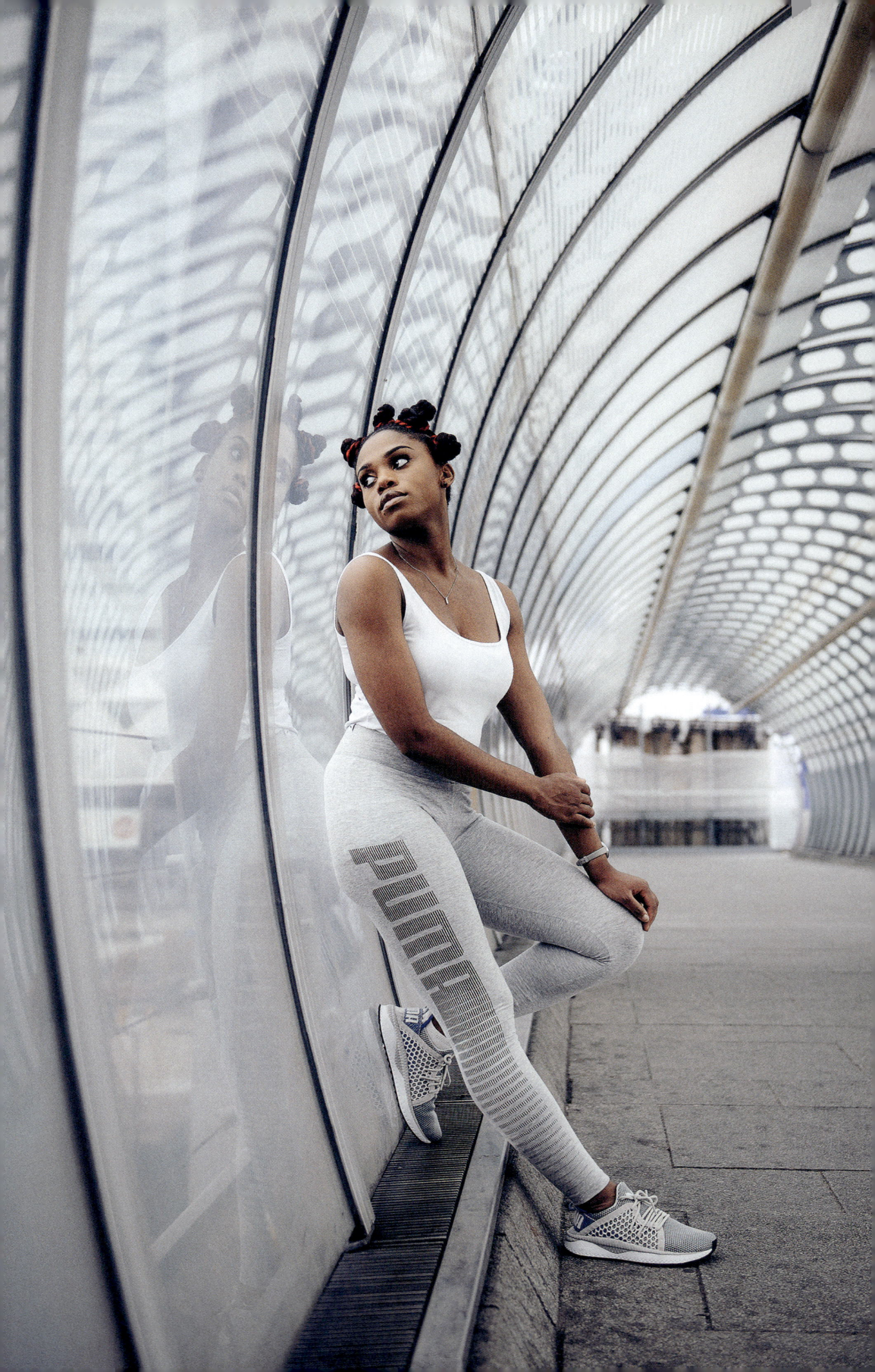

GOOD VIBES ONLY

Photography is documenting life as it happens, it's capturing the decisive, unexpected and unique. I'll forever be in awe of street photography's spontaneity in particular, as it was the style I was introduced to at the beginning of my photography journey. The work of Henri Cartier-Bresson was a massive inspiration for me early on – I was drawn to his way of 'capturing the decisive moment'. I don't think there's ever gonna be anybody as good as he was.

Parallel Lines is sorted into my professional and my personal work. With both, my goal is for viewers to see as extraordinary, even something seemingly ordinary. Setting an image's mood and tone, whatever I do in post-processing, it's all geared toward appreciation for my surroundings and elevation of the everyday. To capture the moment, but in an unexpected way.

No matter what I'm shooting, I spend a lot of time thinking about composition: lines, angles, light, perspective. To produce a good image, these elements – and more – have to work well together. When I get them right, my images can stand out from the rest.

I always look for a way to incorporate lines and have them lead to either the subject or background. Depending on the shot I'm going for, I want the viewer to be drawn in by those lines, to get a sense of depth. Repeated patterns, grids, geometric shapes always catch my eye; I may explore those on their own, or use them to anchor my shots. Of course my angles have to be on point too; different angles give my images a whole new dimension. Experimenting with distances and vantages can create big impact, as well as help my image be interpreted in a better way. Reversing the foreground and background brings the 'ordinary' unexpectedly into focus.

I like to play with light and shadow. Light sets the overall tone, mood and atmosphere. If light is too harsh it may not be good for the subject, so I always take the time of day into consideration before heading out to shoot. Complementing the subject takes precedence.

As all my elements come together, I always ask myself, 'Is this shot worth me pushing the shutter?' We live in a digital age, but I still tend to treat my DSLR like a film camera; I'm mindful about each and every shot I take. I don't like to take any images that I feel won't be good enough.

I try to capture visually appealing images that bring a good vibe to the viewer, or at least an interest in knowing or seeing more. I'm always looking to show positivity. I'm not always successful in achieving this – you can't please everyone – but at the end of the day if I have a good feeling about what I'm shooting, that's what matters, right?

My commercial work gives me a great sense of achievement. I'm not just shooting for myself; I'm shooting for an entire brand or company. There's so much riding on what I produce. It also gives me great joy knowing that brands like Adidas, Puma, Huawei and BMW specifically wanted my style of work.

I do a ton of planning for my brand work. I have to look at their target audience, what they're trying to say. I stay true to my own style, it's just a different mindset, more a process in thinking through the subject, the angles, the mood, the lighting.

My personal work, on the other hand, is a free-for-all. I thrive on travelling the world and connecting with people, and this work is just mine – 100% what I want to shoot. I explore farther, I take more risks, just to see if something works. I can be more instinctual. I'm only pleasing myself, after all.

Total honesty with my subjects is important to me, though, and I think the connections I make come through in the pictures. Even with my street photography, I always let my subjects know why I'm taking photographs, what they're for. I have to come correct and be very mindful in order for them to be comfortable with me; I don't ever want to be invasive.

I find a smile goes a long way. Even when there's a language barrier, I can use it to communicate how much I love what I do. I tend to show the images to subjects after; when I'm totally transparent with them, they can see my passion for my work and share it with me, even if just for a few moments.

The photograph in this book that means the most to me is one of my personal shots, the image of my grandmother. My parents were born in Nigeria, but this was my first trip there, my very first time meeting her in person. There was a bit of culture shock – there are so many things I take for granted living in London, like reliable electricity. Her life isn't glamorous, it isn't easy, but she's happy, and it was amazing to capture her in her home, in her element. I have so much respect for her and the way she is so content with what she has. It was a powerful and humbling experience, and I think the emotion of that moment really comes through.

It's so important to never lose passion to continue doing what you love, even when things aren't so positive. Consistency really is the key. I've found the more you do something, the better you'll get, people will eventually see your desire, and everything else will follow.

Ope Odueyungbo

PARALLEL LINES

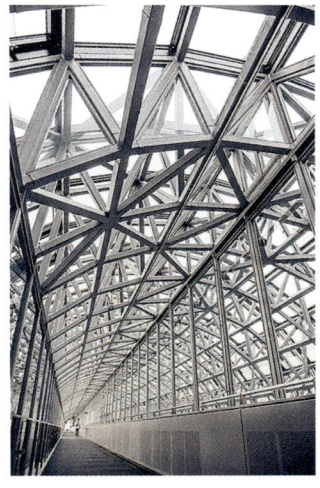
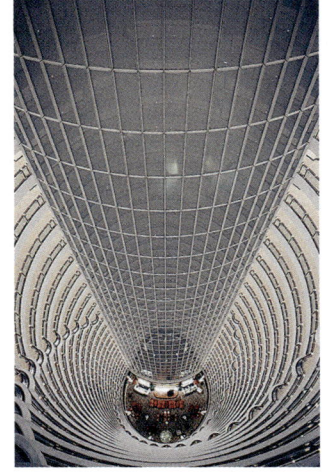
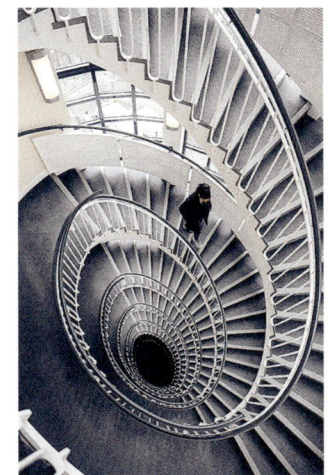
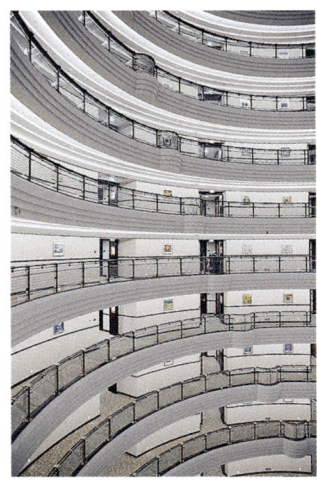
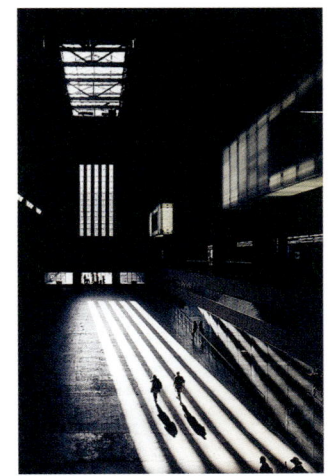

**ALL
ABOUT THE
LINES**

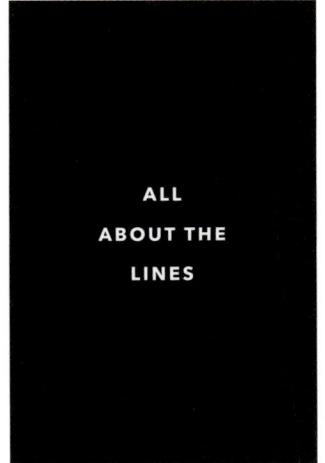
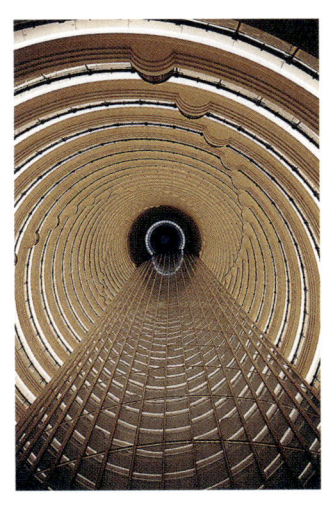
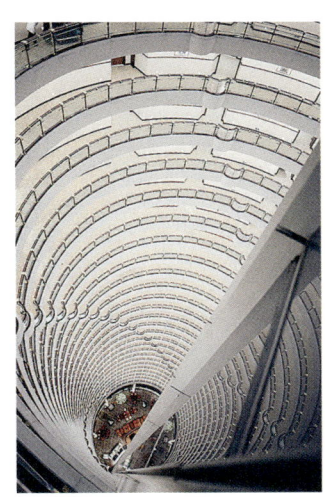
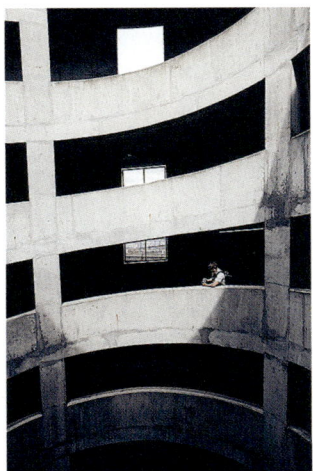

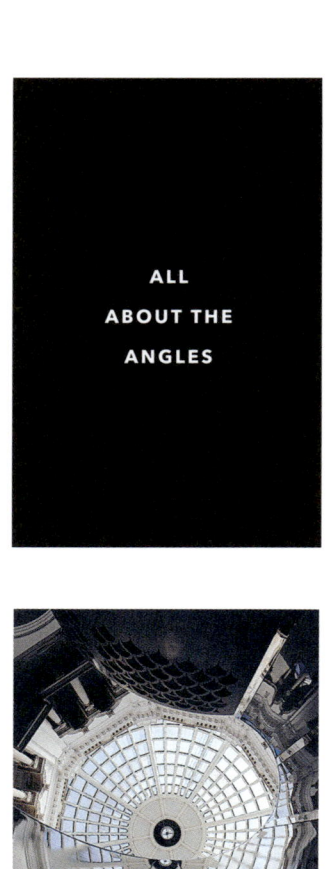

**ALL
ABOUT THE
ANGLES**

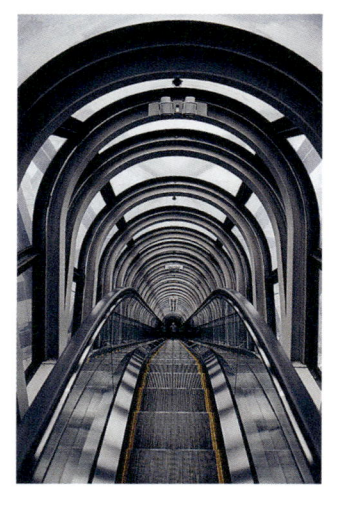

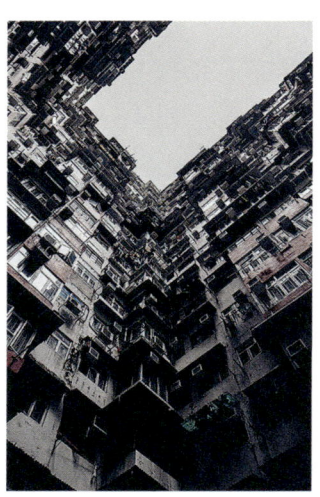

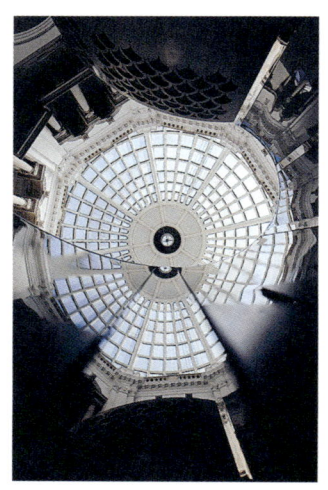

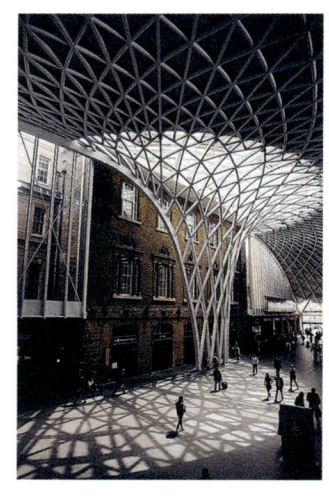

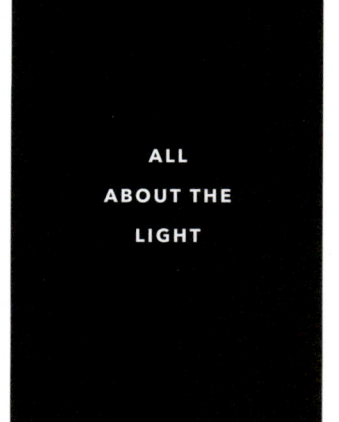

**ALL
ABOUT THE
LIGHT**

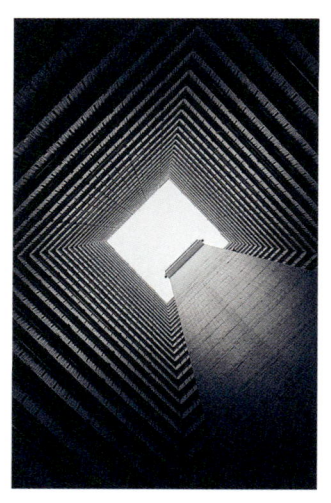

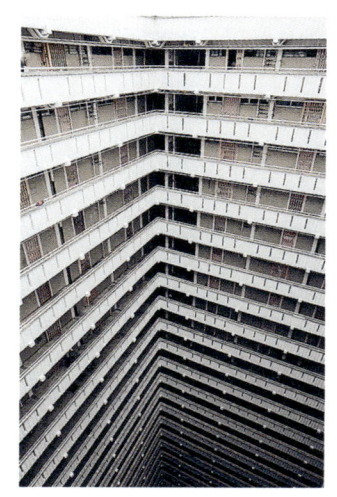

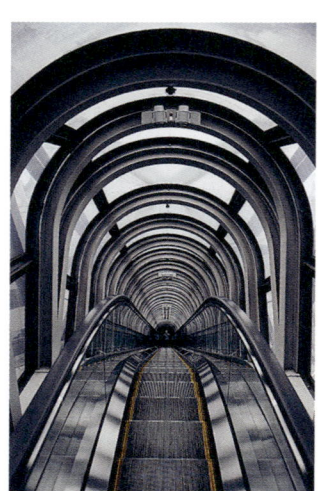

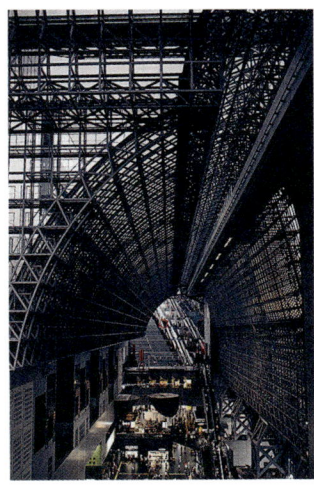
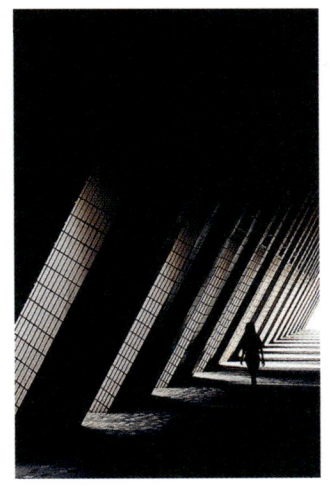
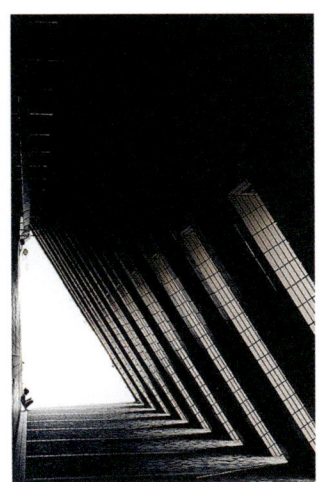
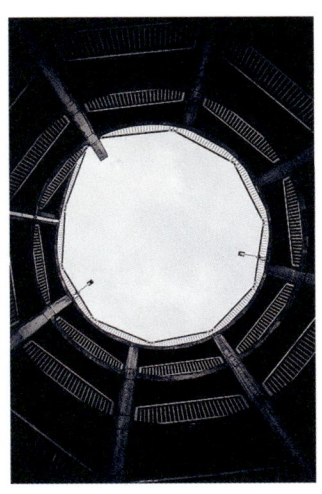
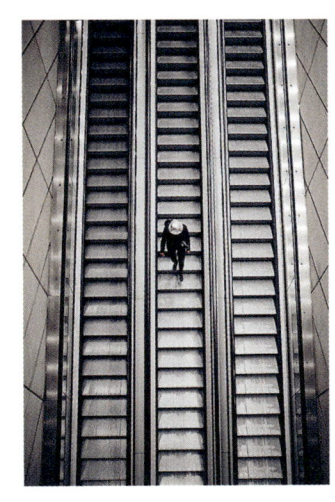
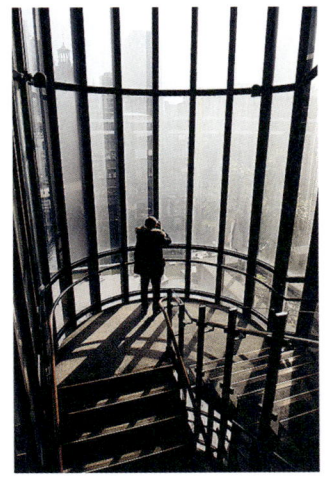
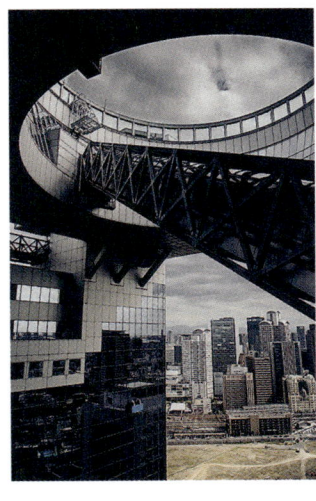
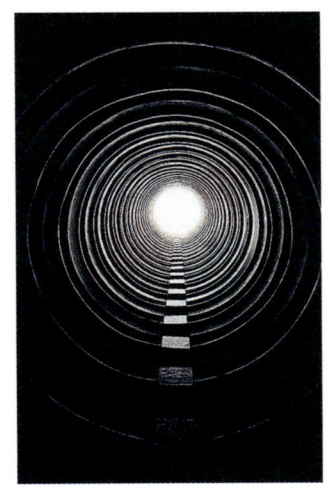
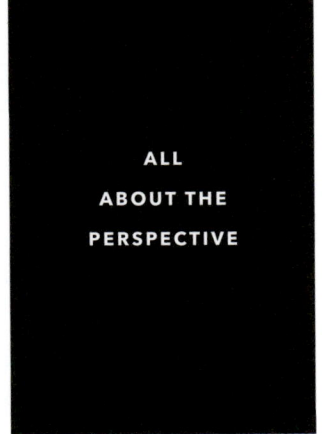

**ALL
ABOUT THE
PERSPECTIVE**

SOMETIMES IT'S THE JOURNEY THAT TEACHES YOU A LOT ABOUT YOUR DESTINATION

WORK
WITHOUT
CONTEMPLATION
IS
NEVER
ENOUGH

@GREATARSENAL

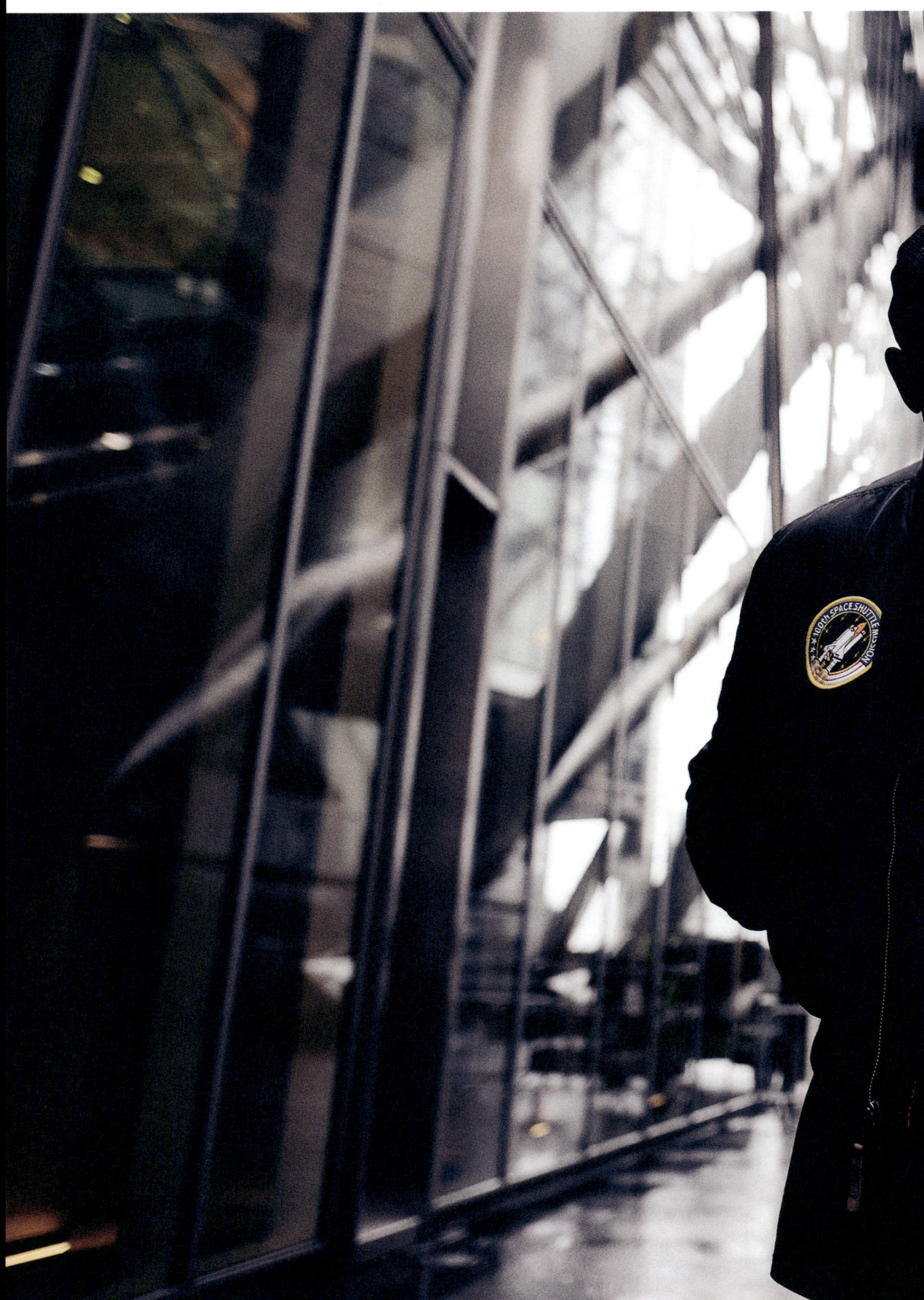

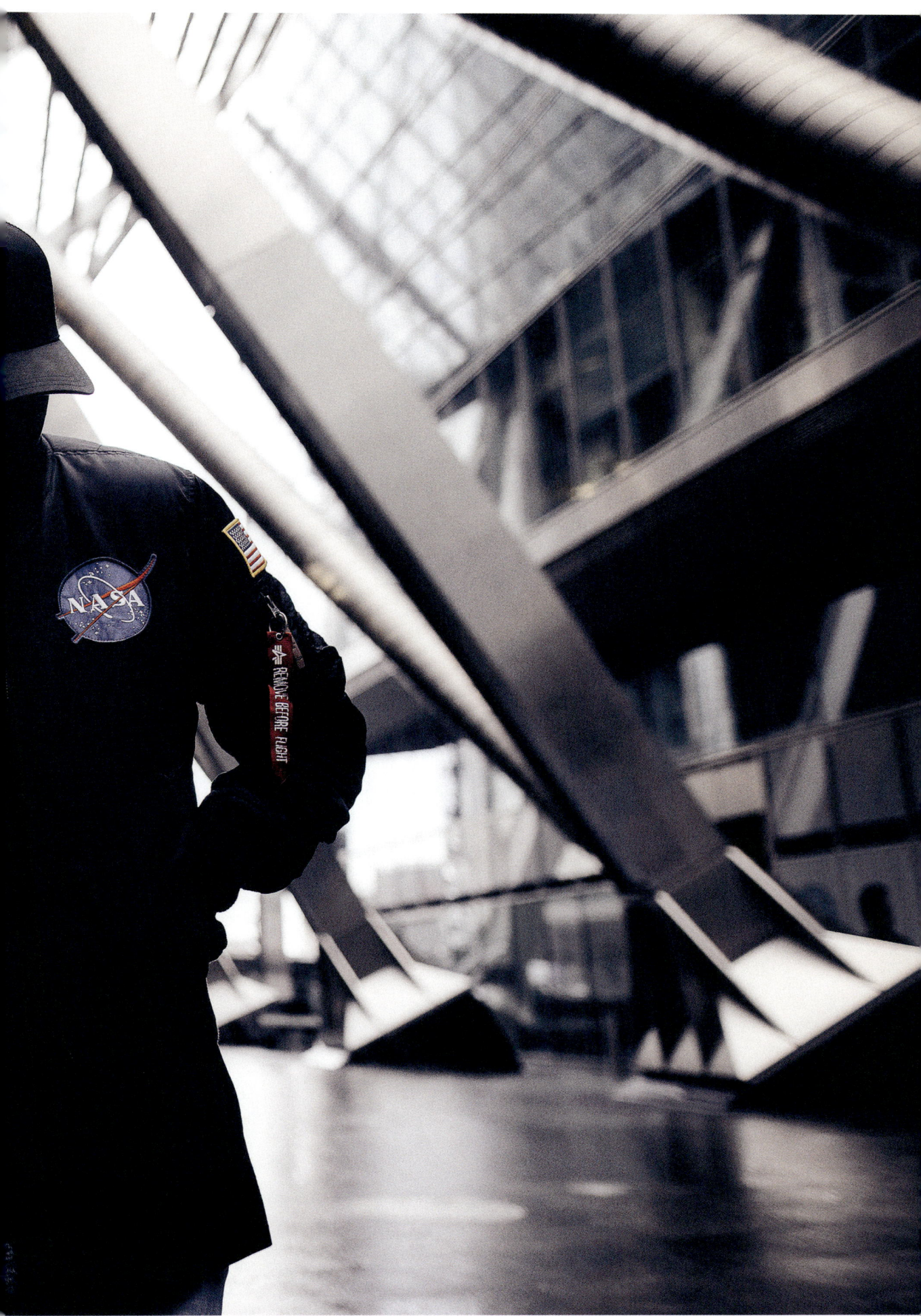

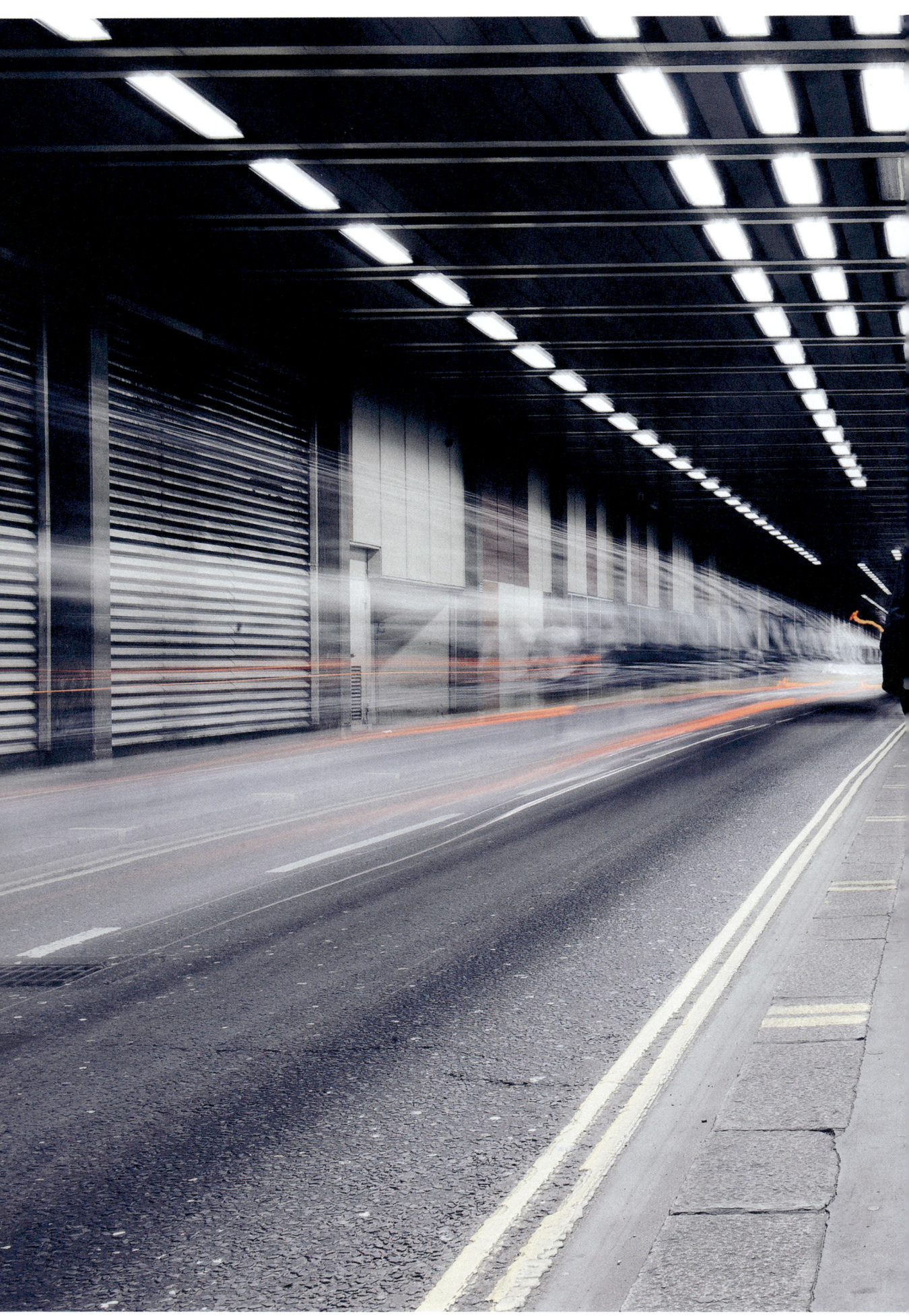

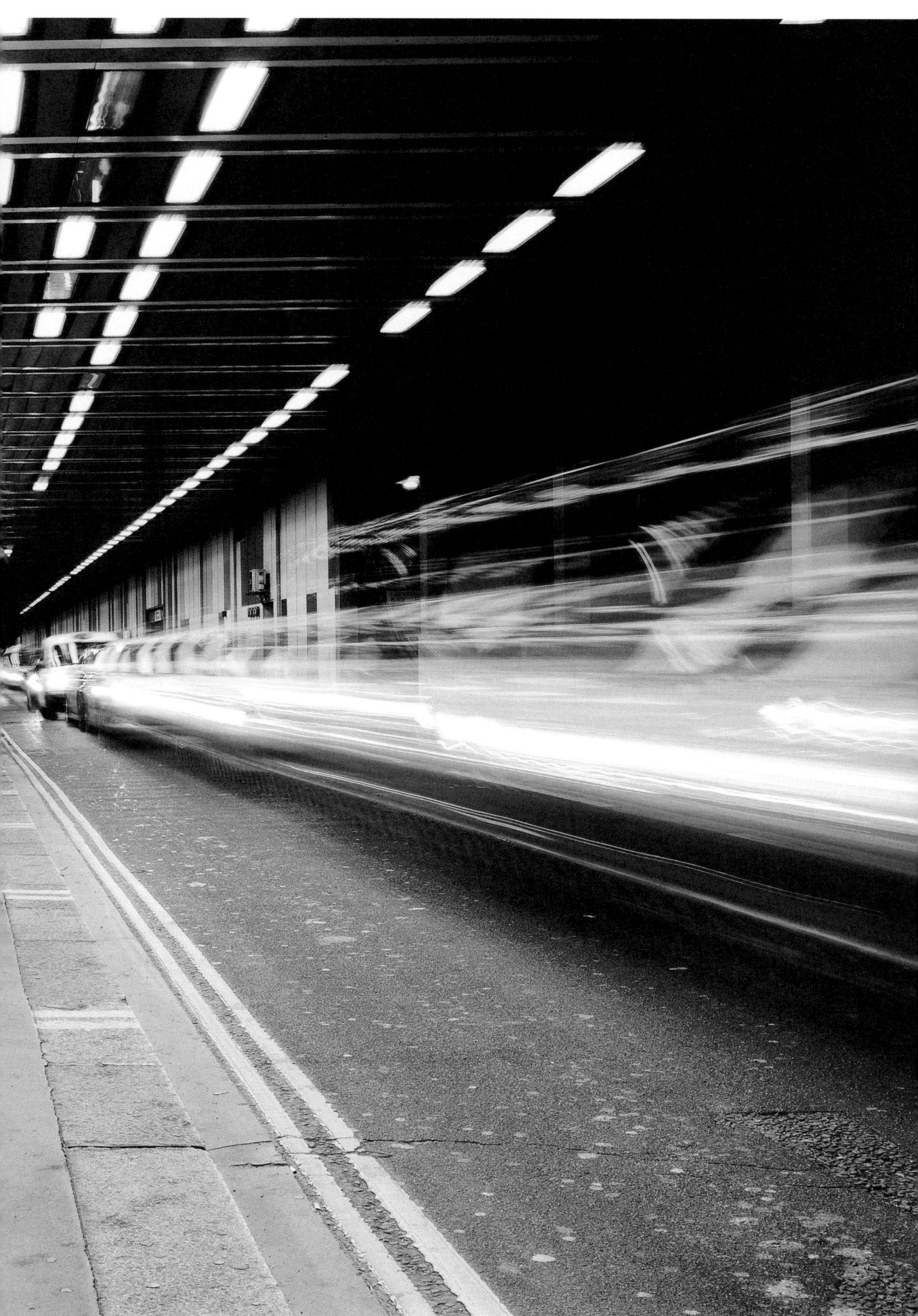

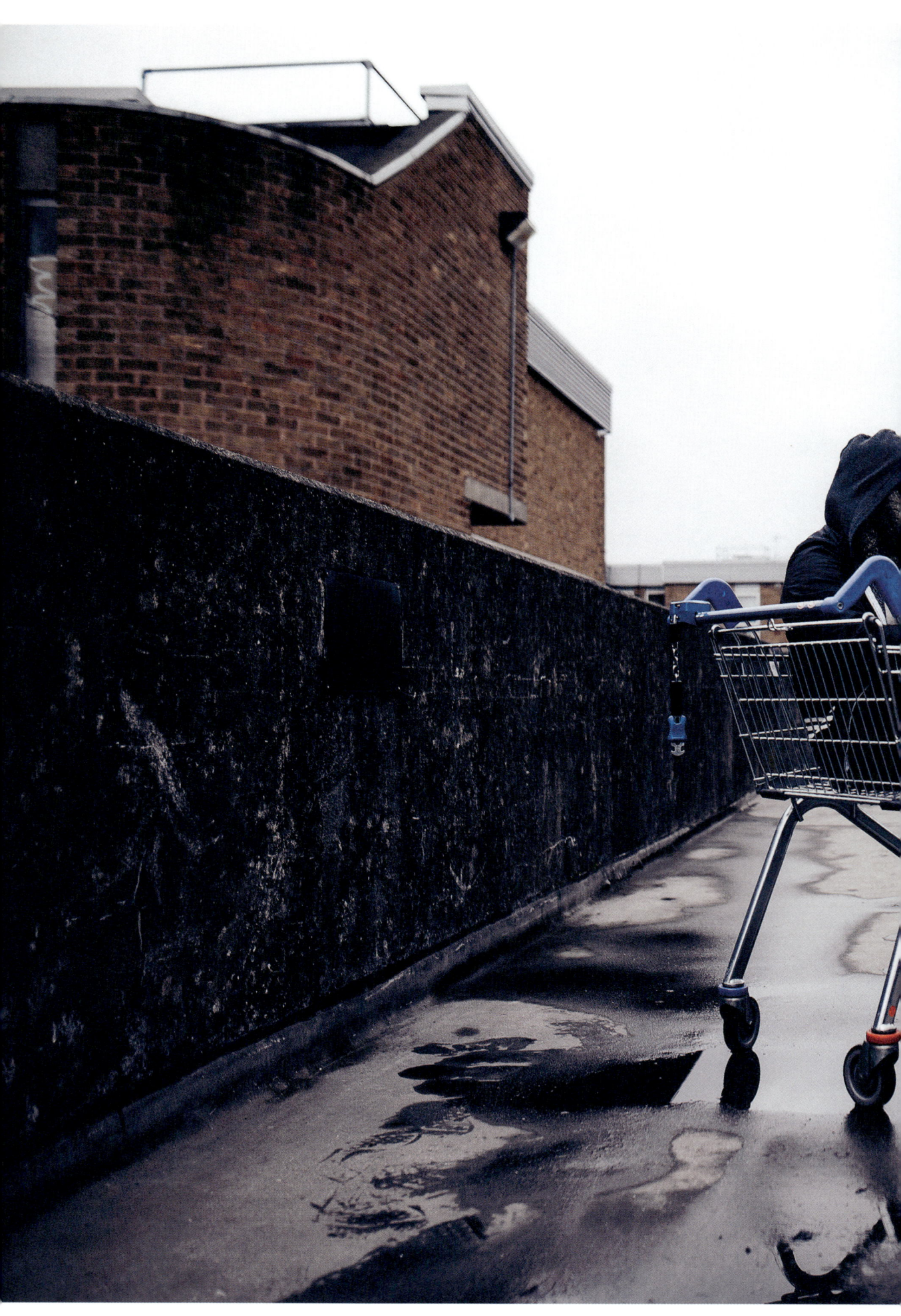

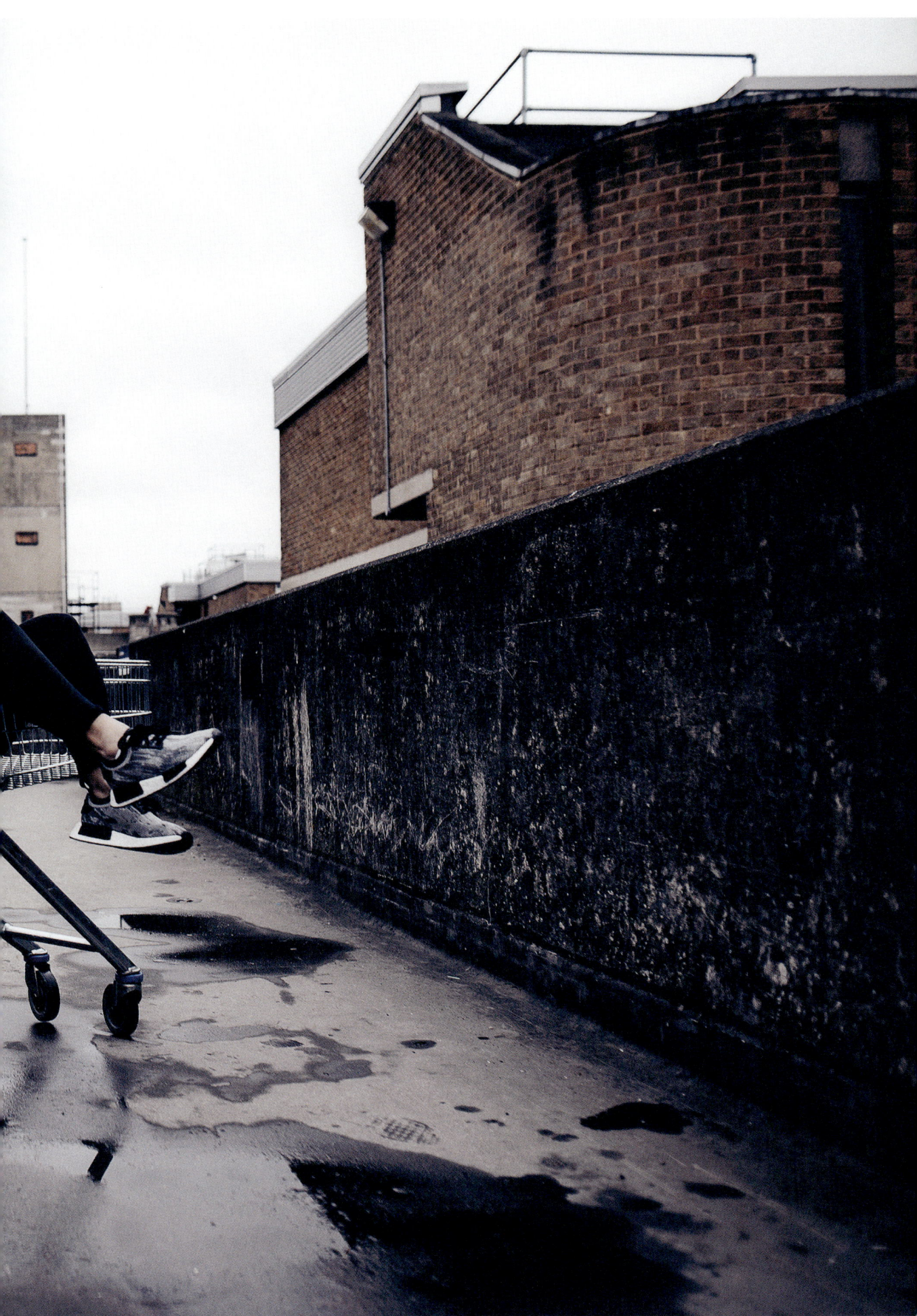

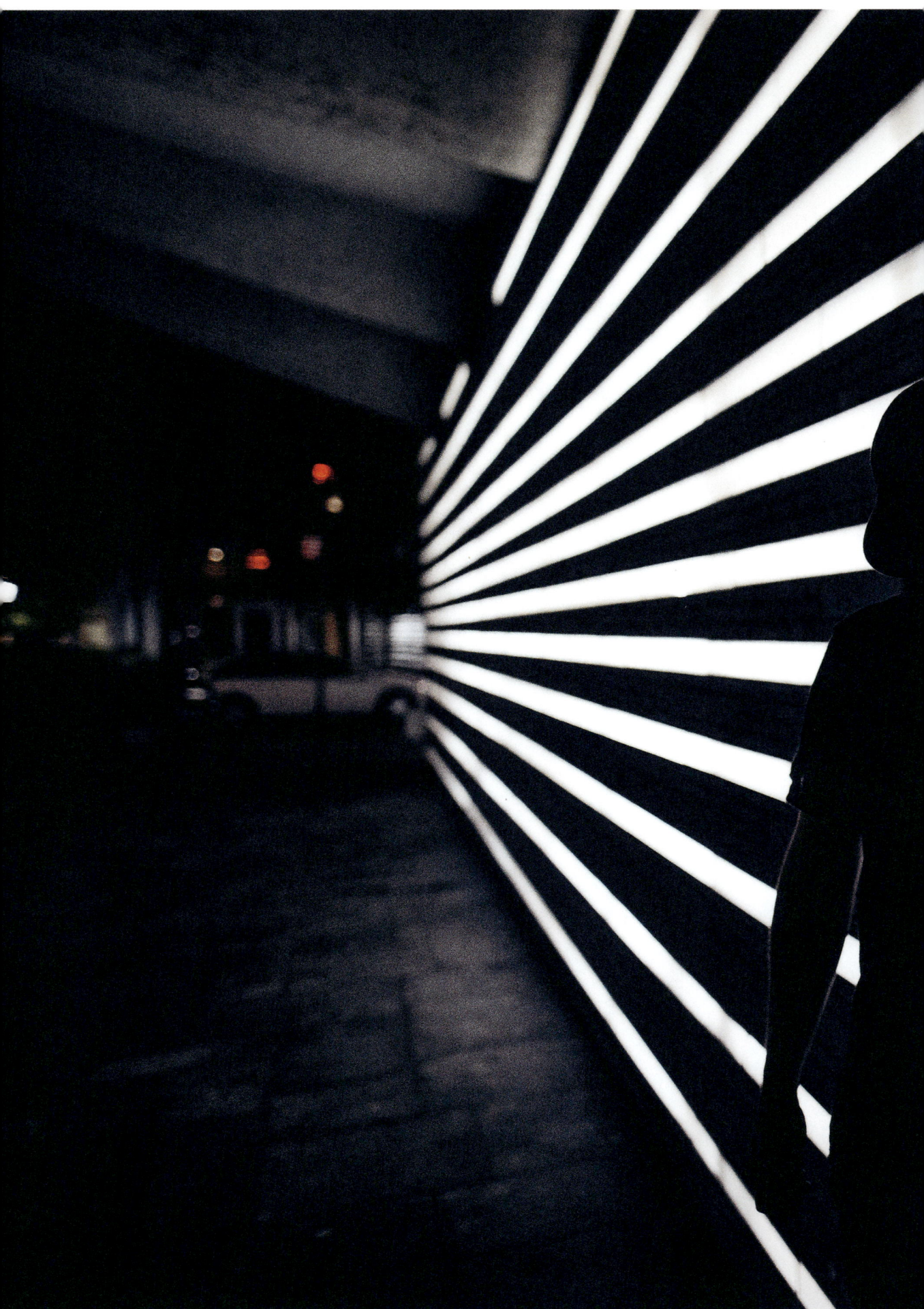

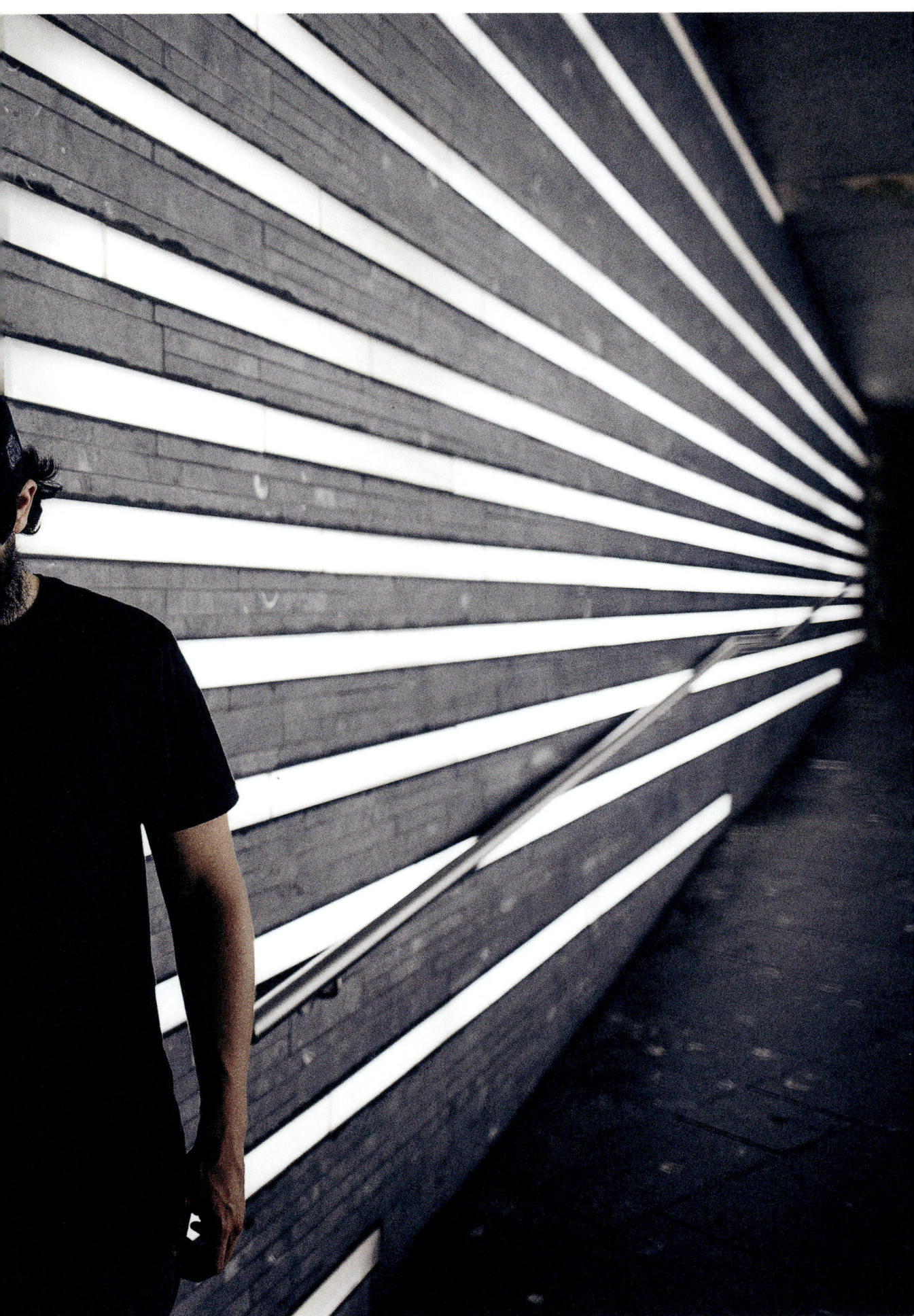

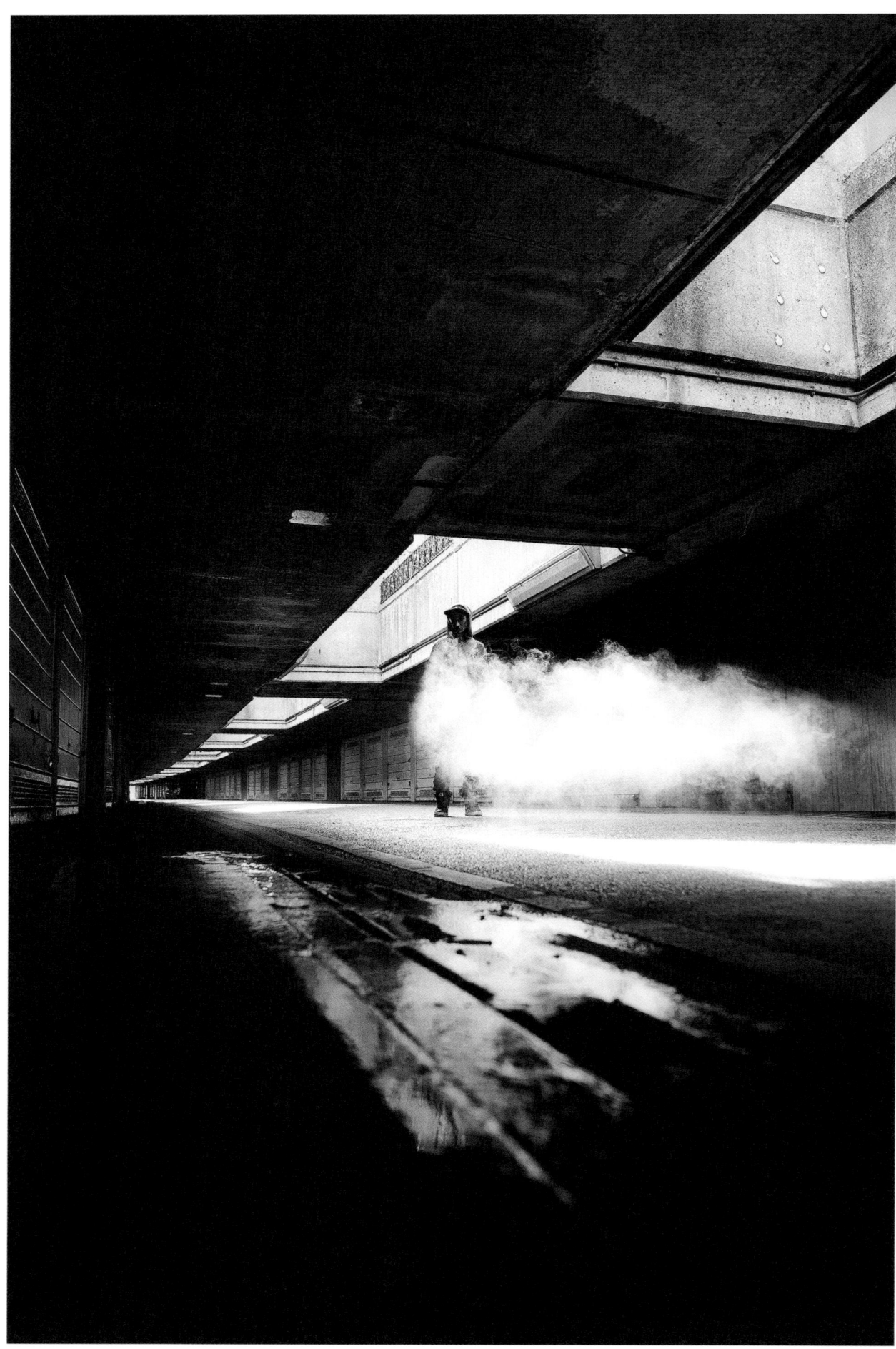

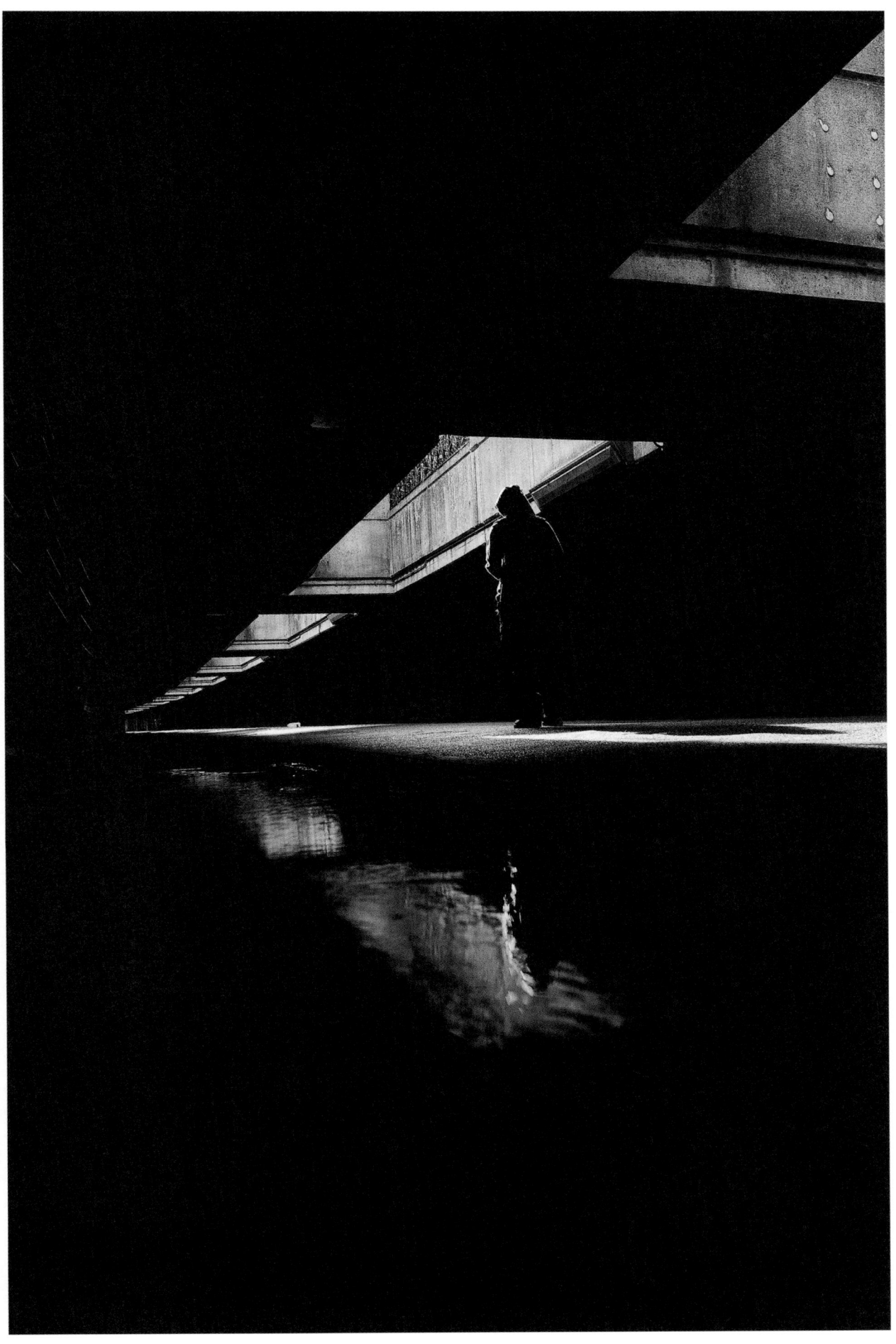

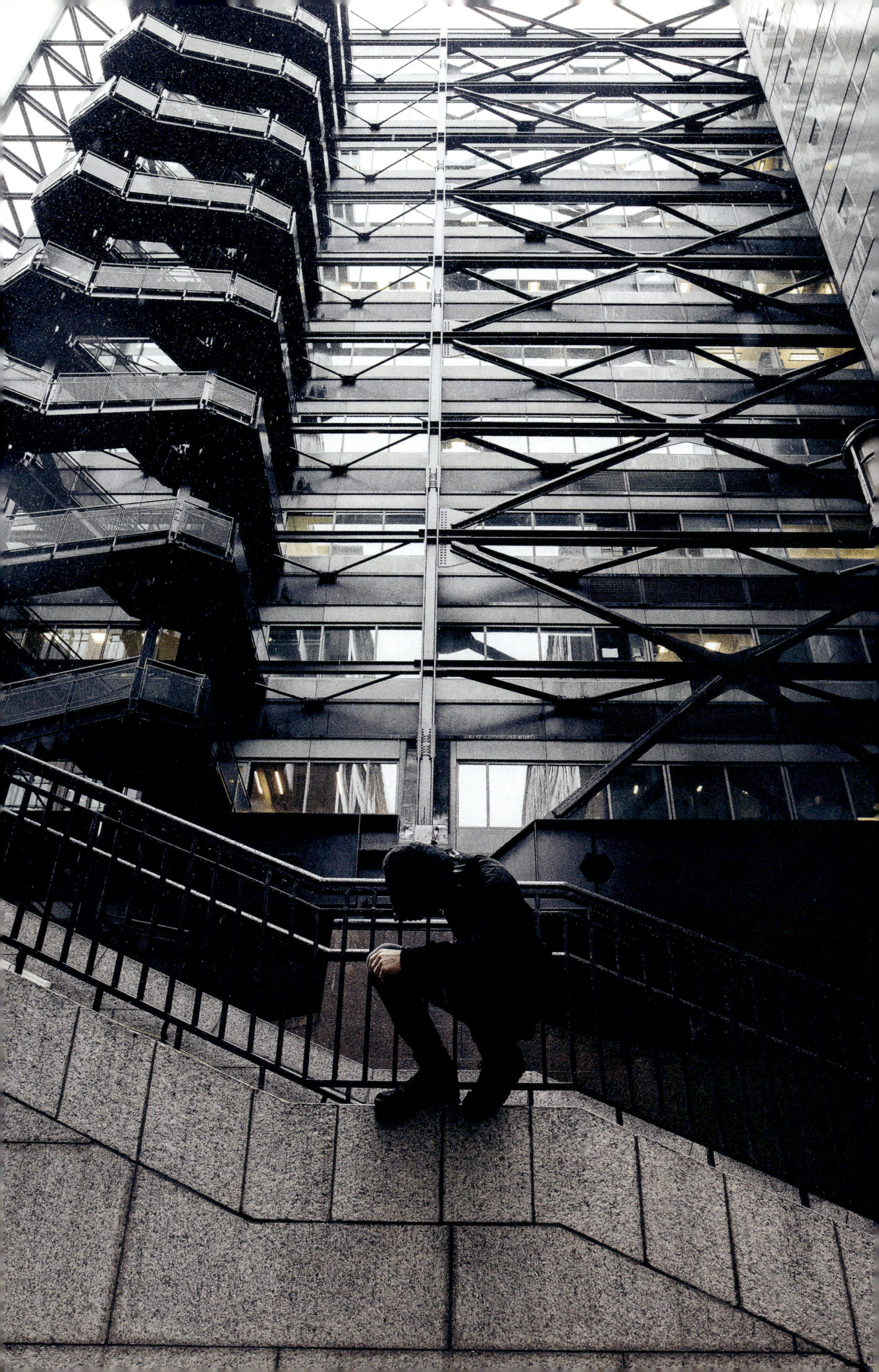

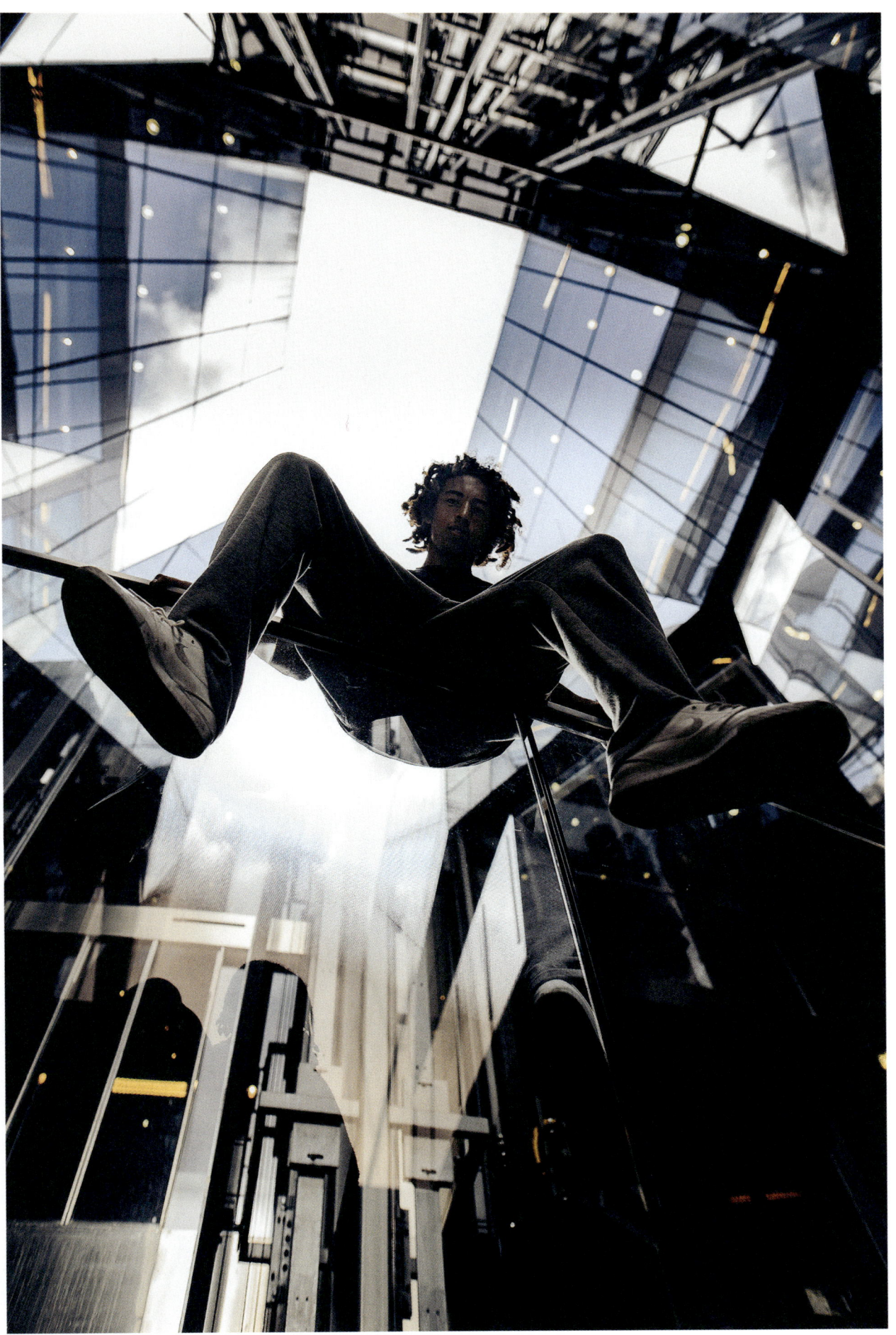

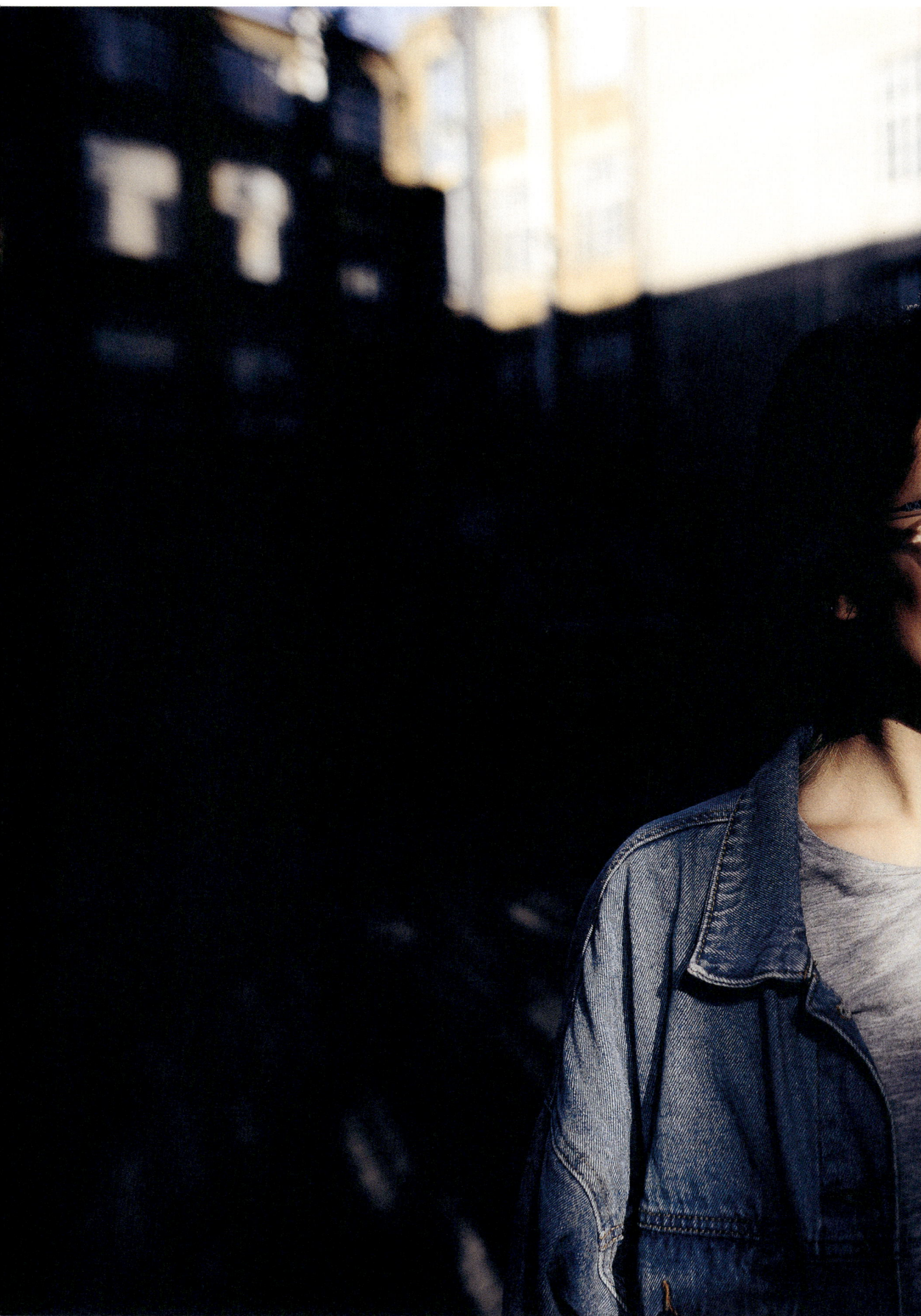

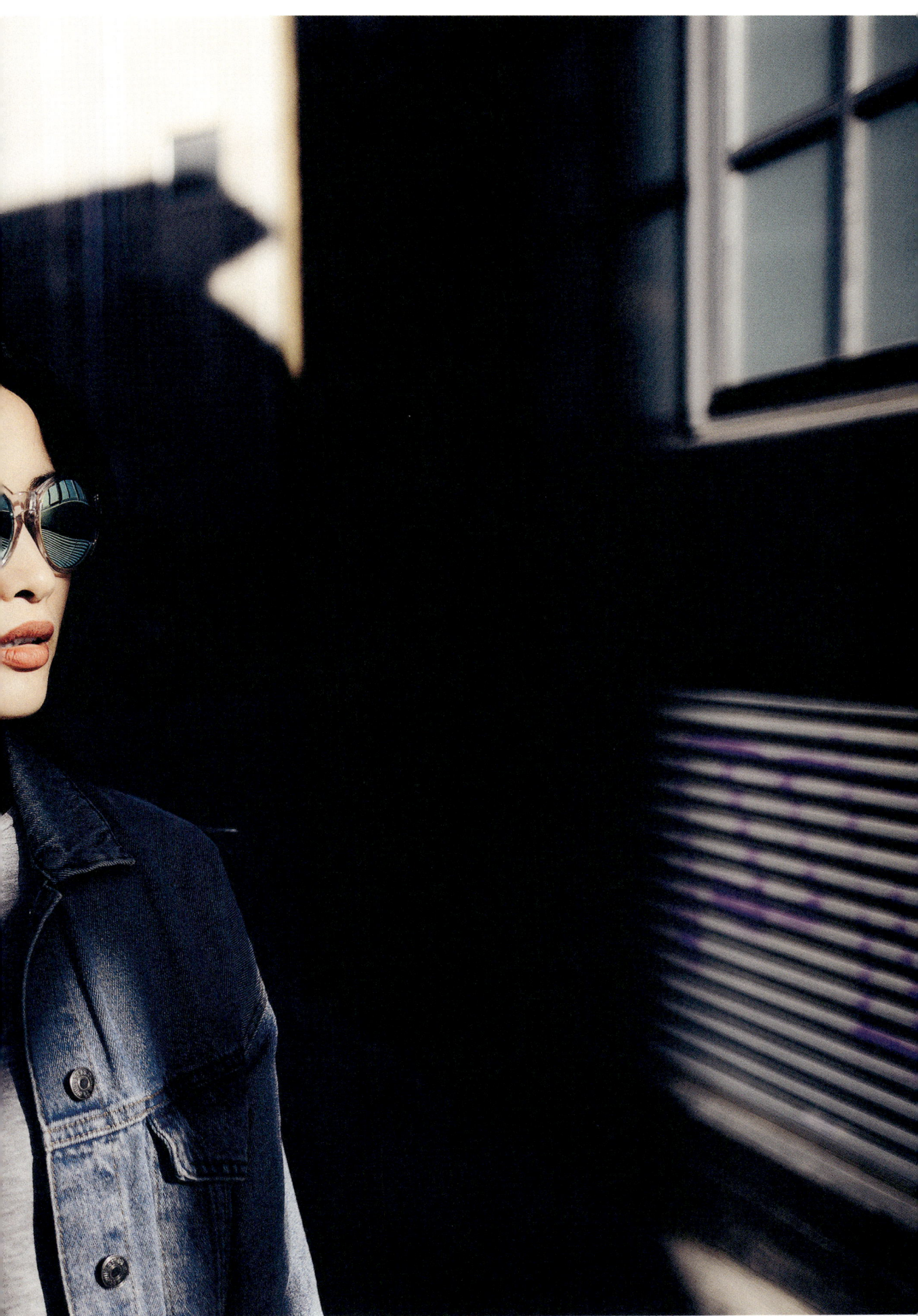

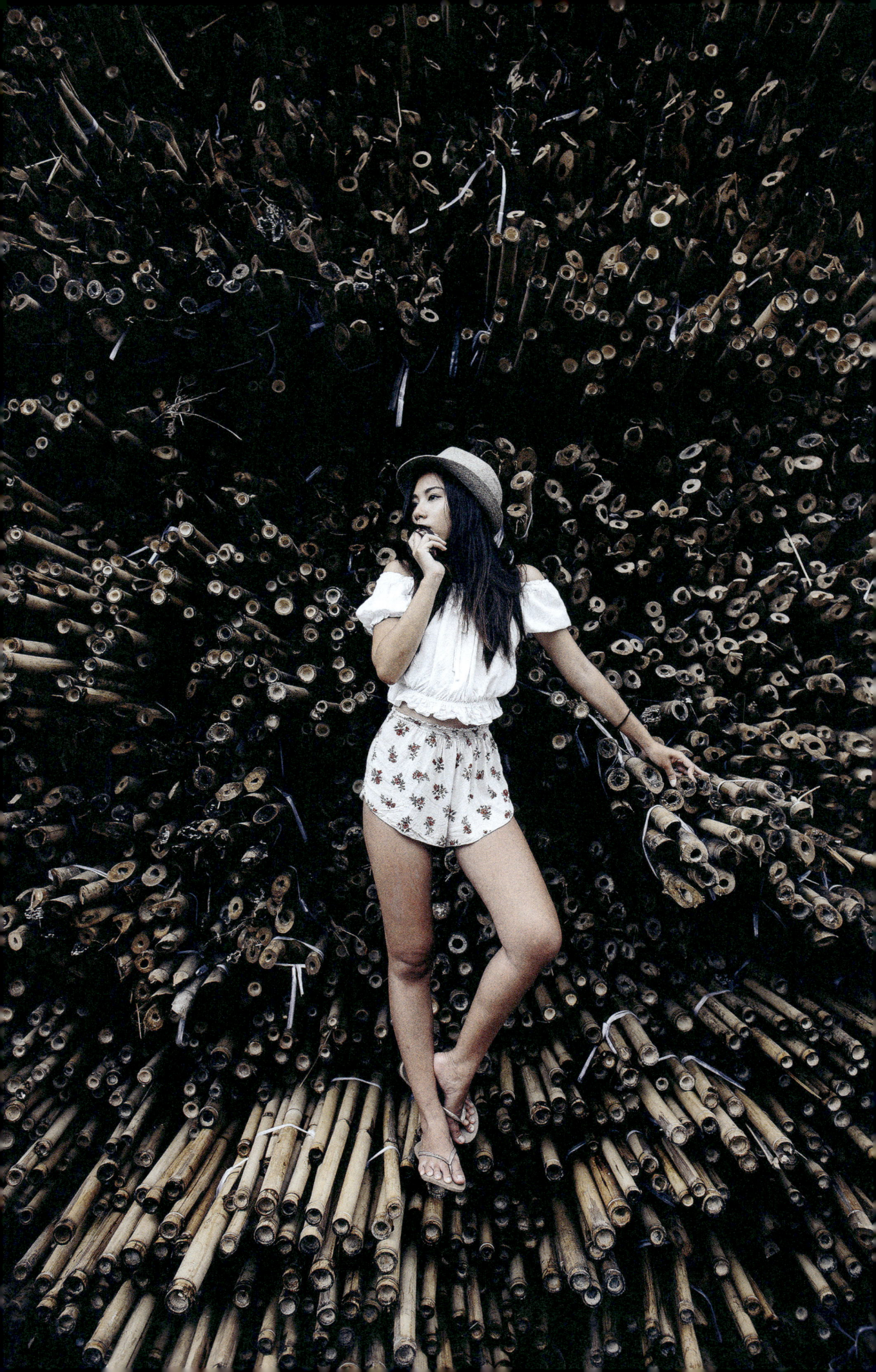

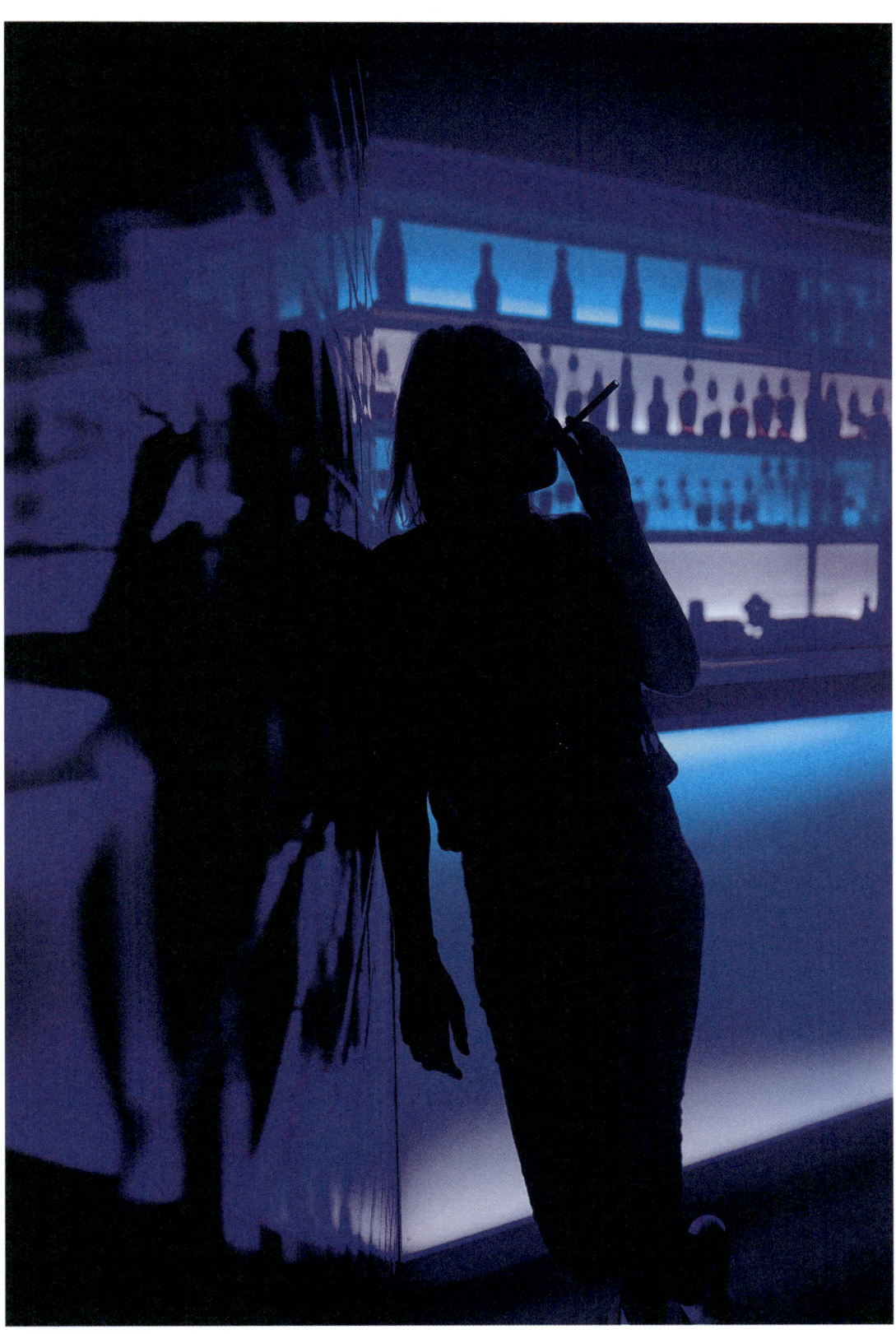

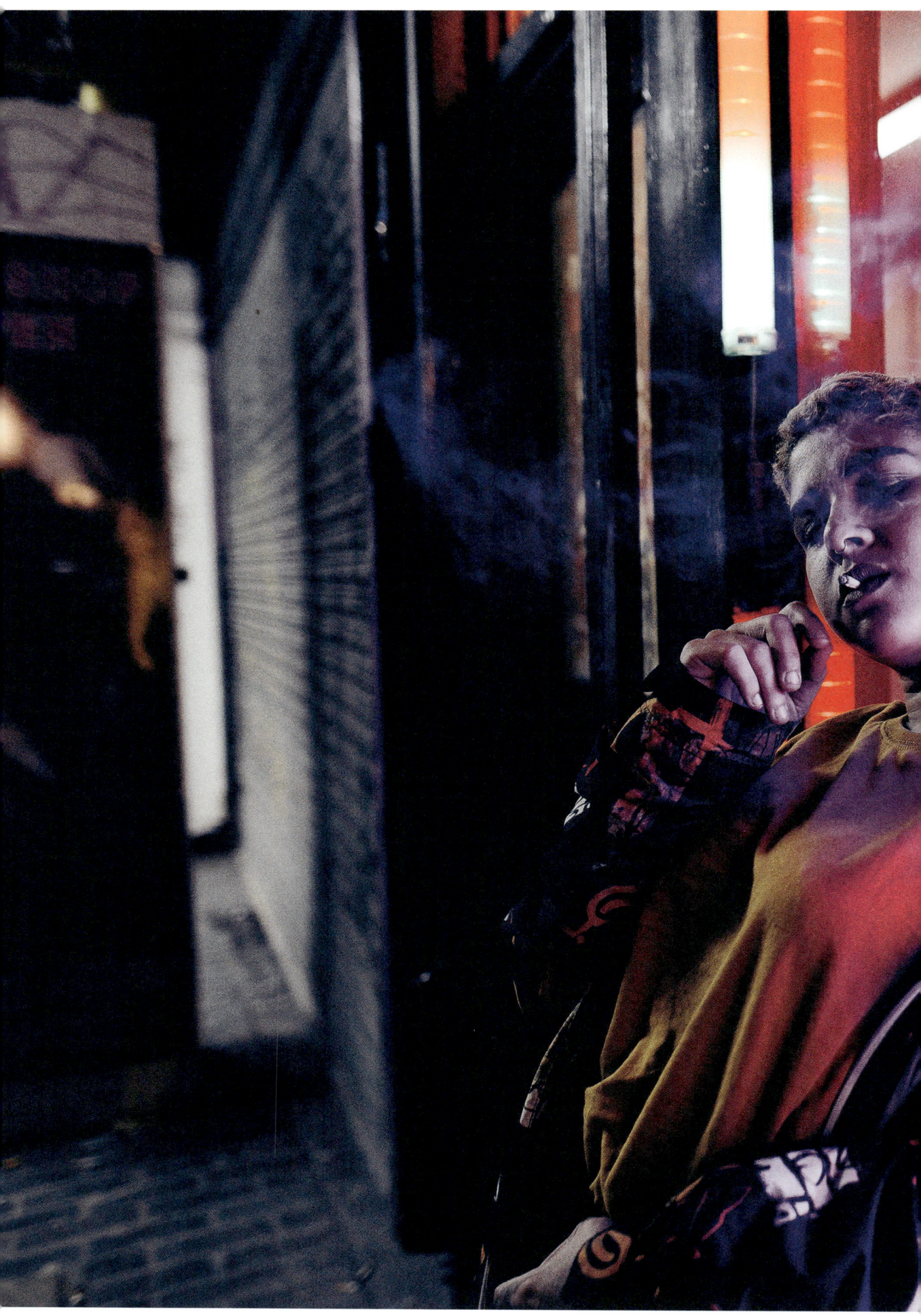

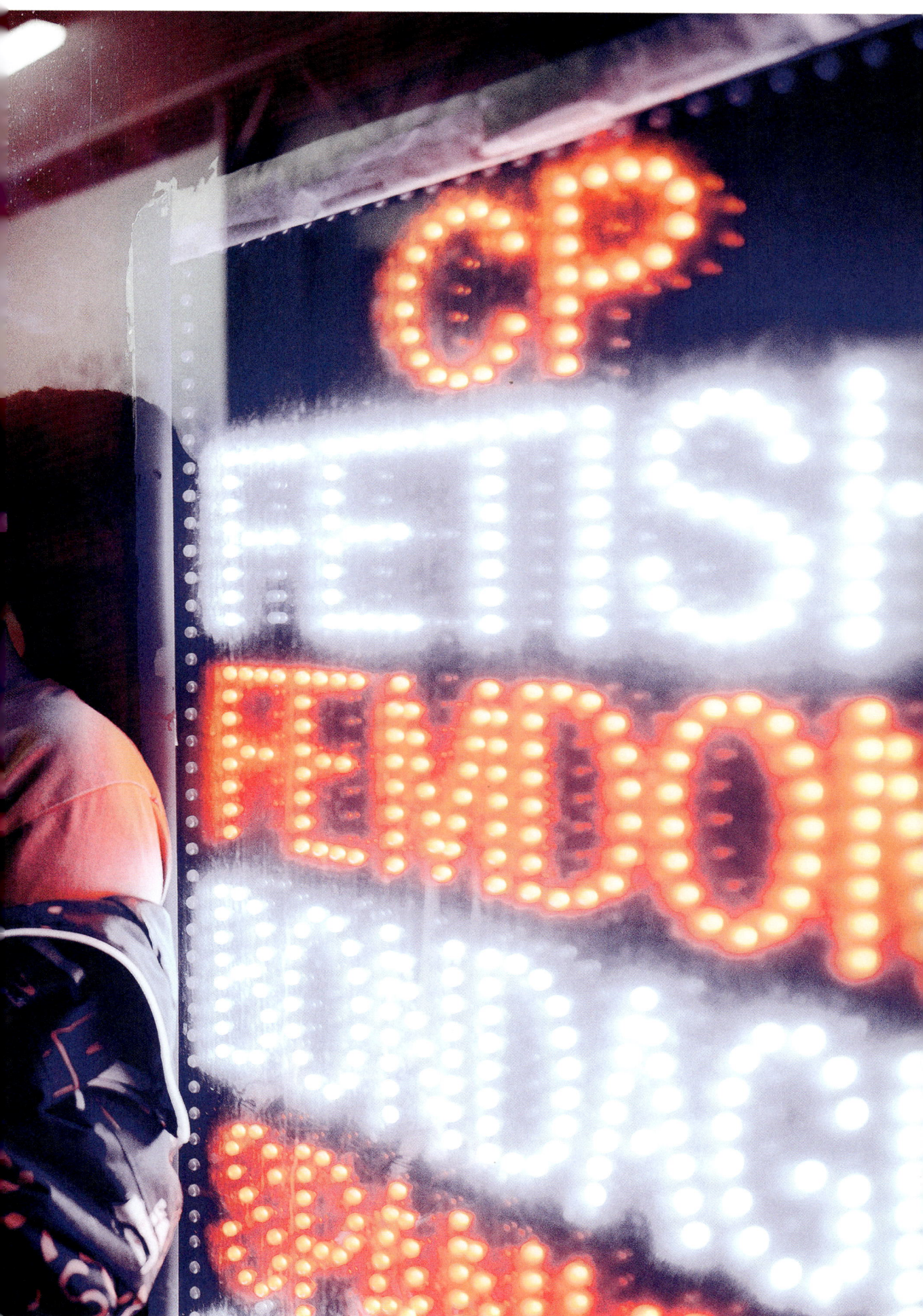

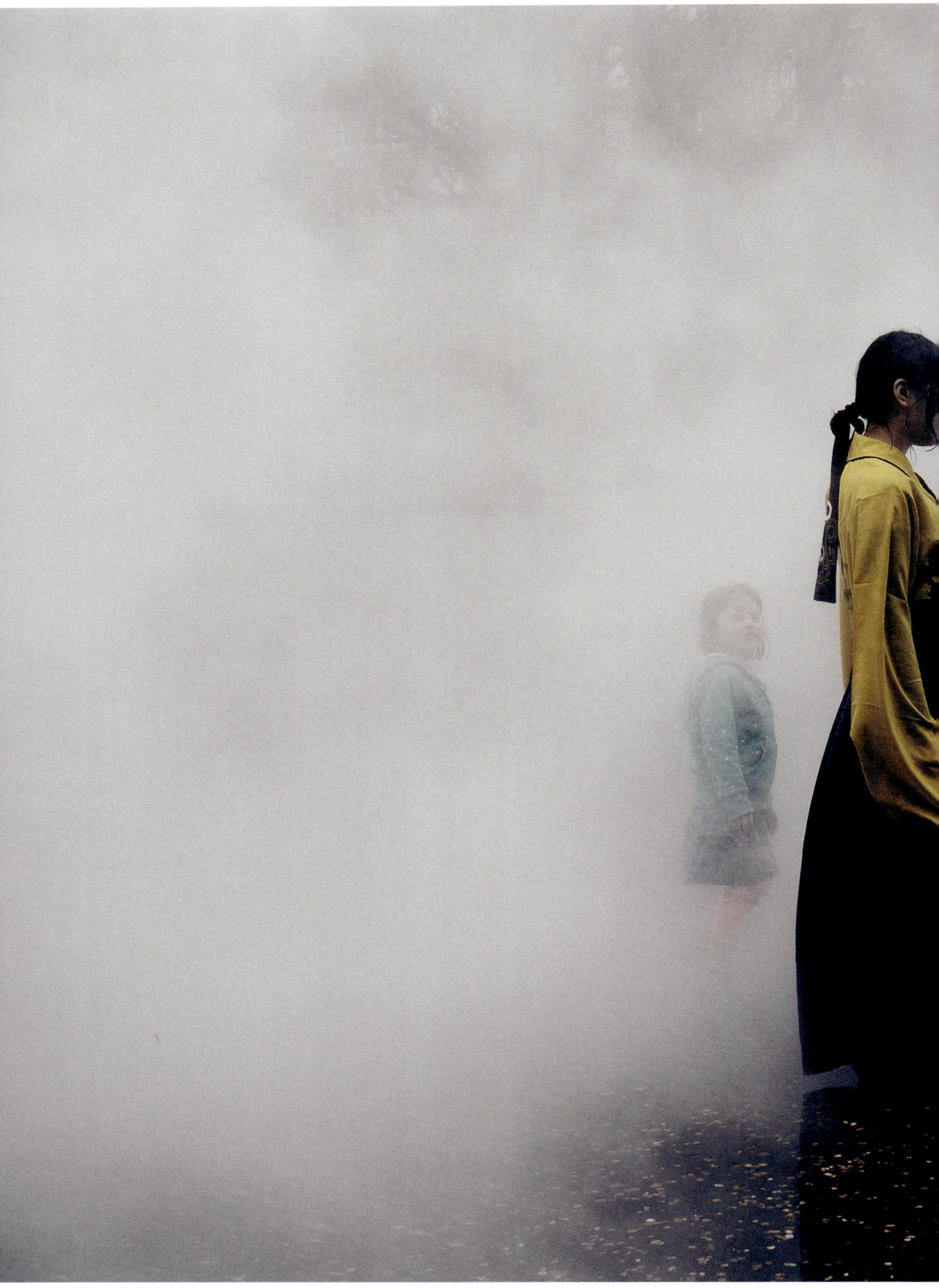

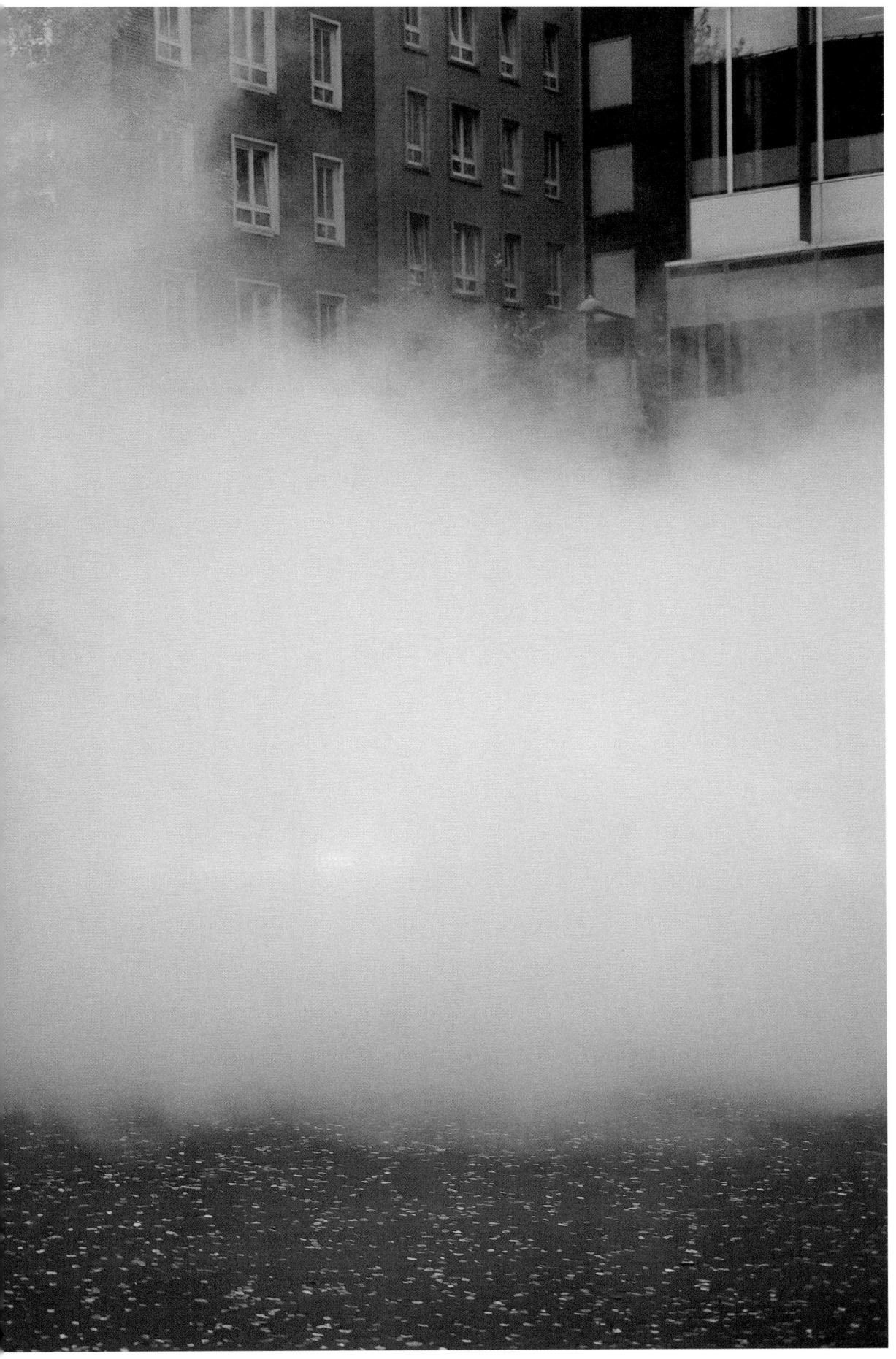

ALWAYS REMEMBER, YOUR FOCUS DETERMINES YOUR REALITY

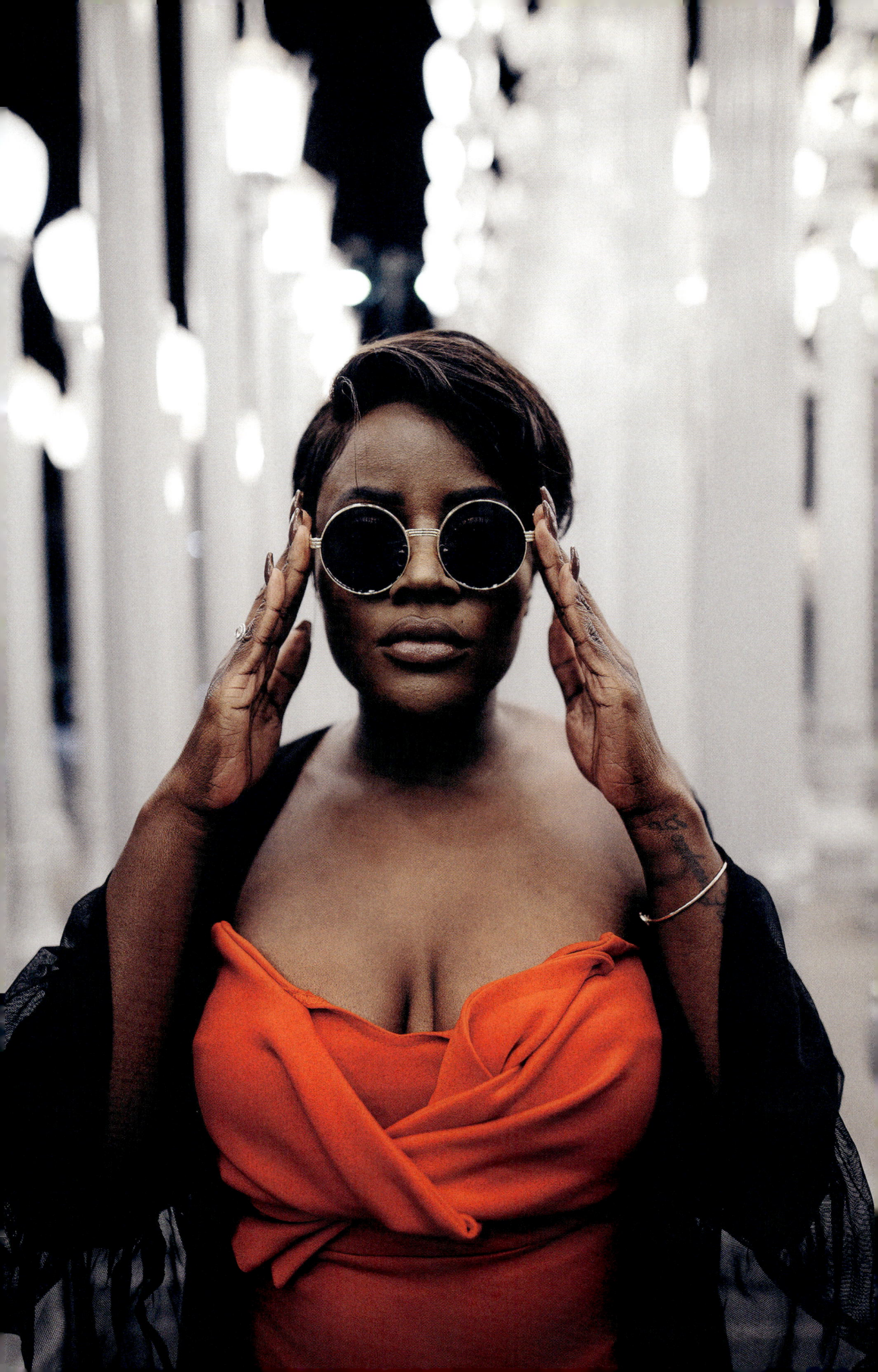

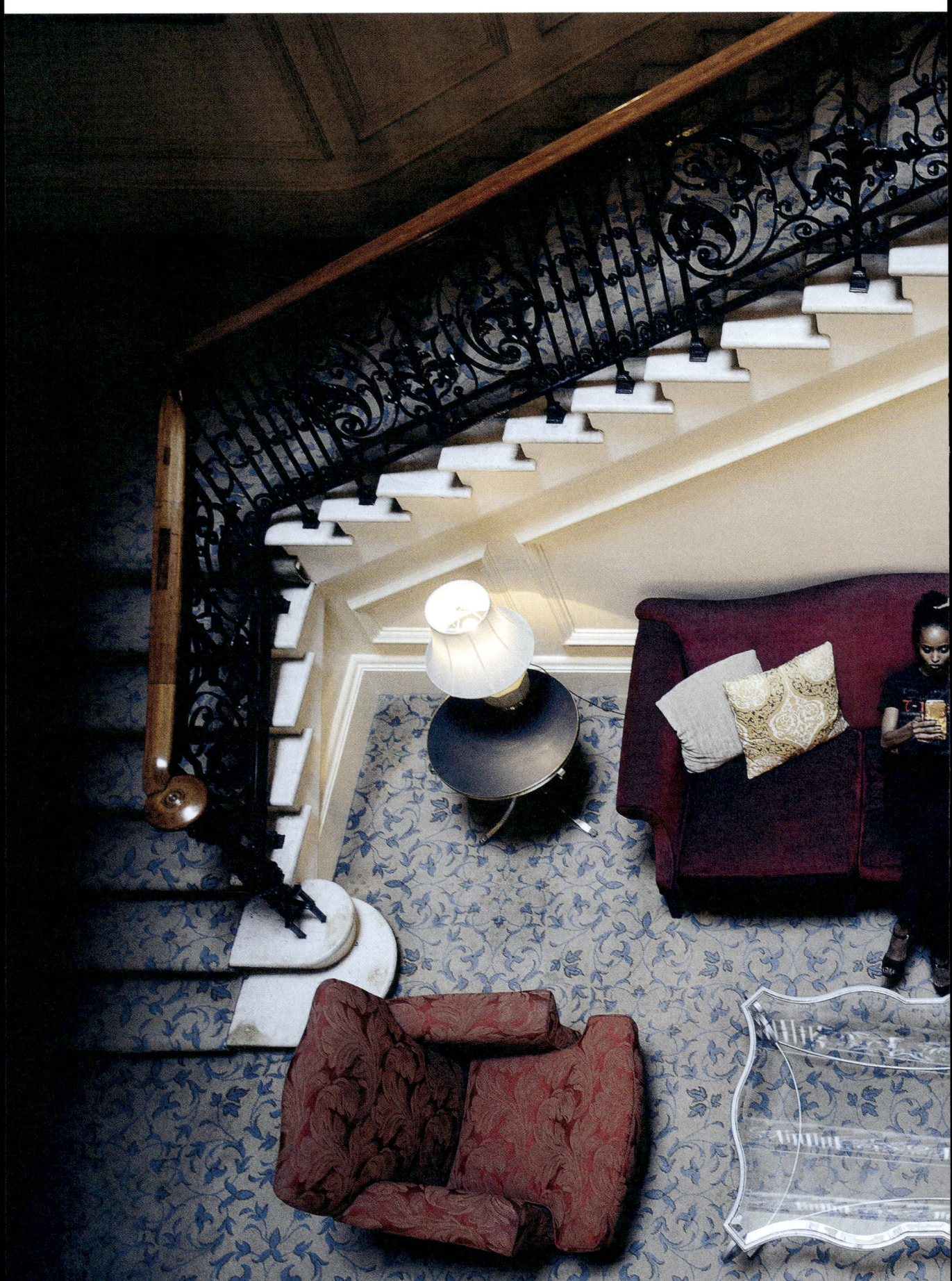

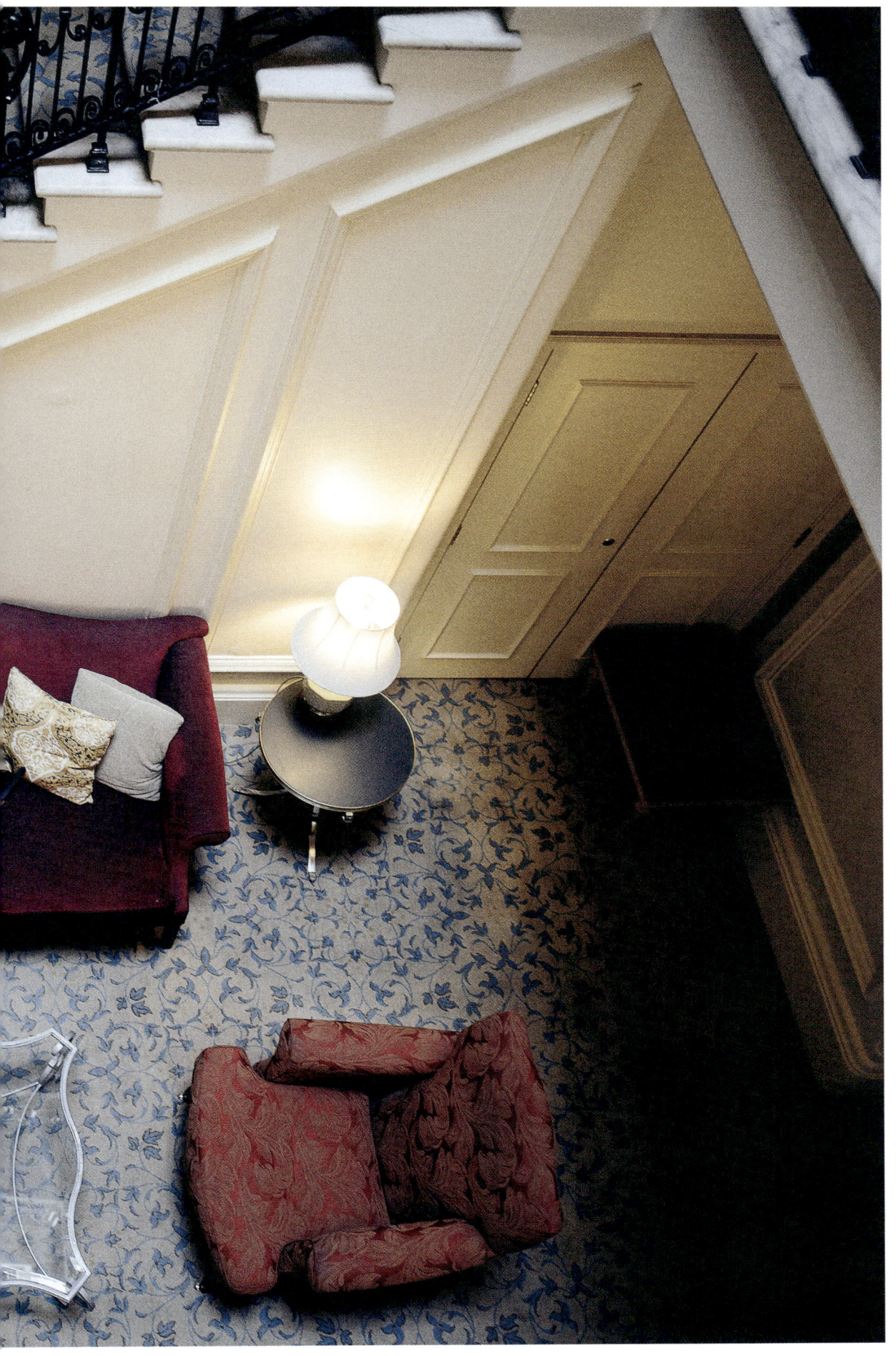

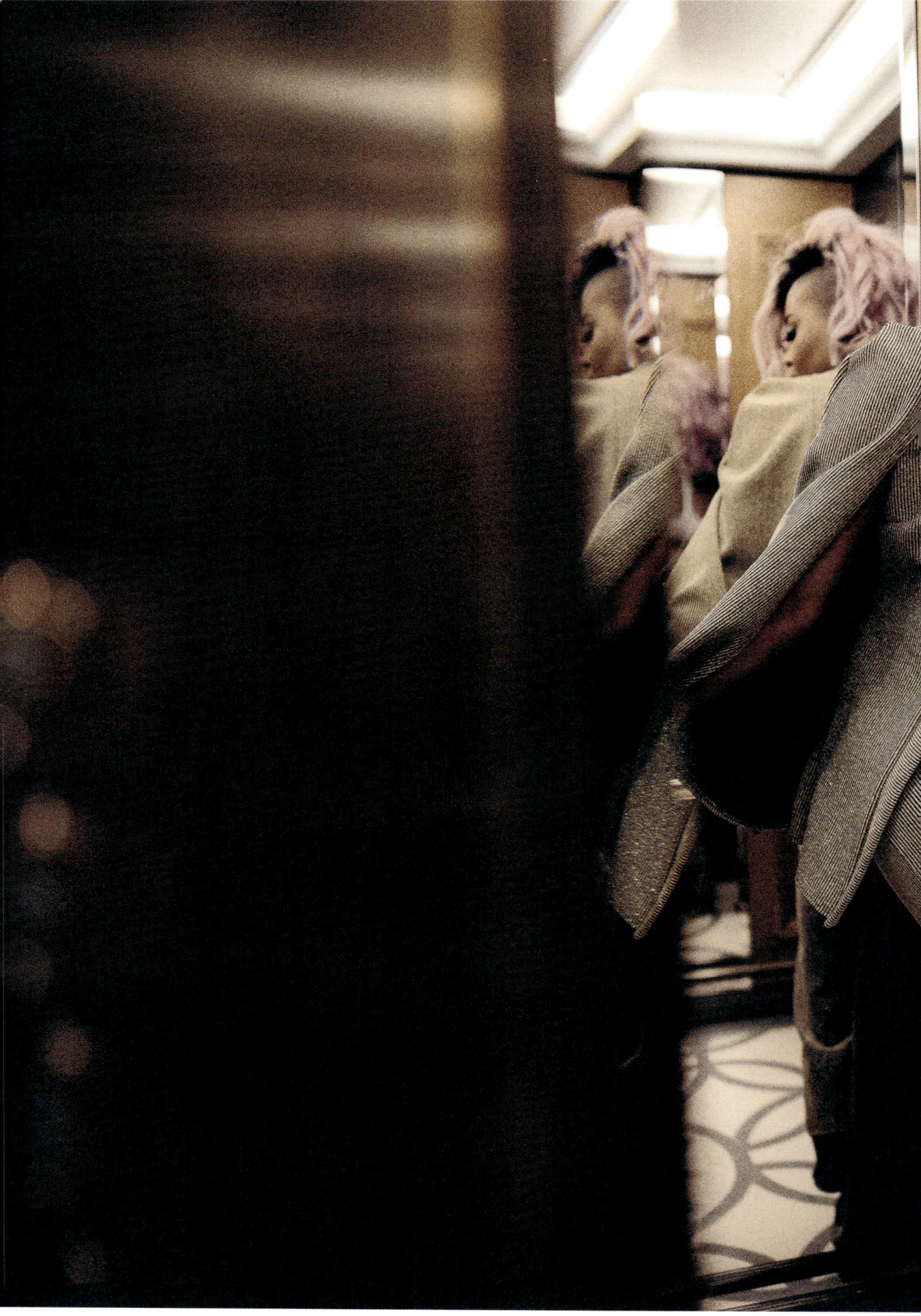

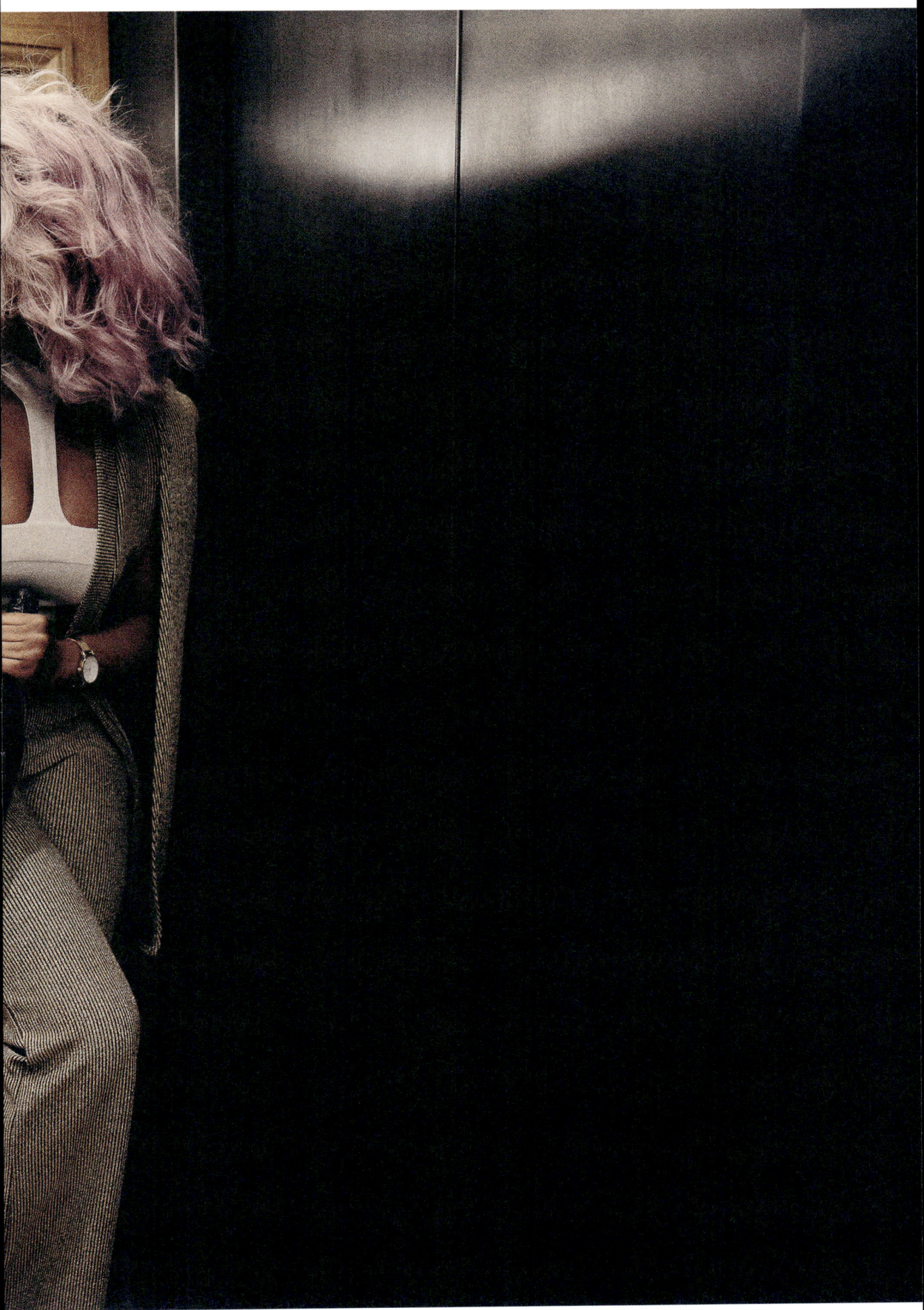

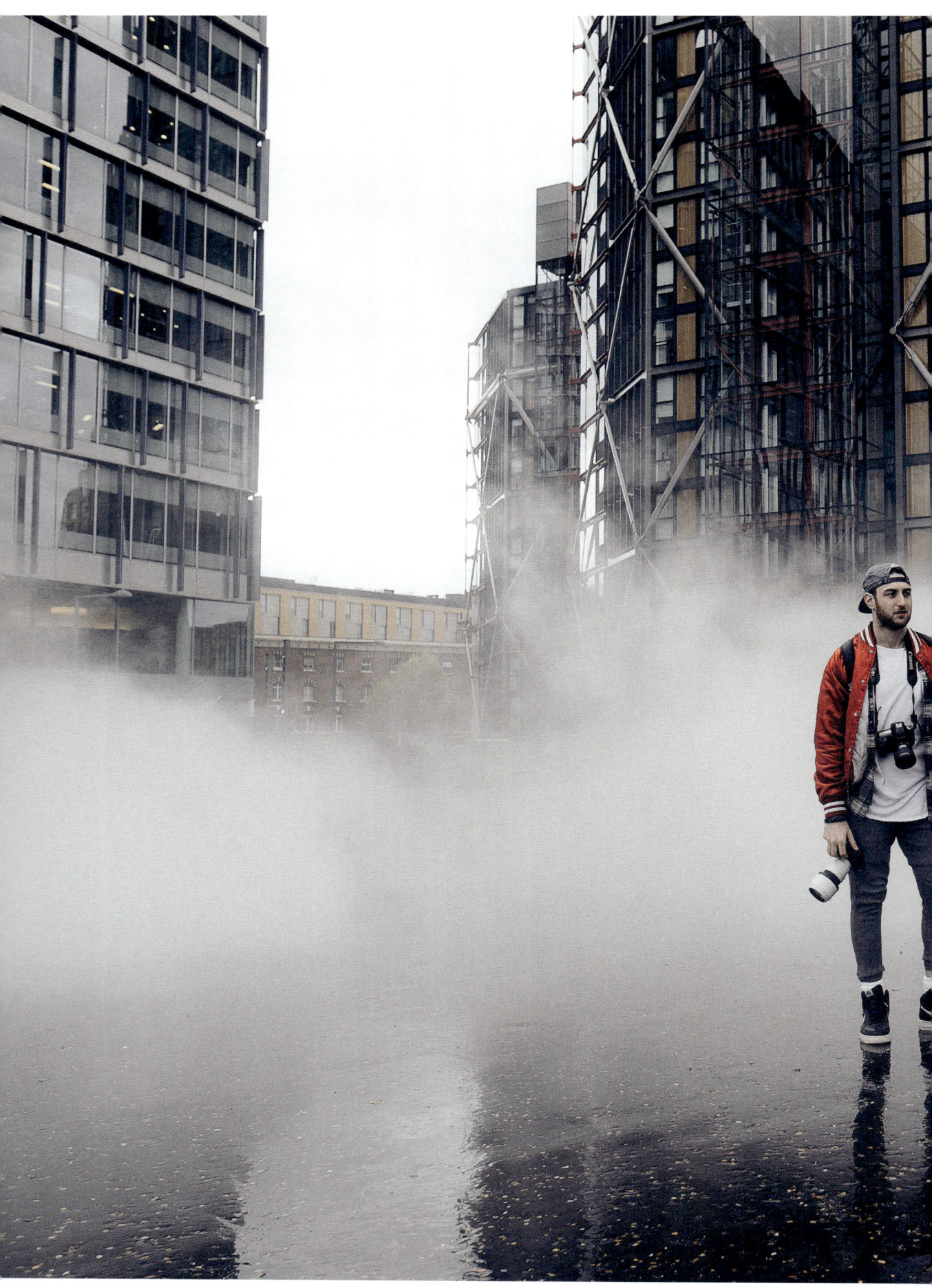

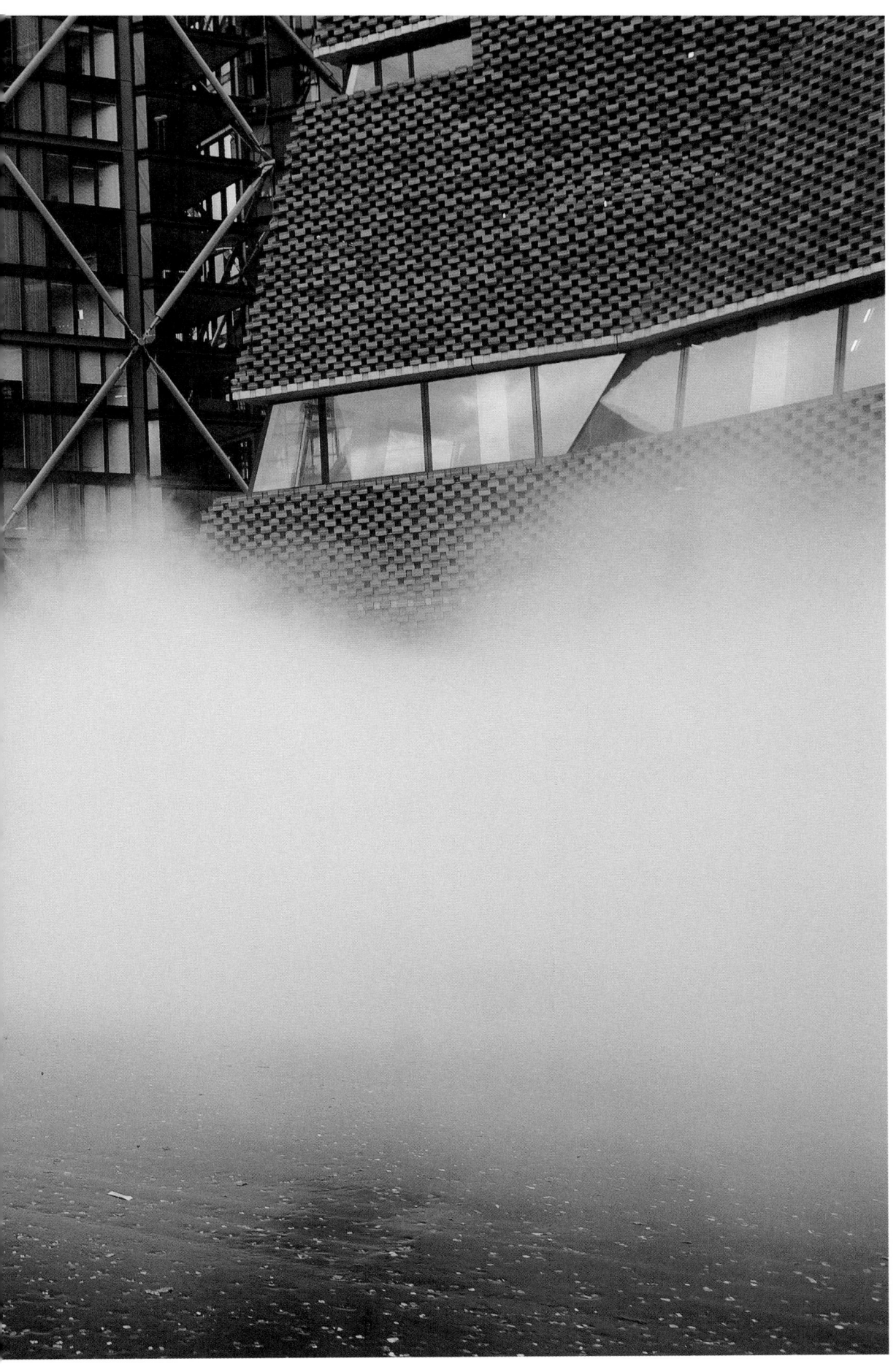

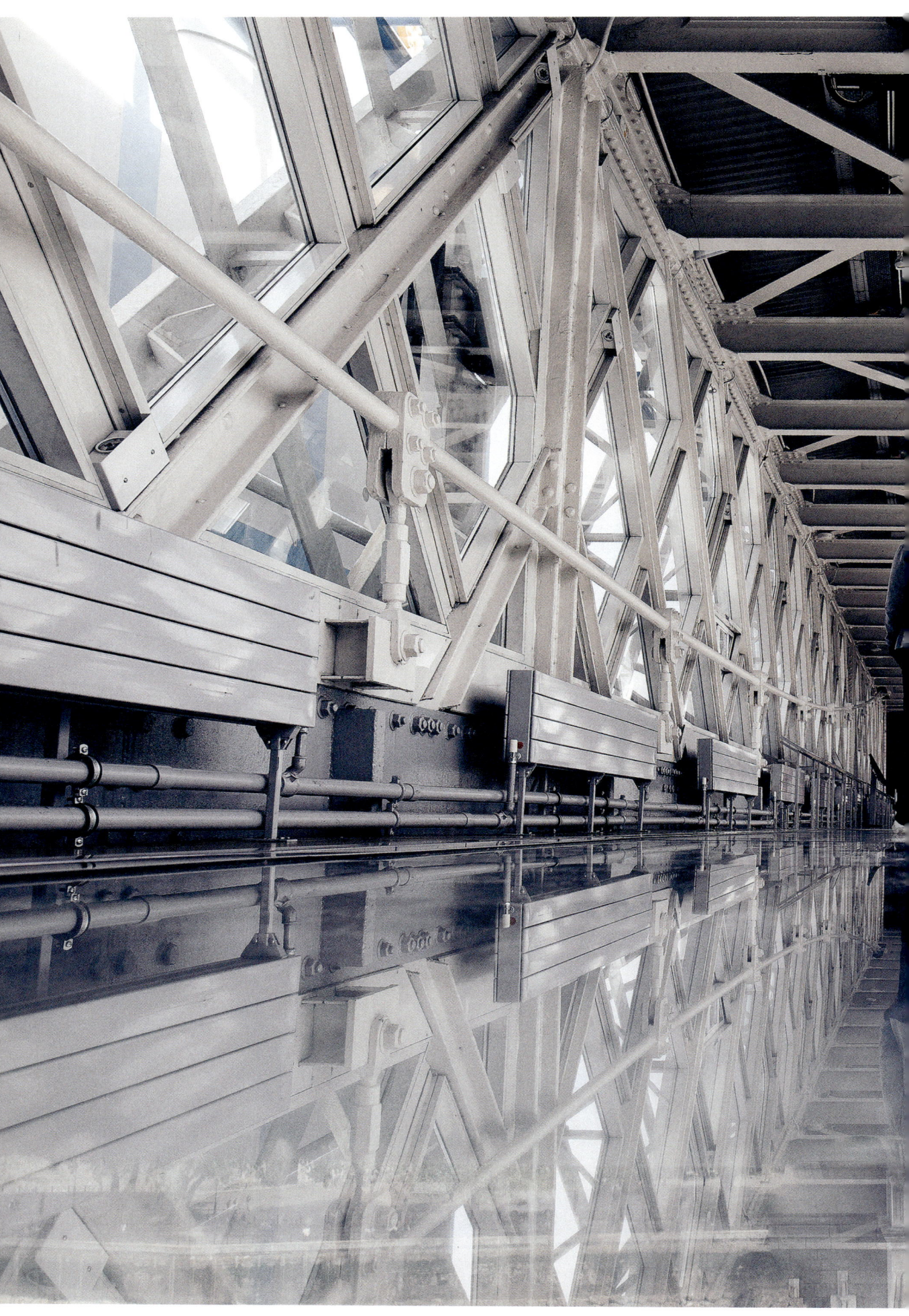

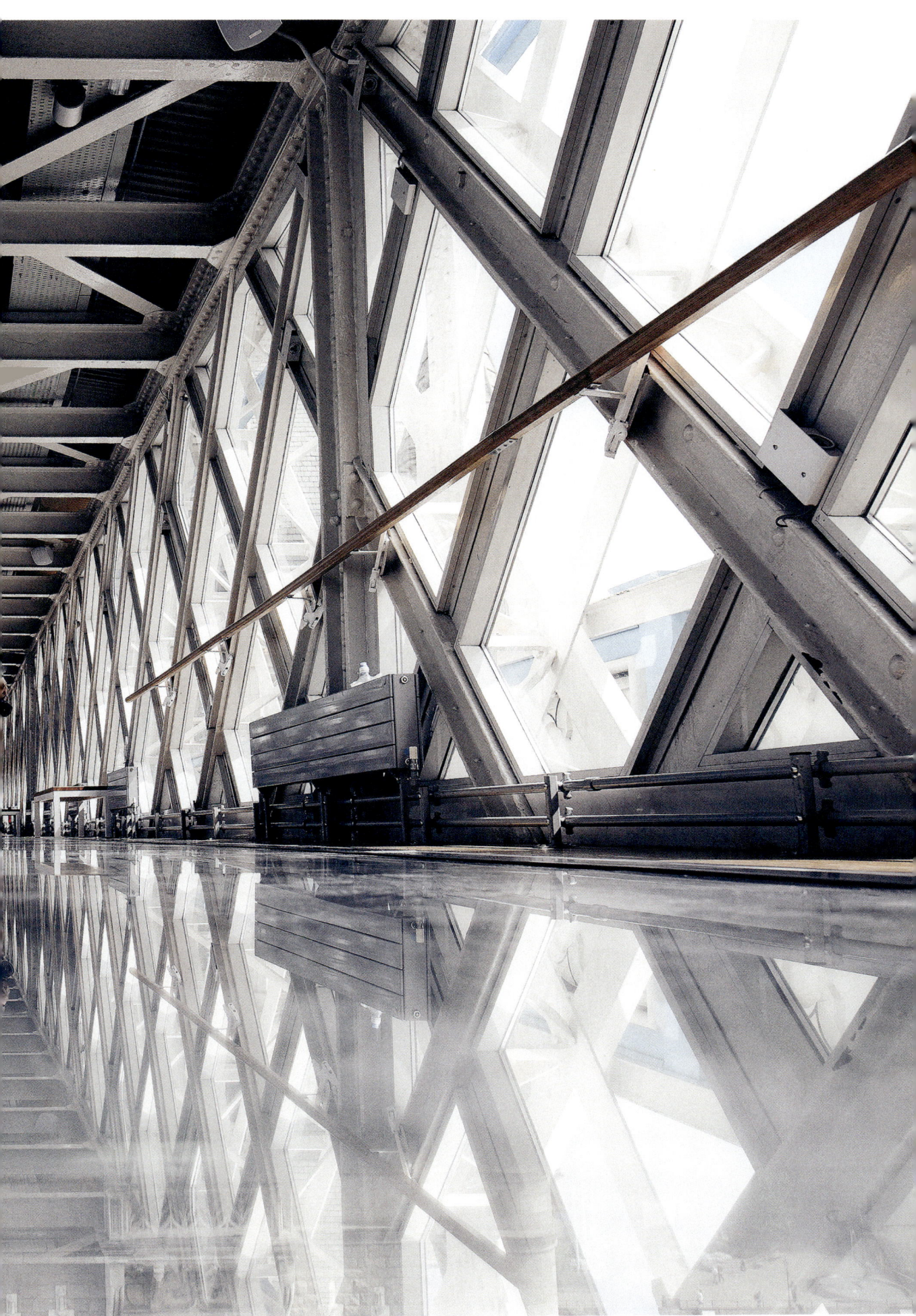

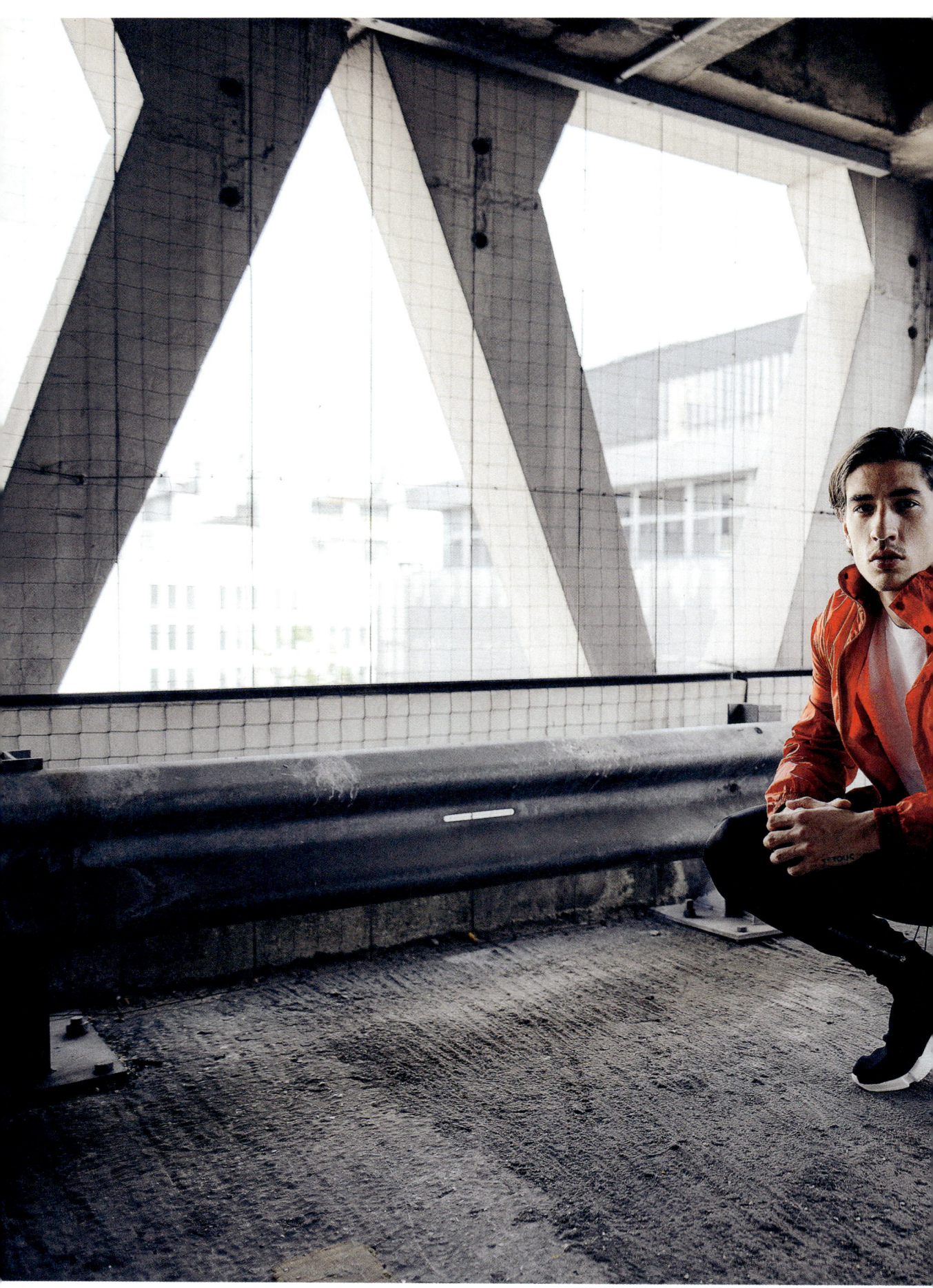

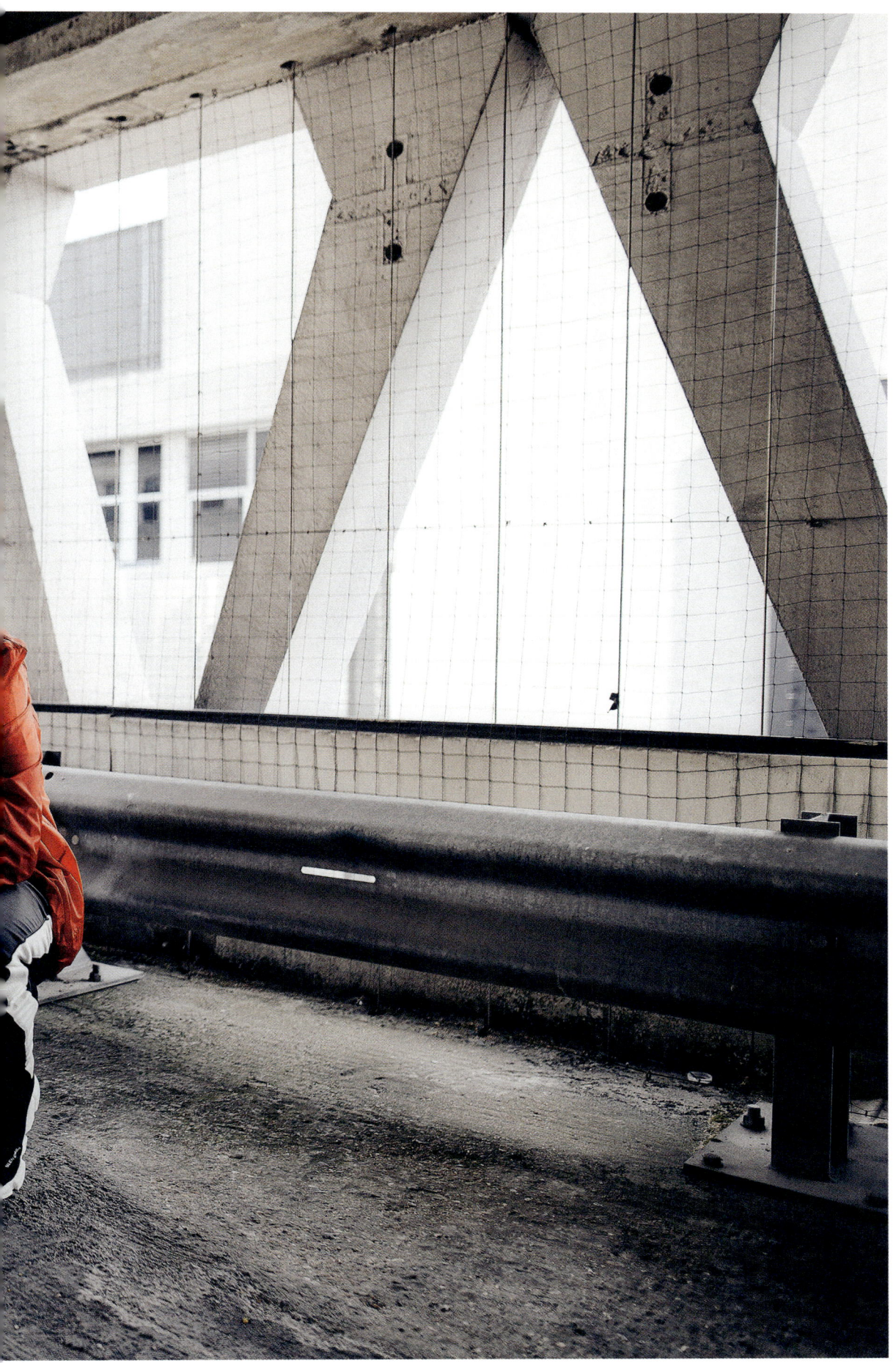

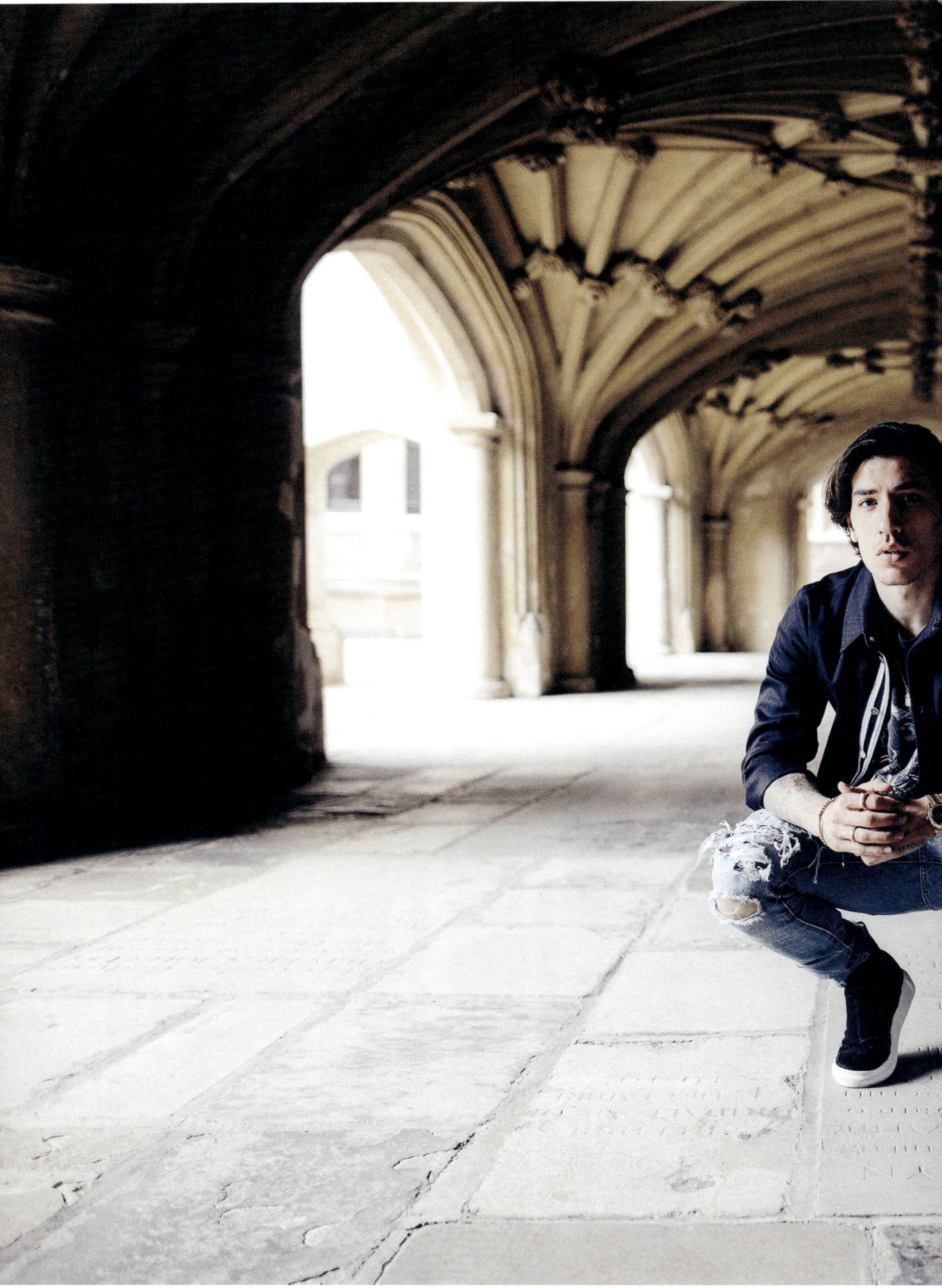

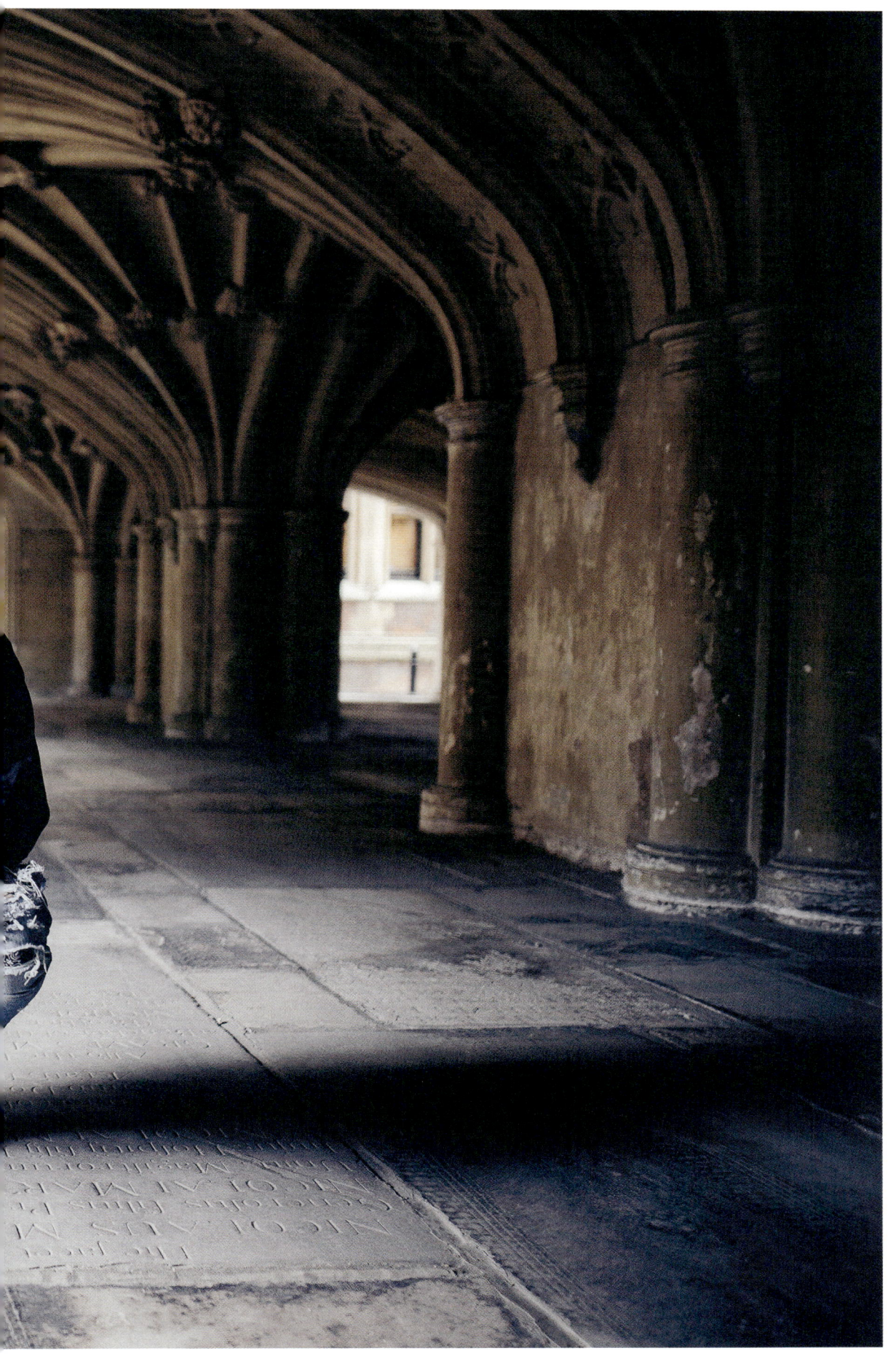

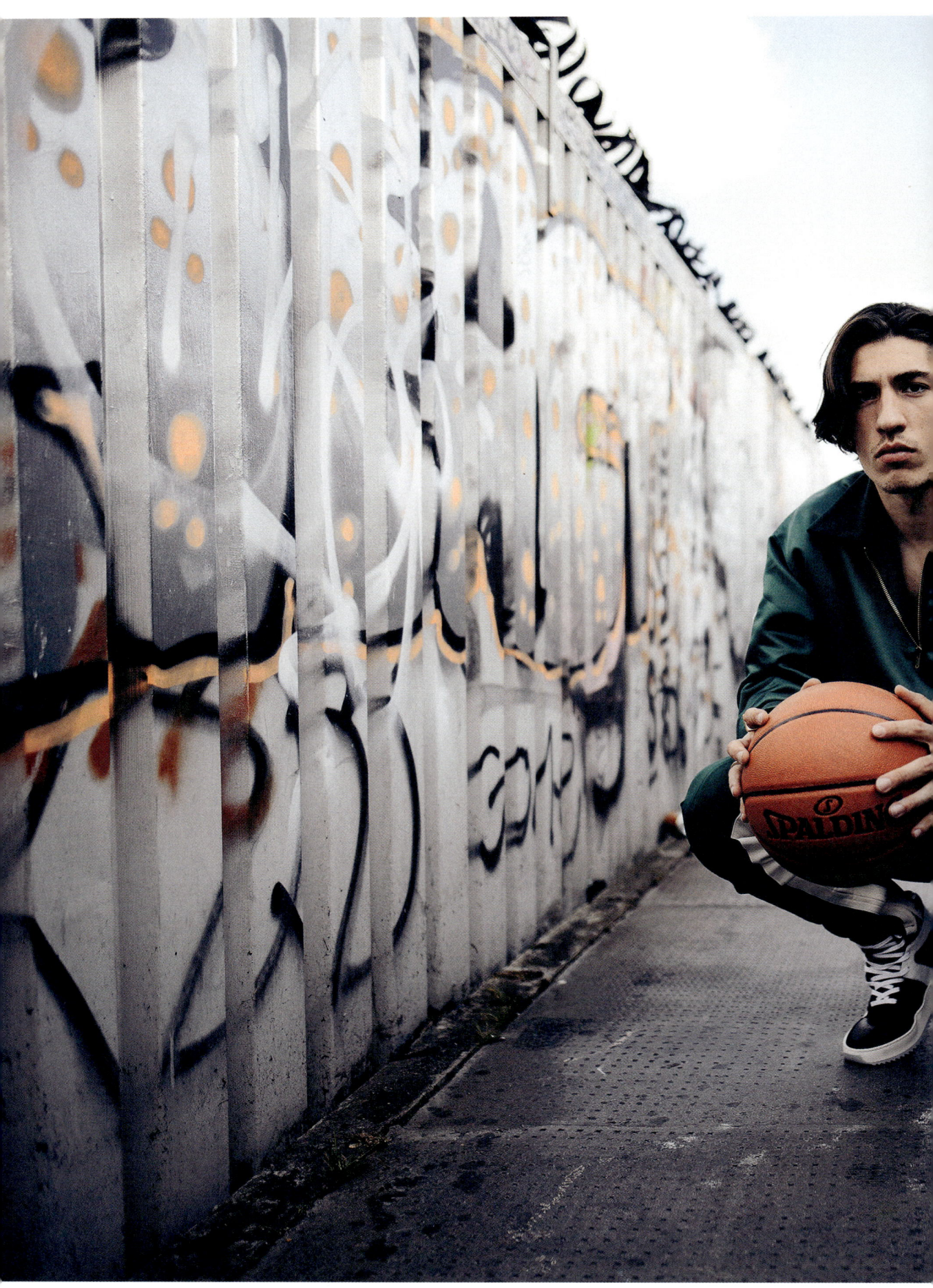

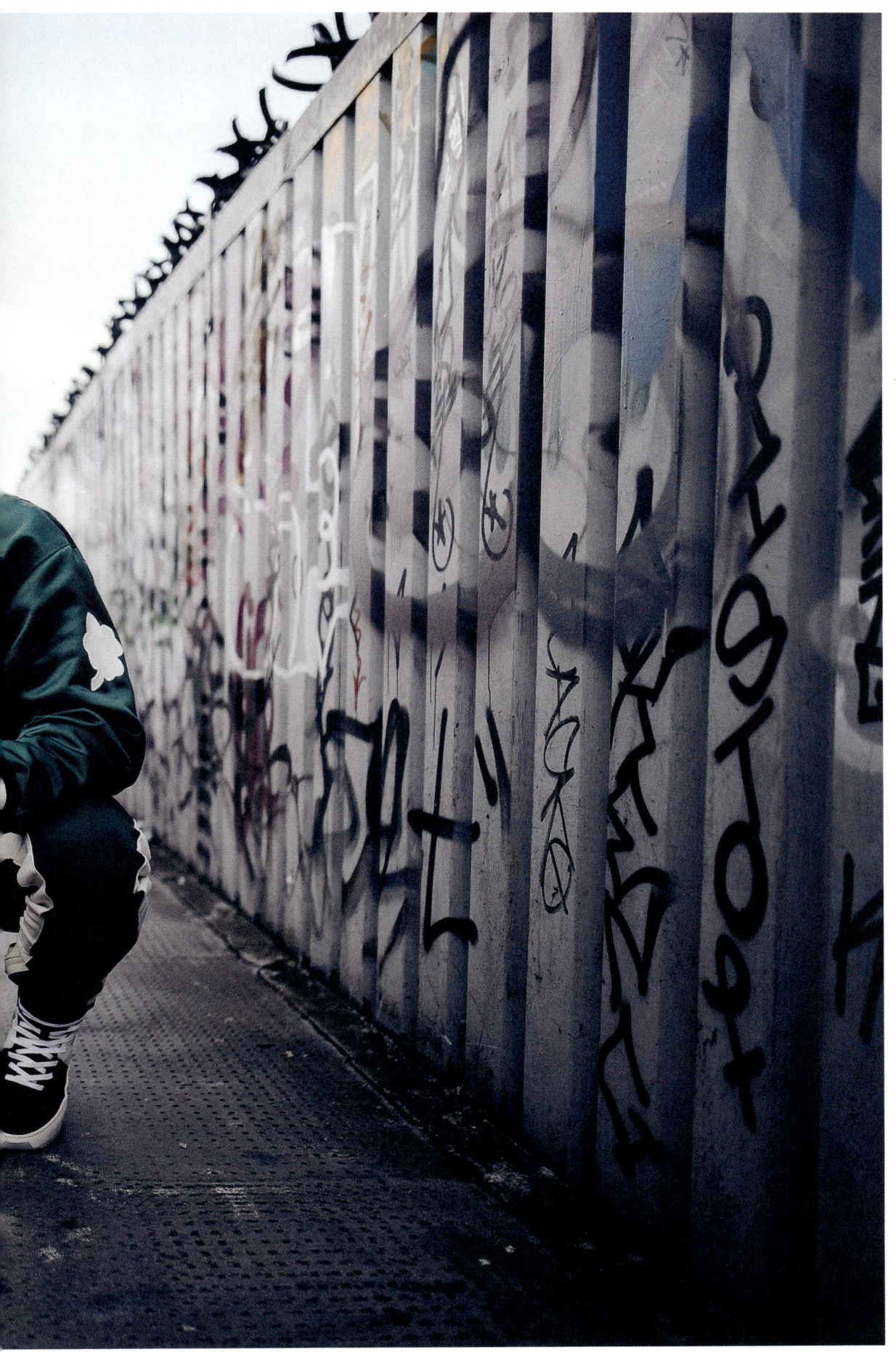

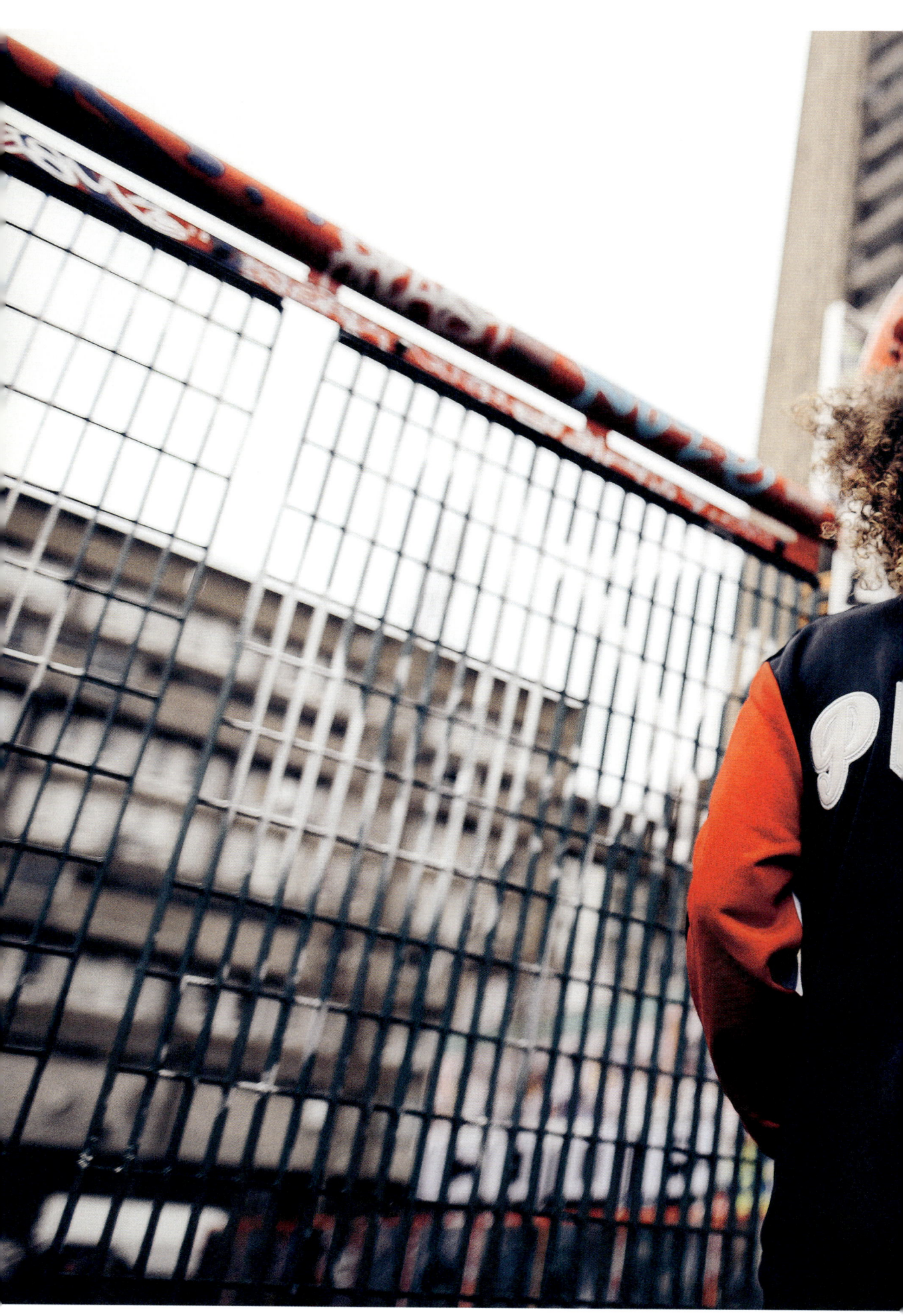

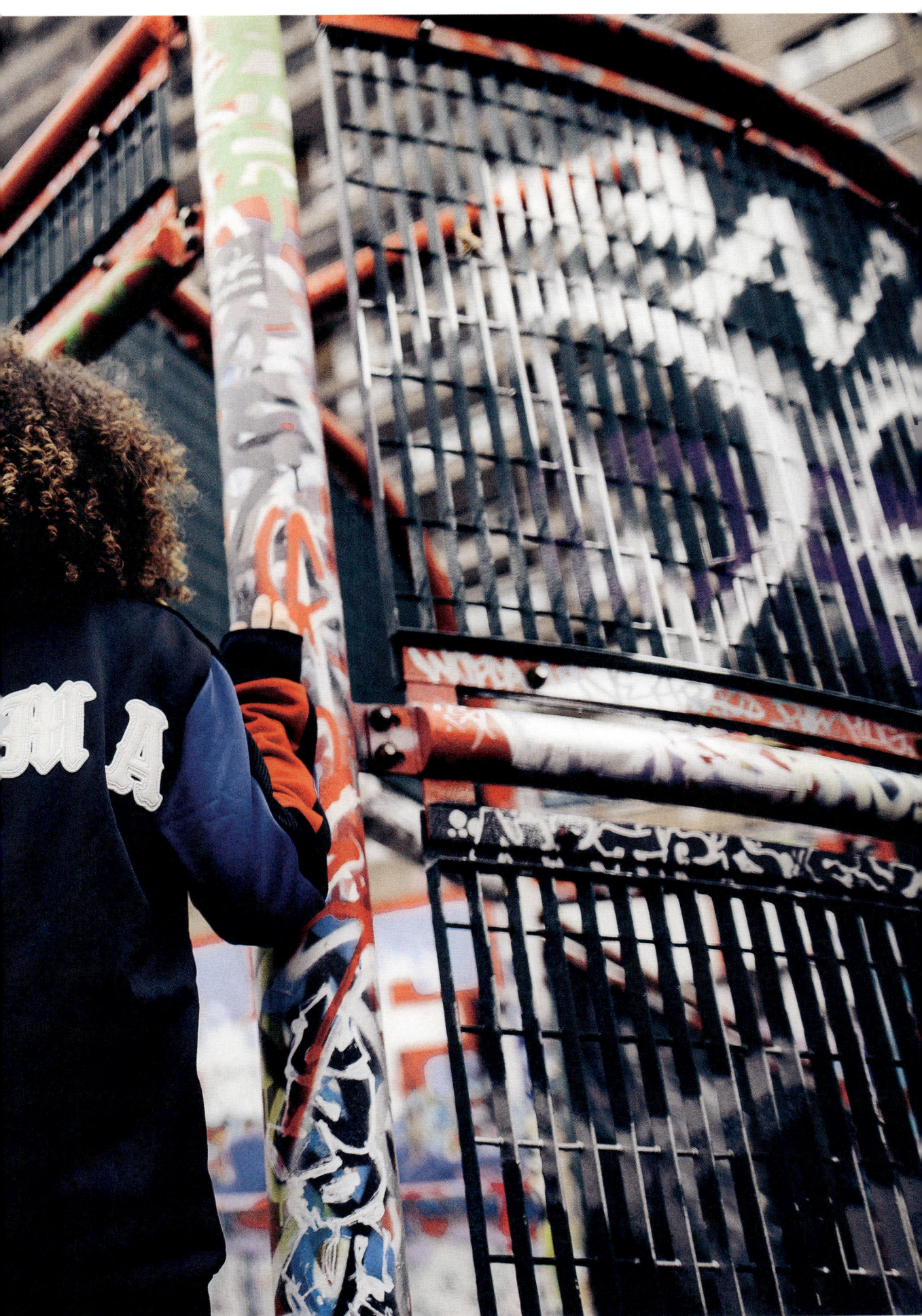

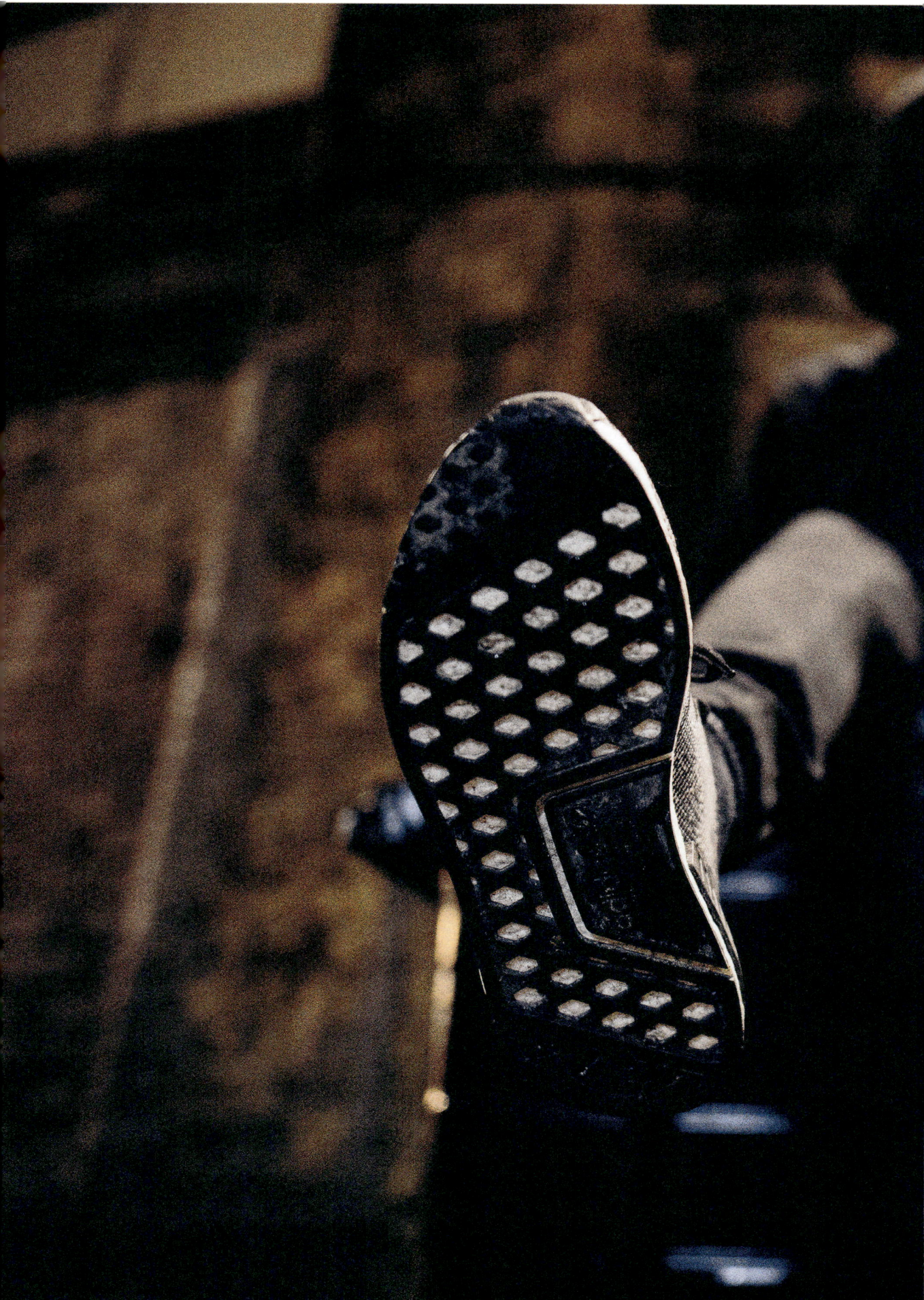

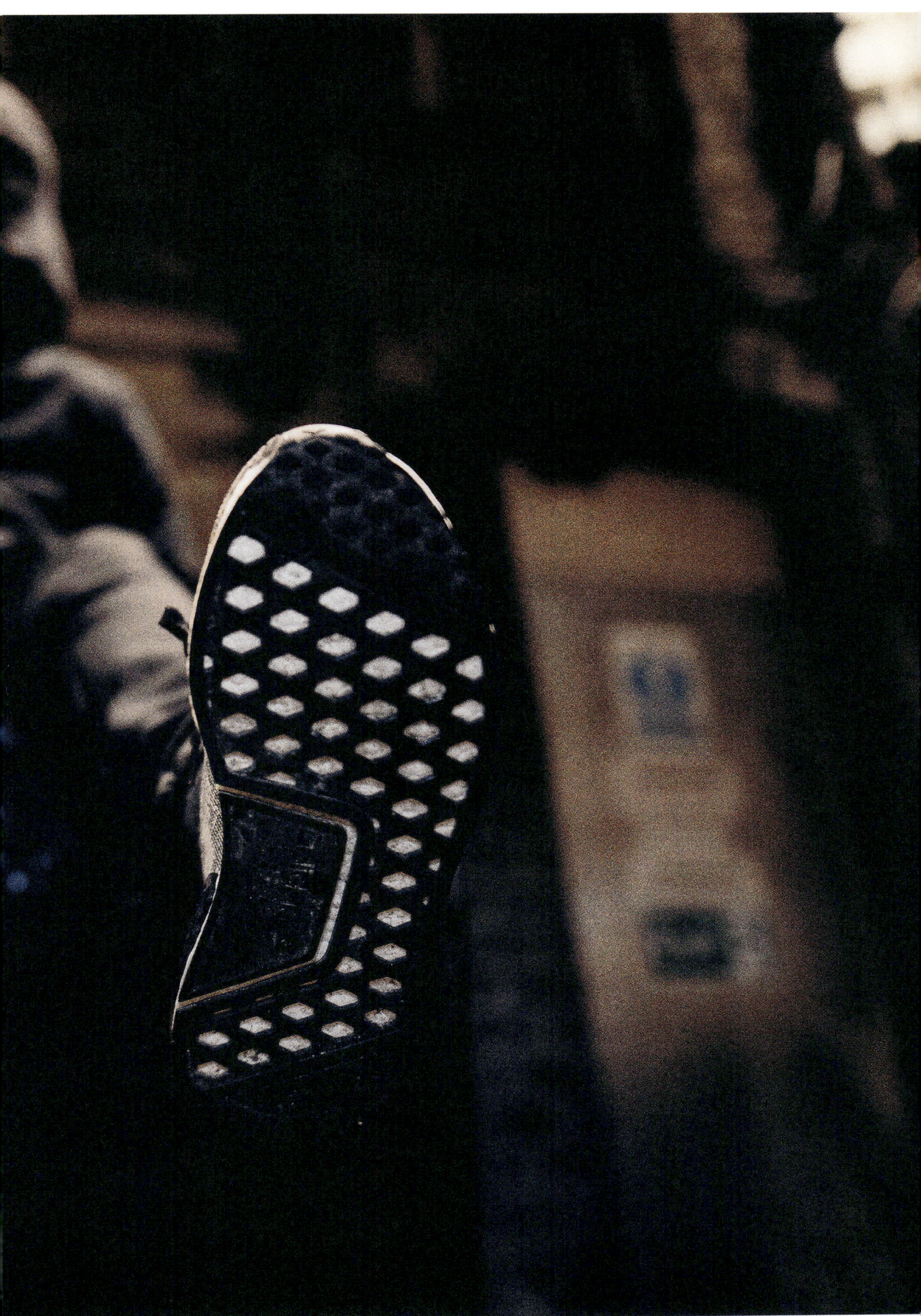

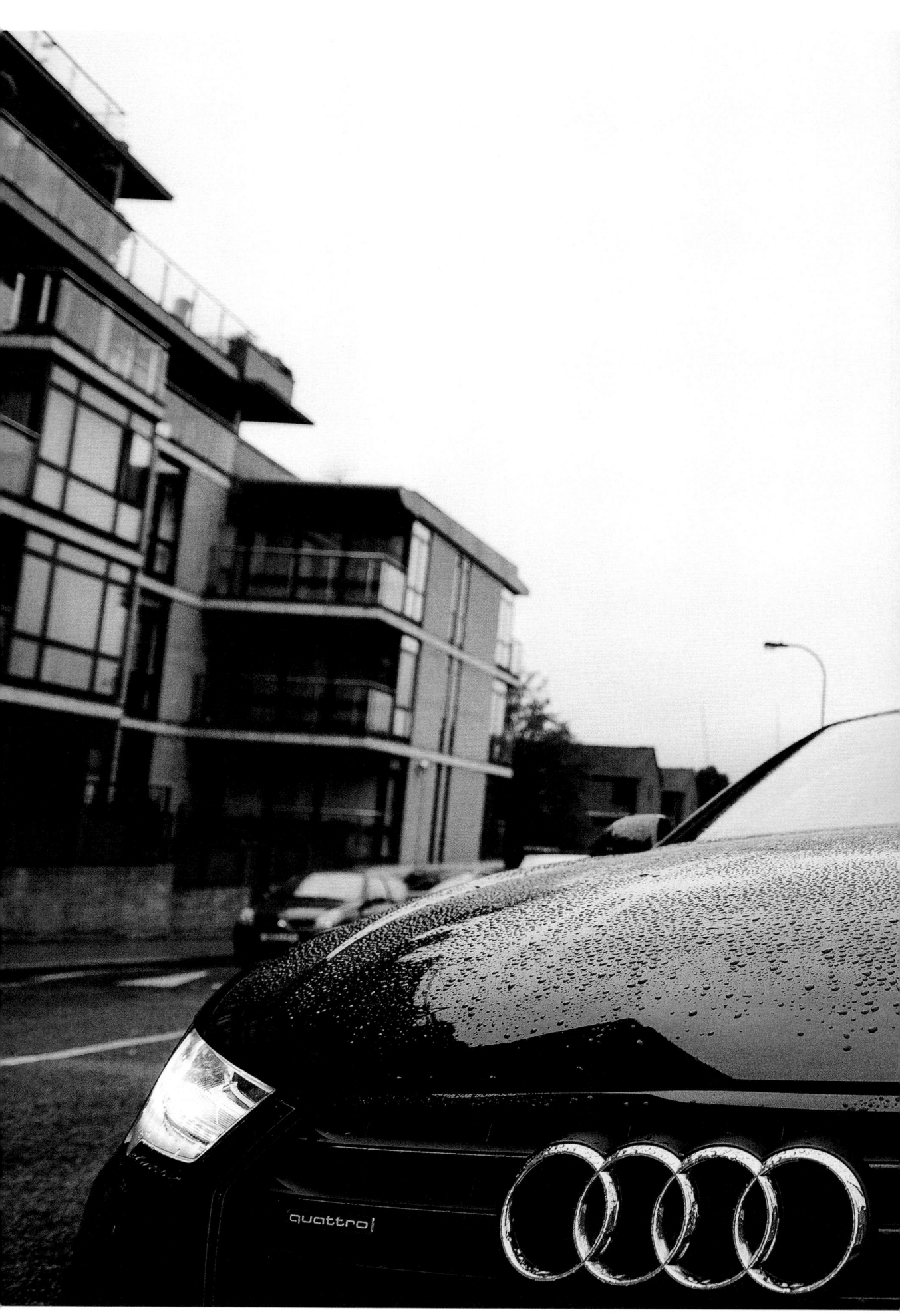

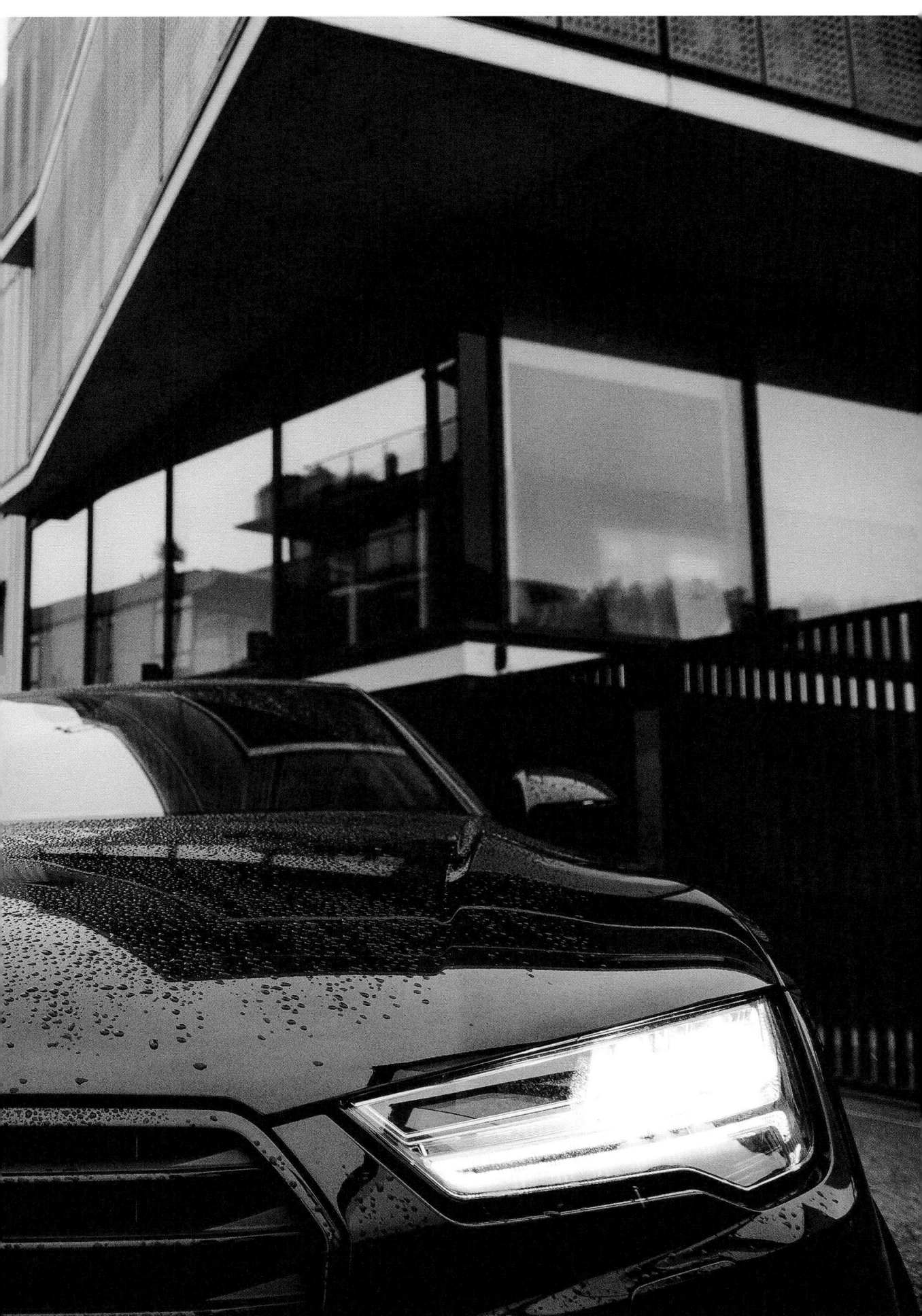

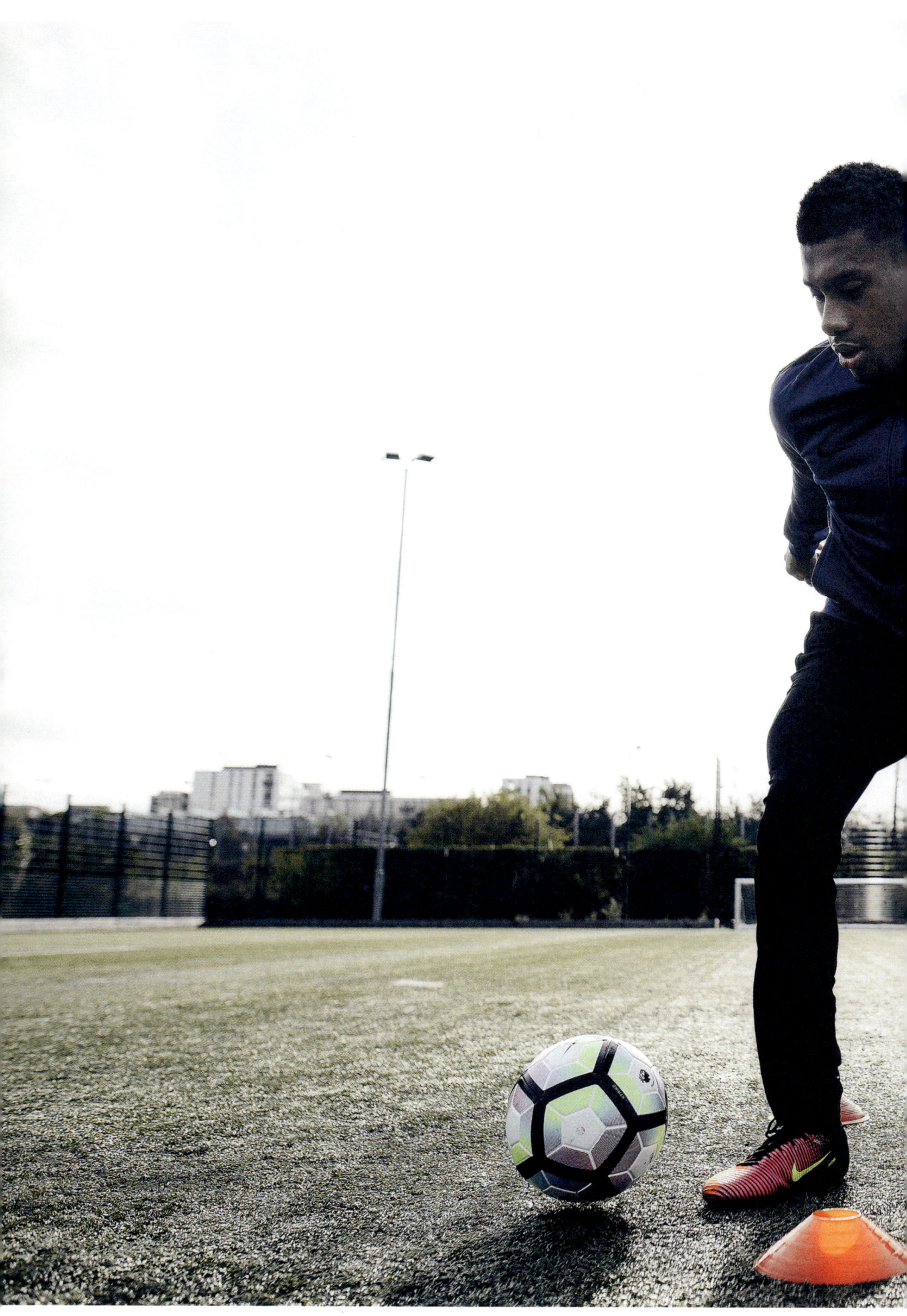

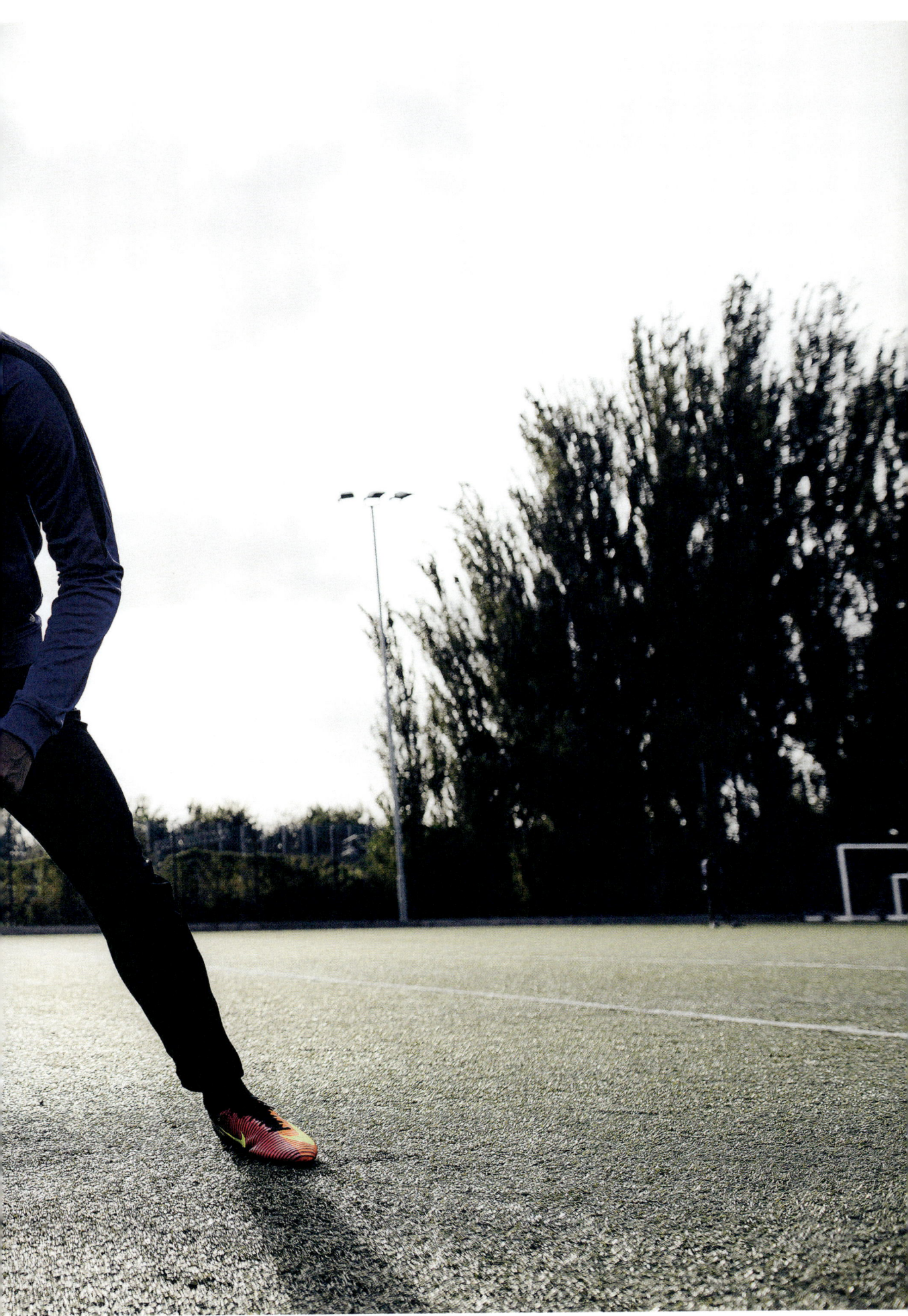

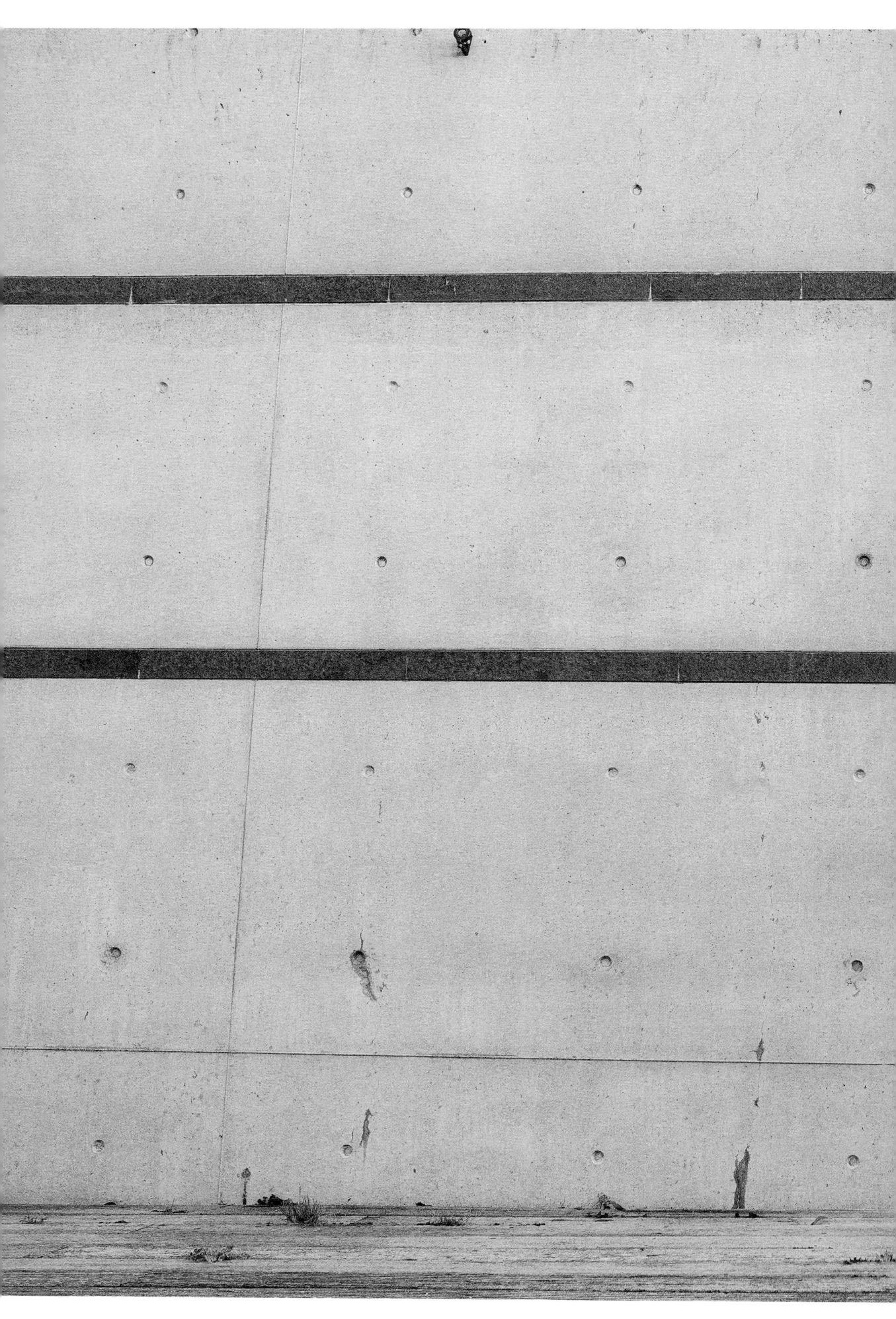

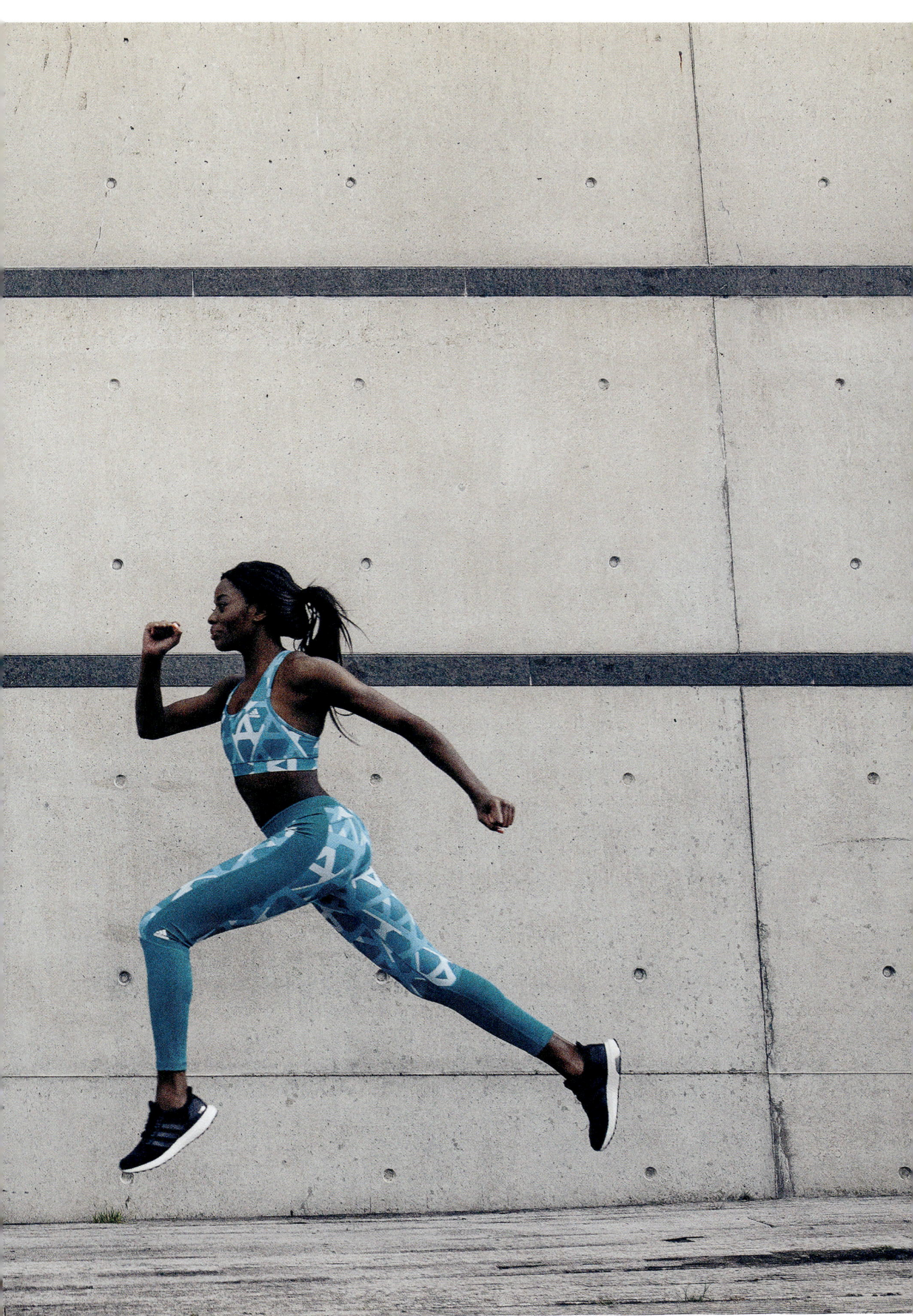

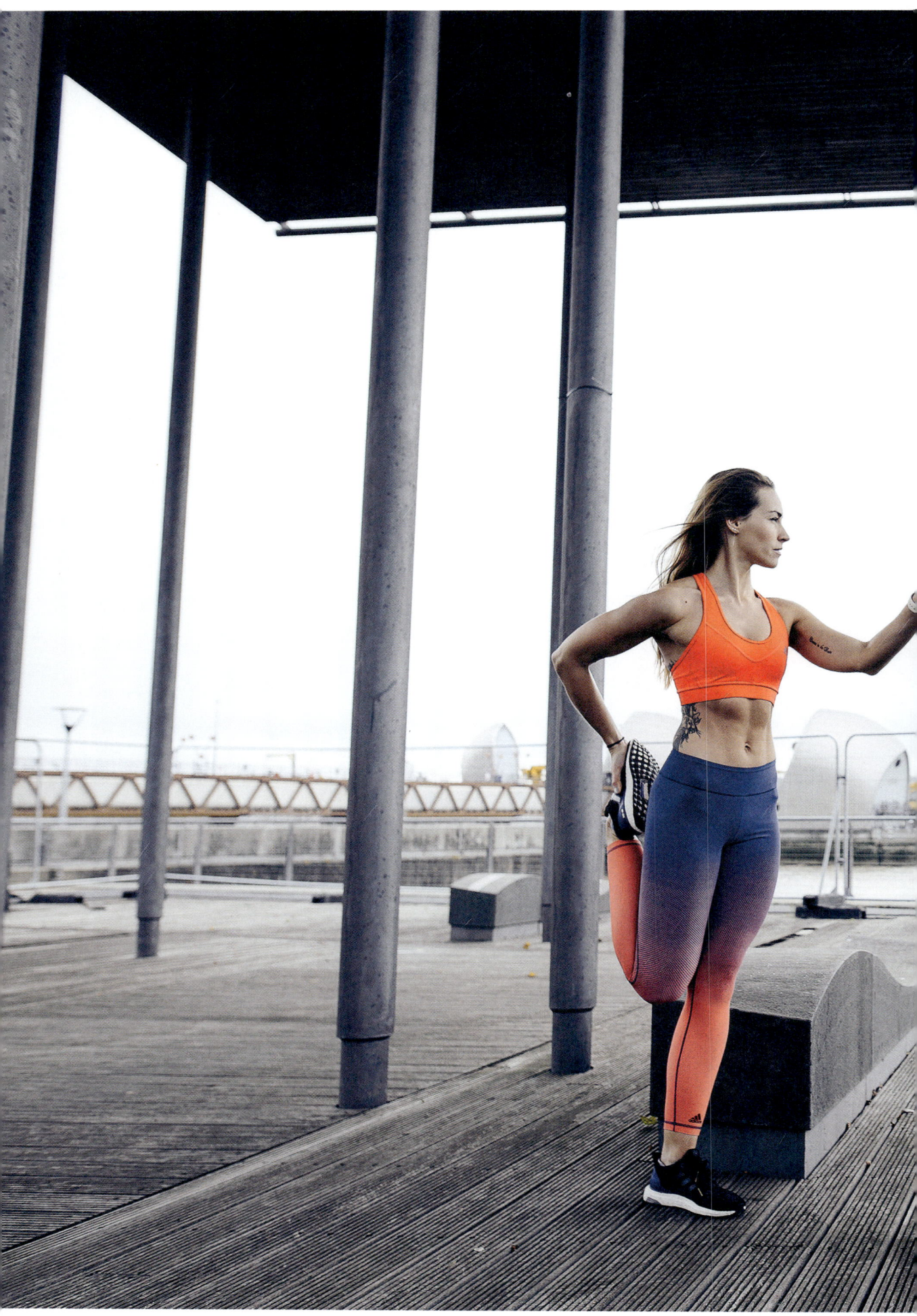

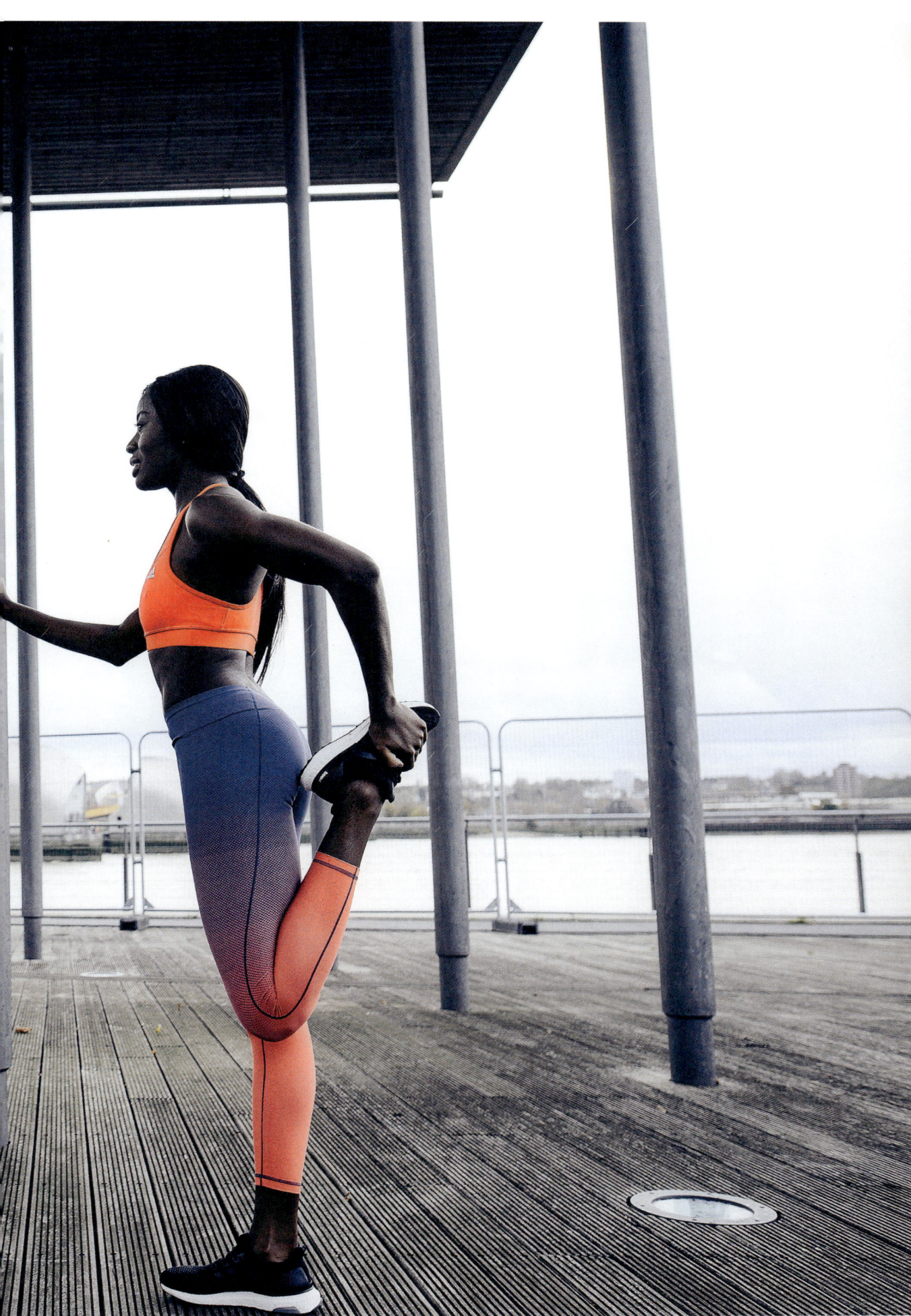

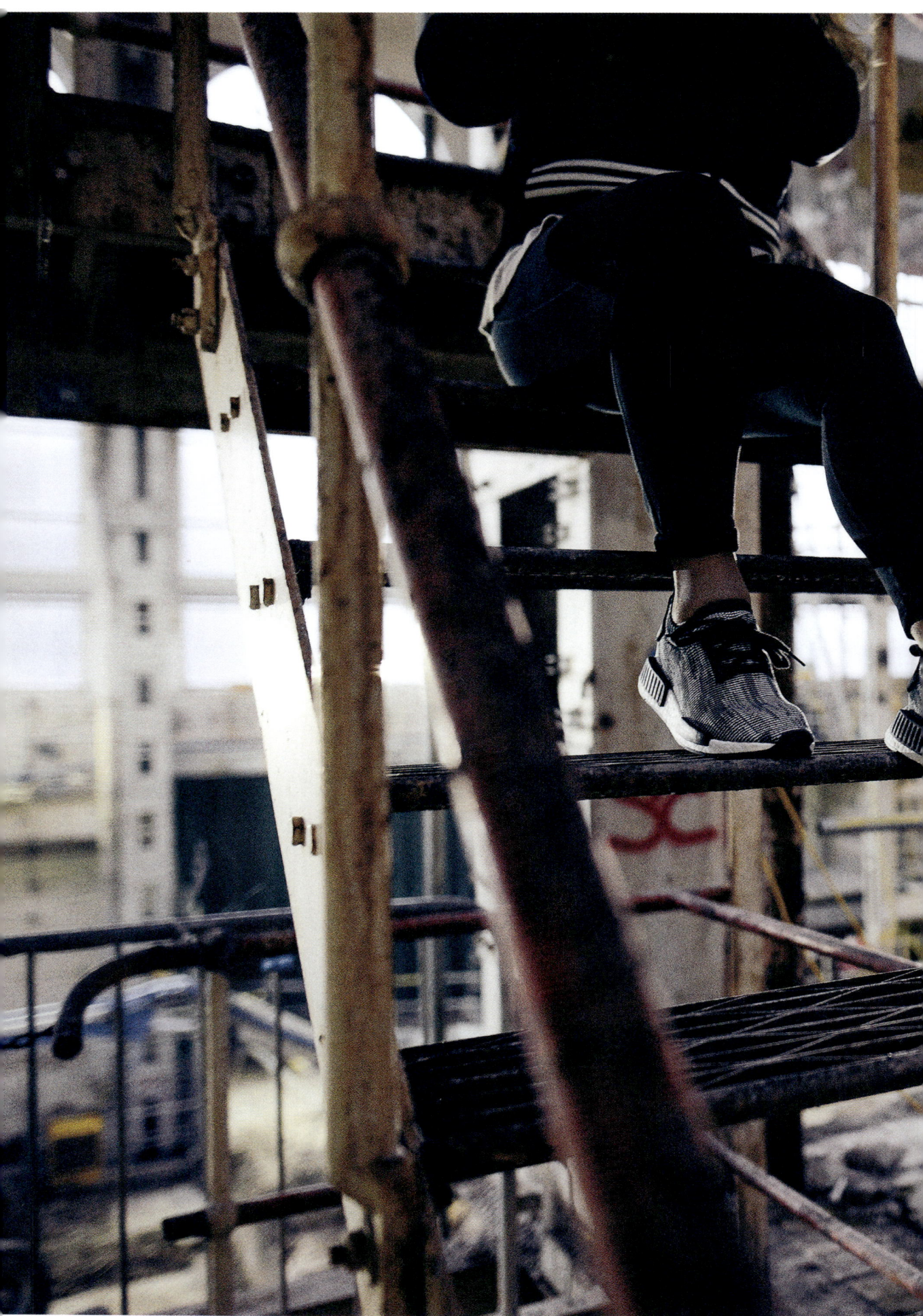

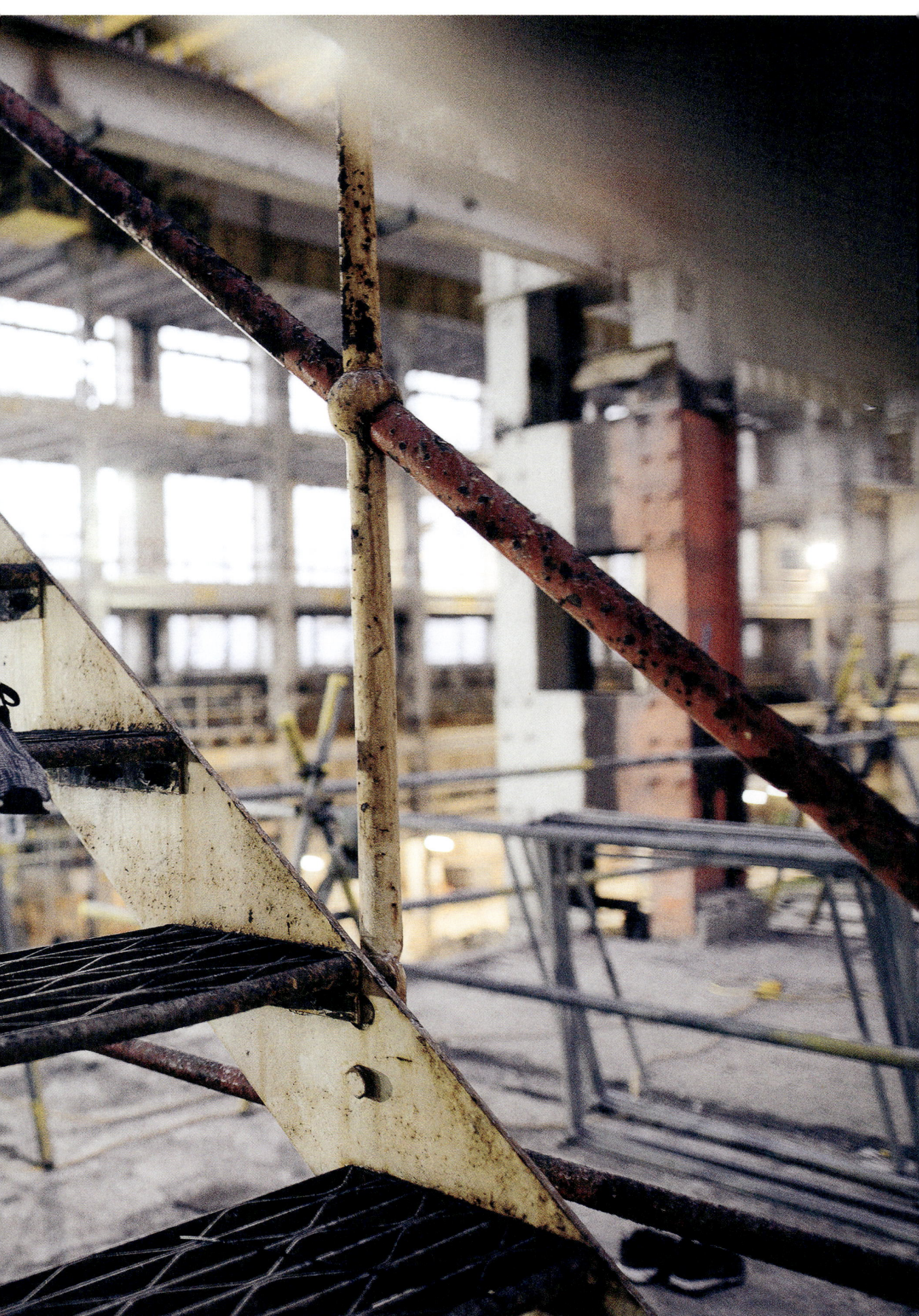

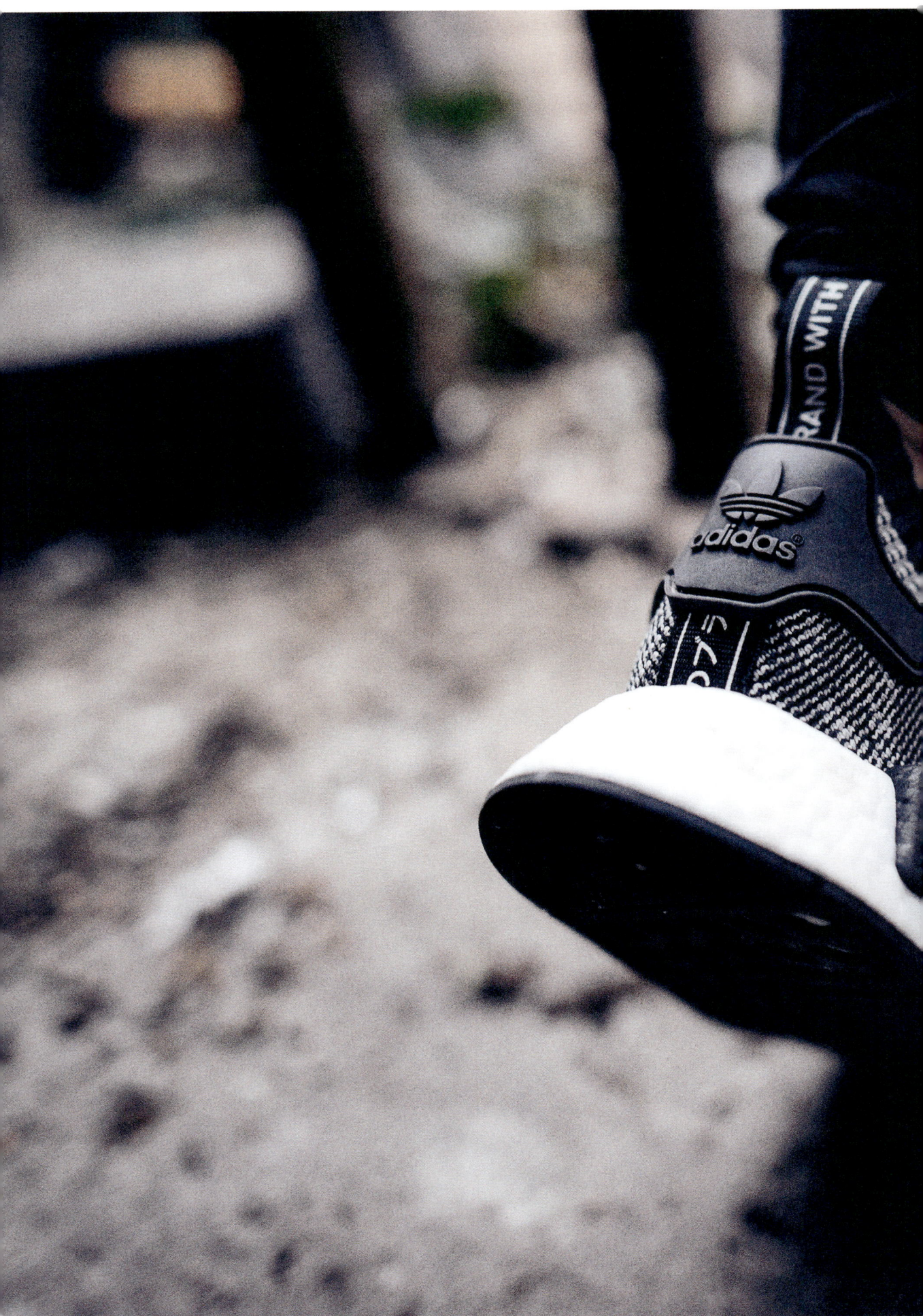

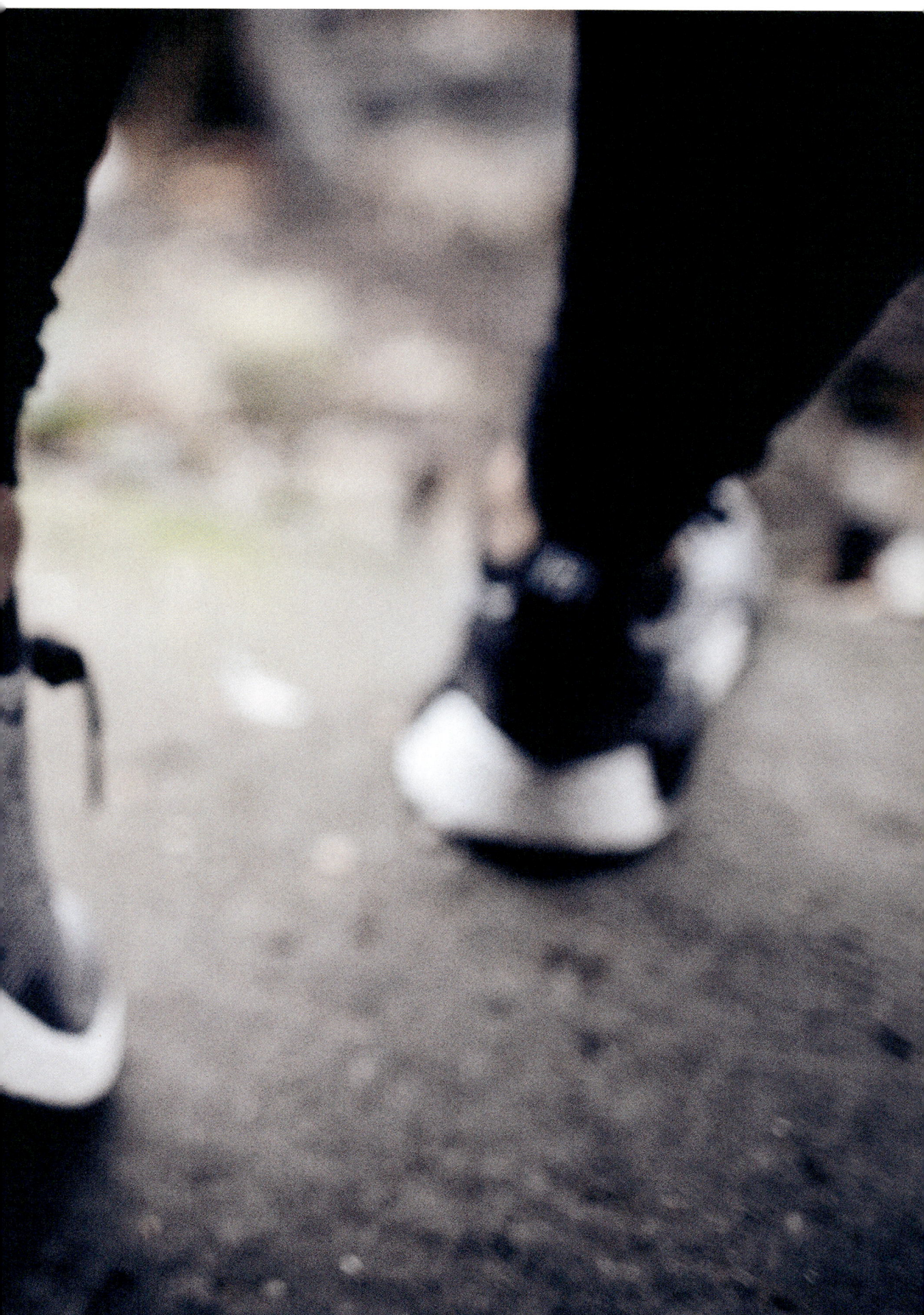

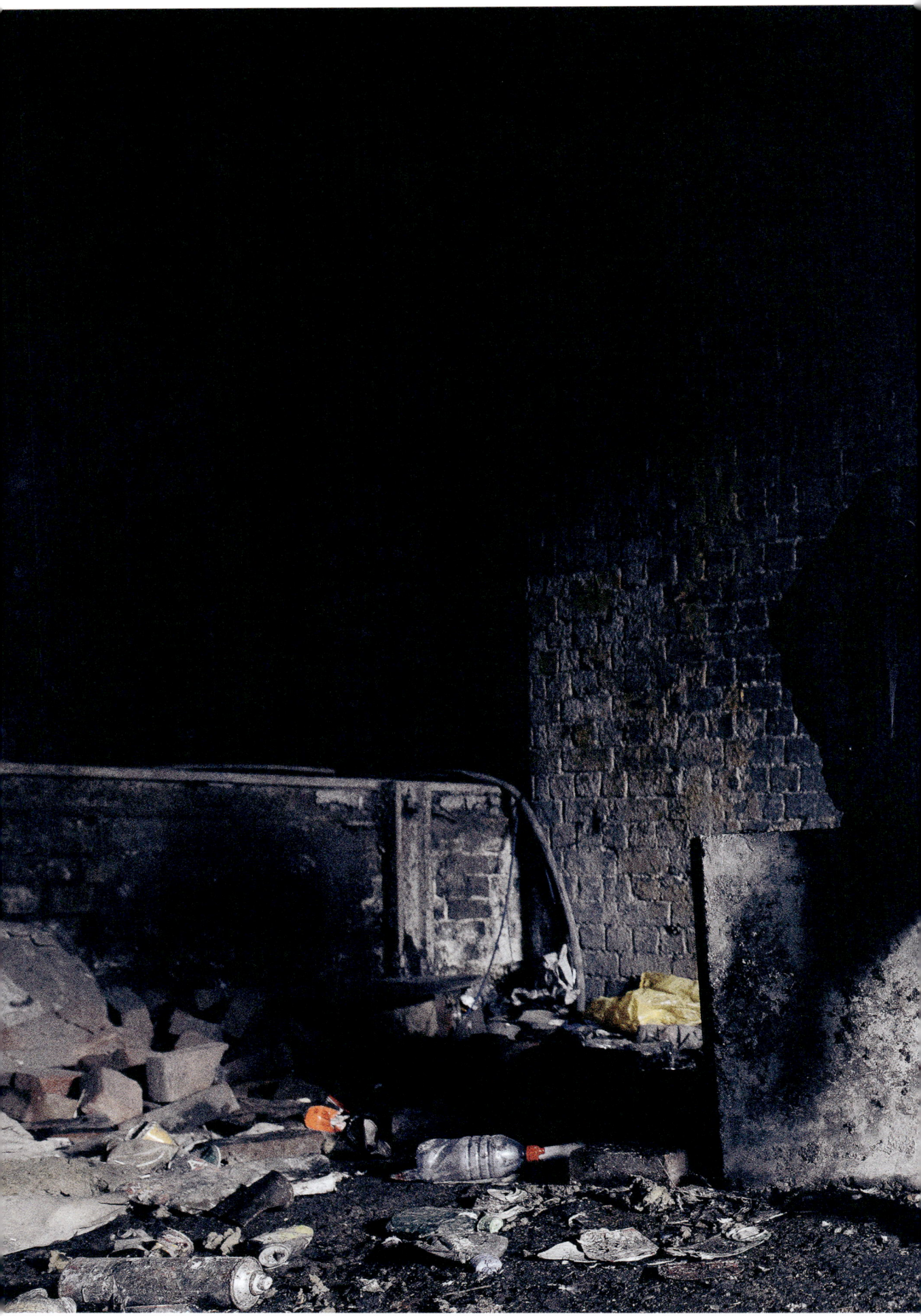

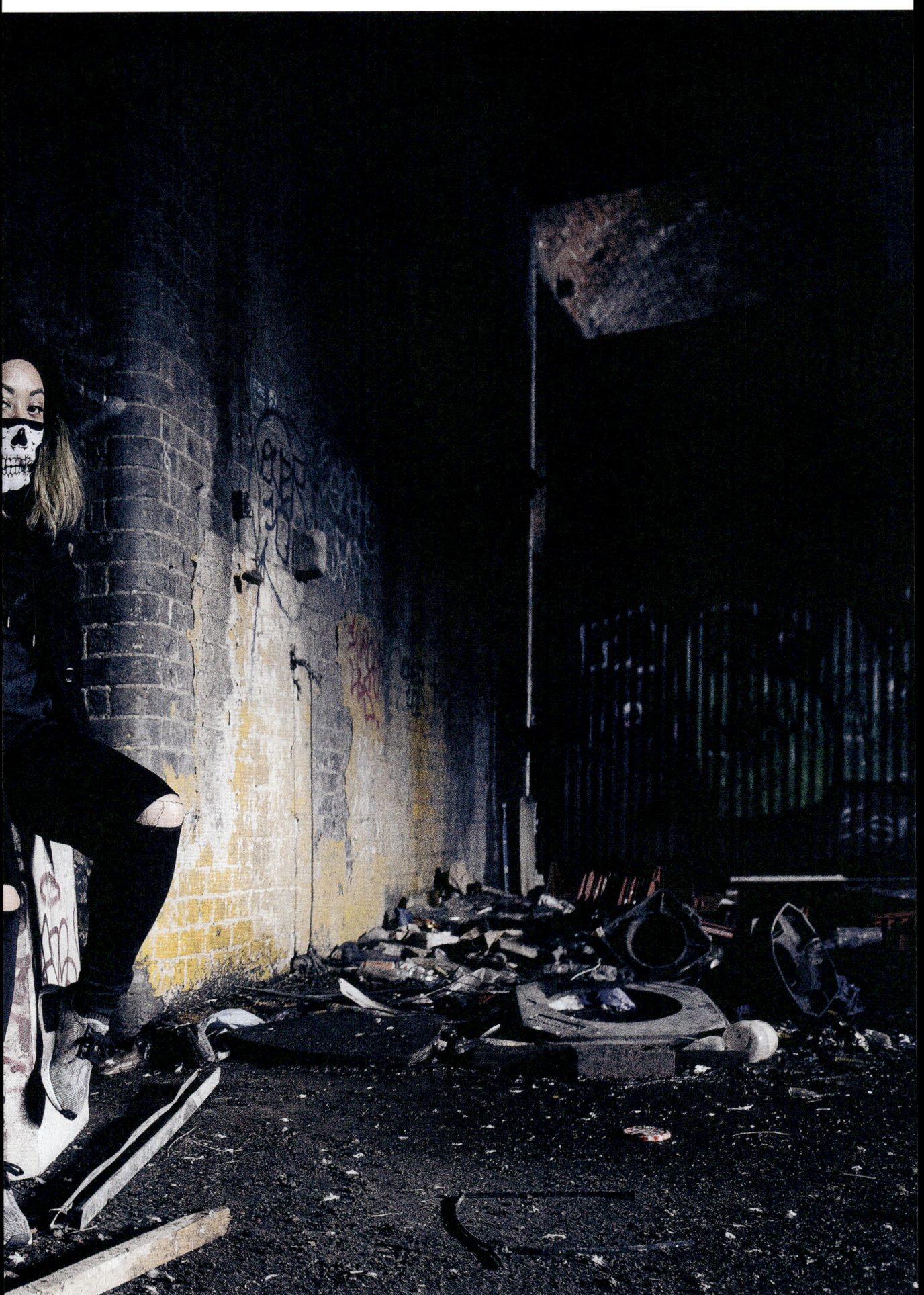

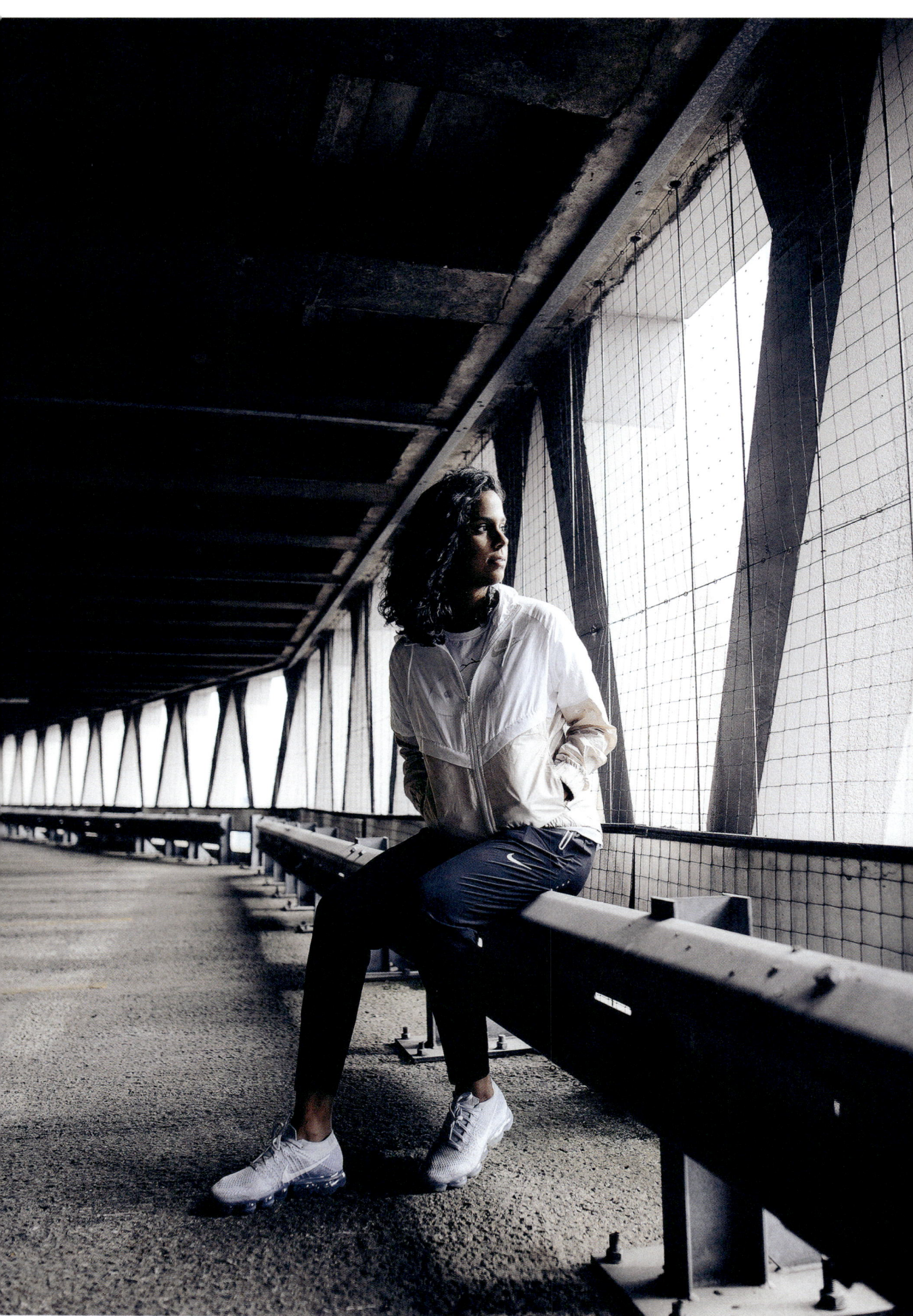

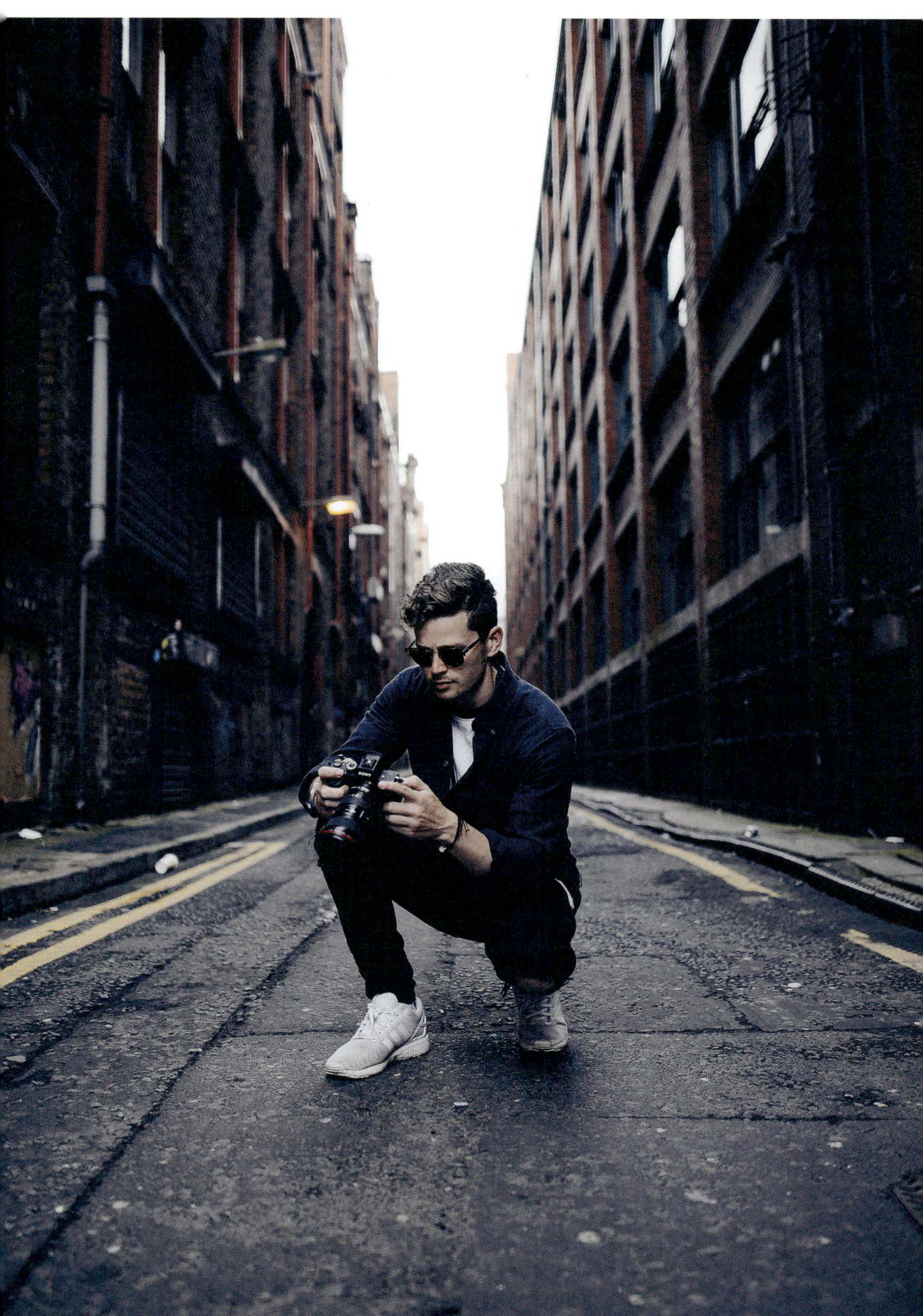

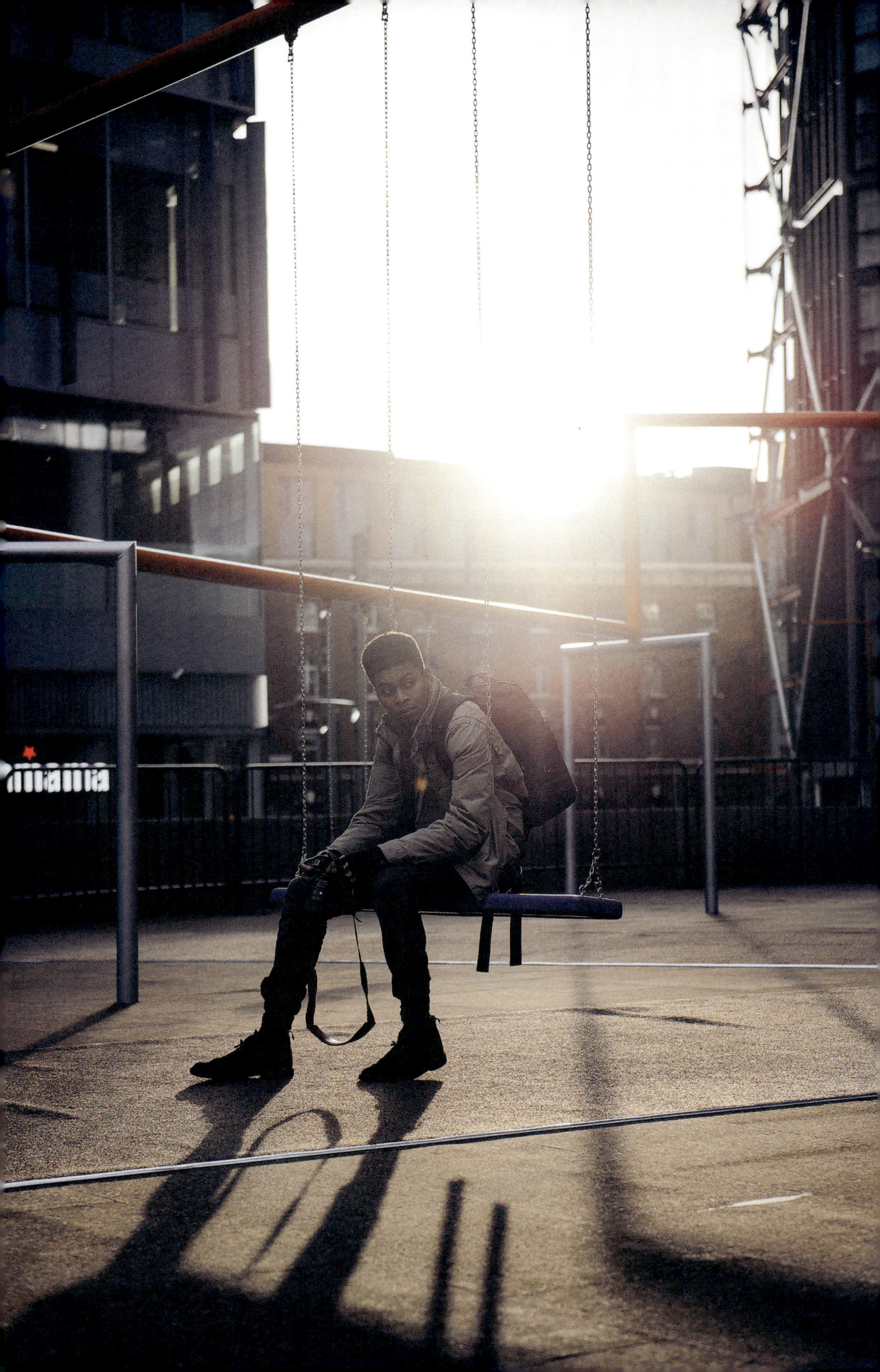

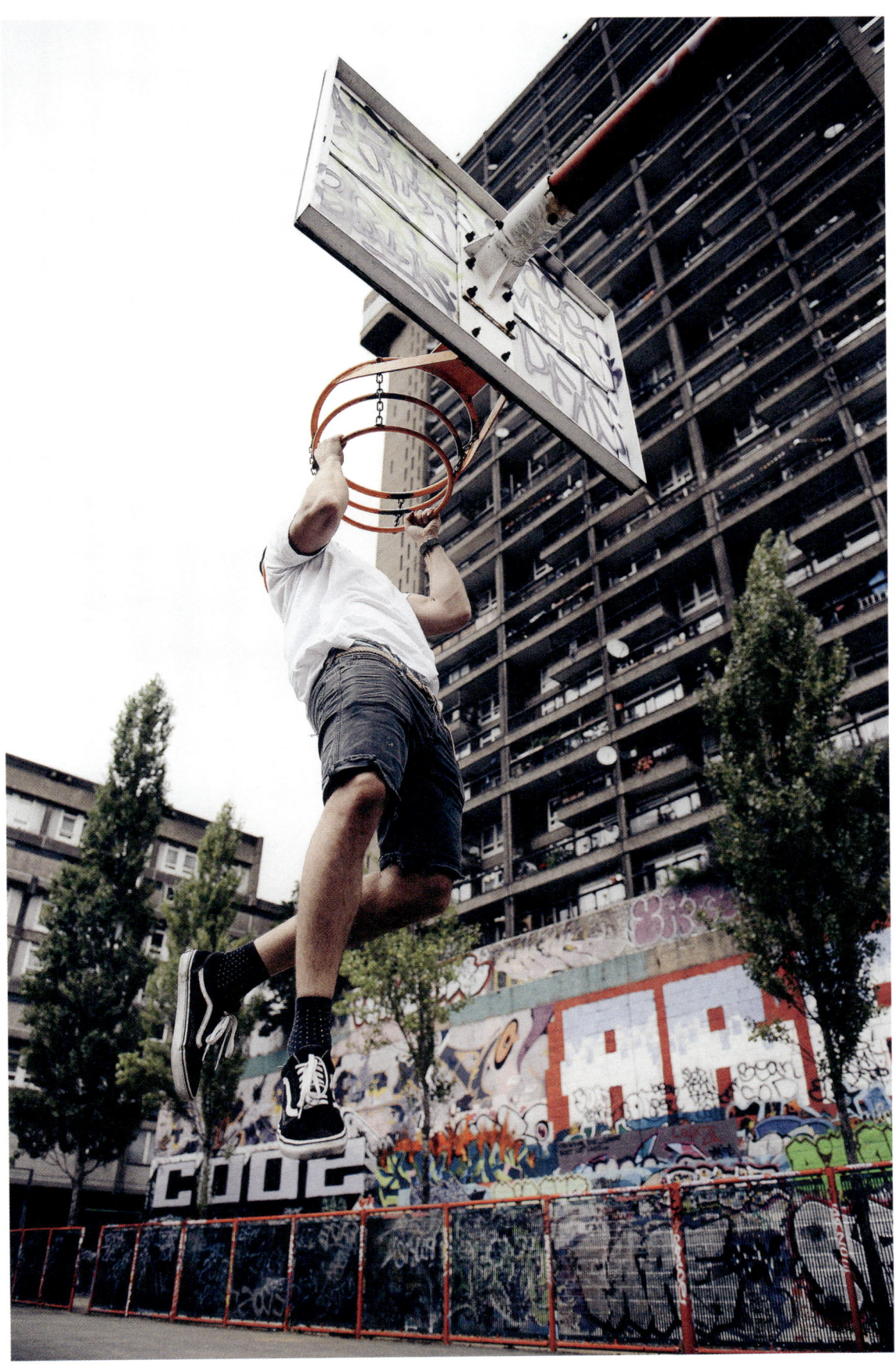

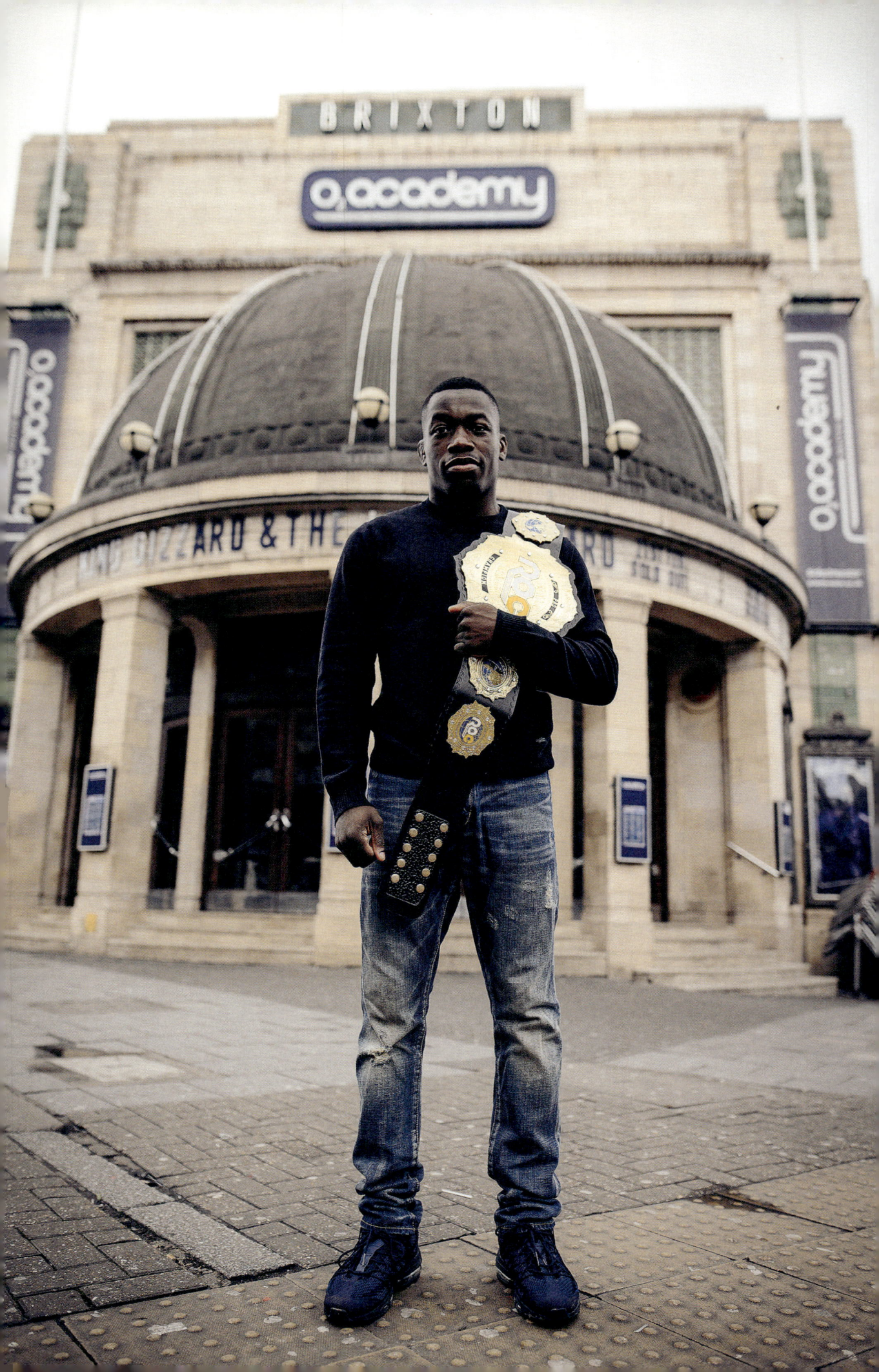

THE ONLY IMPOSSIBLE JOURNEY IS THE ONE YOU NEVER BEGIN

WE
CARRY
INSIDE US
THE WONDERS
WE SEEK
OUTSIDE
US

@GREATARSENAL

OPE ODUEYUNGBO

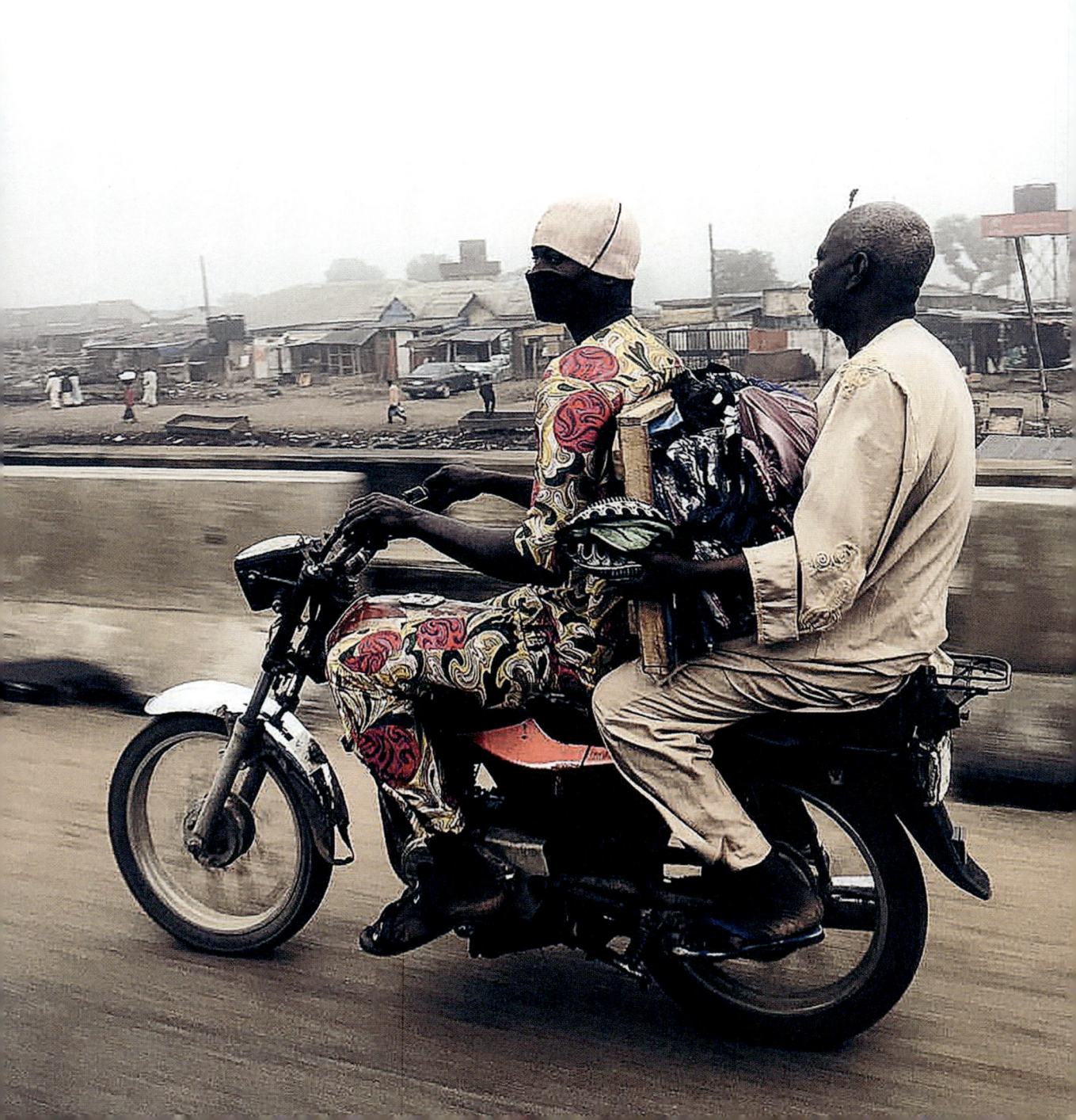

FROM NIGERIA WITH LOVE

I will never forget my first experience in Nigeria, for so many reasons! Not quite sure why I didn't visit sooner, considering it's the birthplace of both my parents. But I was super excited to finally experience more of the culture and traditions I was taught so much about during my childhood.

Growing up in London, my siblings and I would always speak to our grandmother, so I was accustomed to hearing her voice through the phone. Getting to see and talk with my grandmother face-to-face for the first time was a really good feeling, as well as getting to photograph her in her element.

When it came to exploring outdoors I was a little nervous, as I found that the locals almost knew I wasn't from the area before I could even open my mouth. I wasn't going to allow this to keep me from taking photographs, though. I did get a few looks of suspicion, but others were very welcoming. I wish I was able to explore and capture a lot more than I did, but I knew it wasn't going to be easy – it was my first time there, and I was required to meet family and friends nearly every day. I'll be sure to capture twice as much on my next visit!

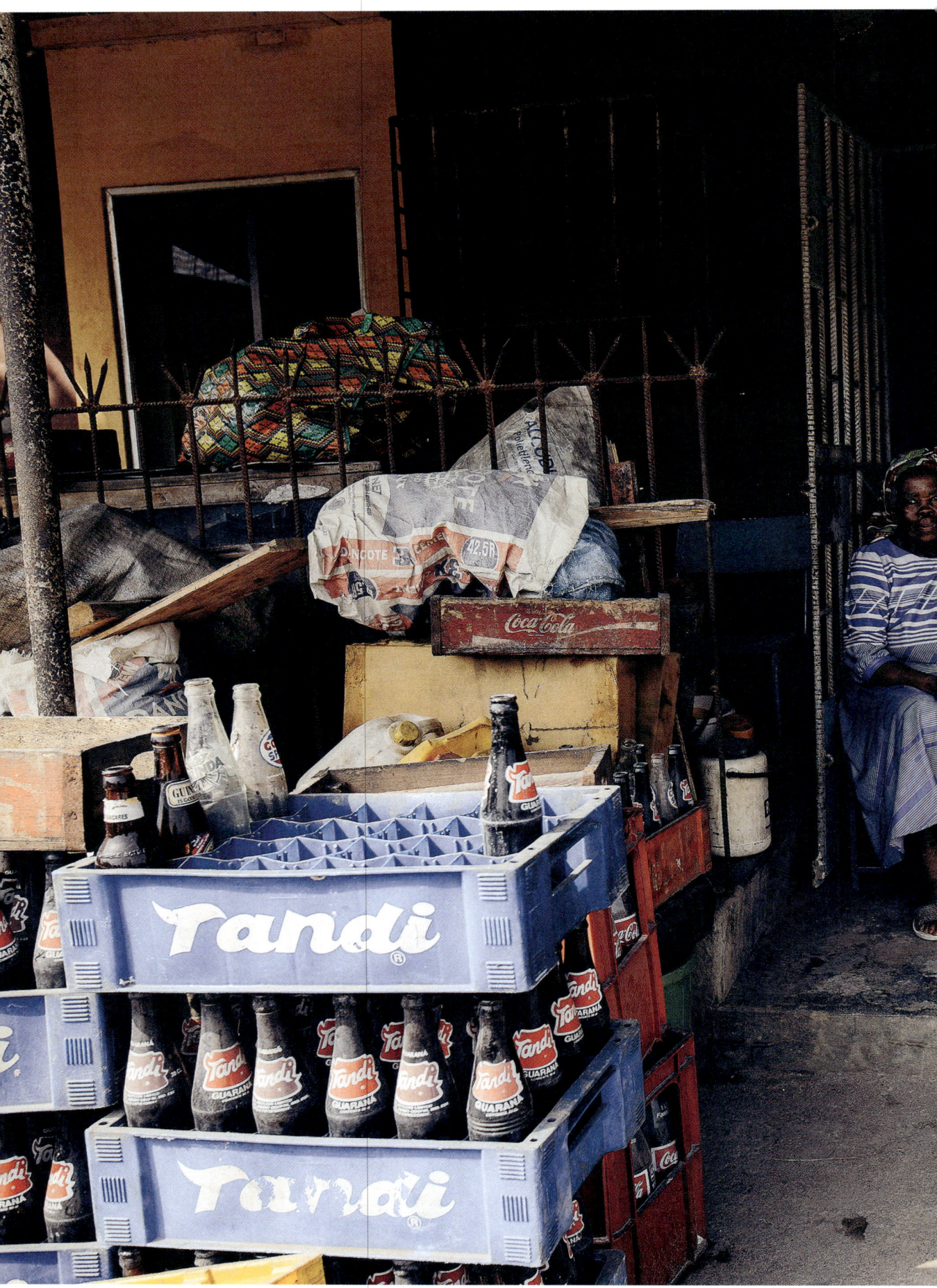

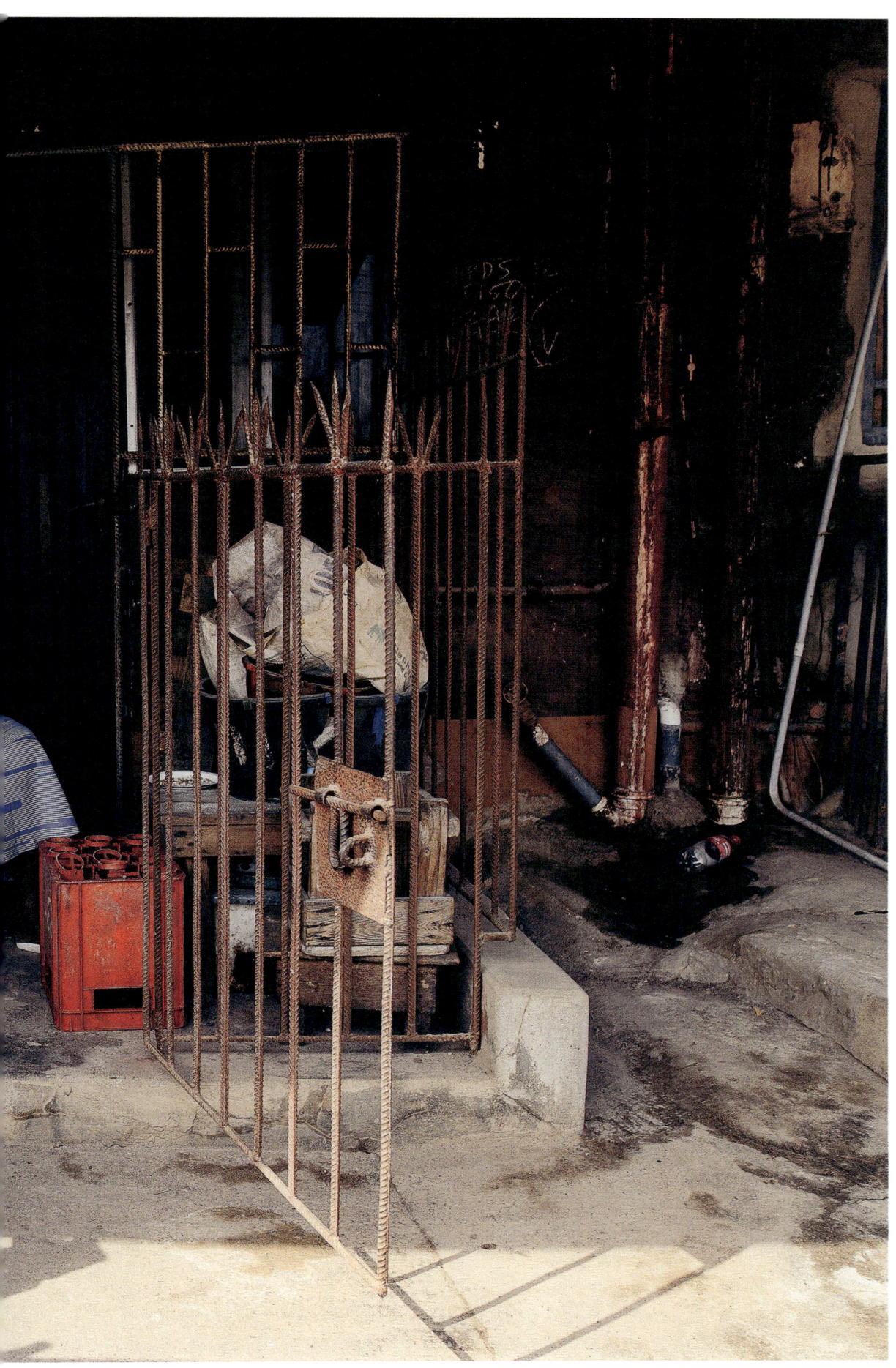

Very humbling to meet my grandmother for the very first time. It meant so much to me to see what she sees when she walks out of her door every day.

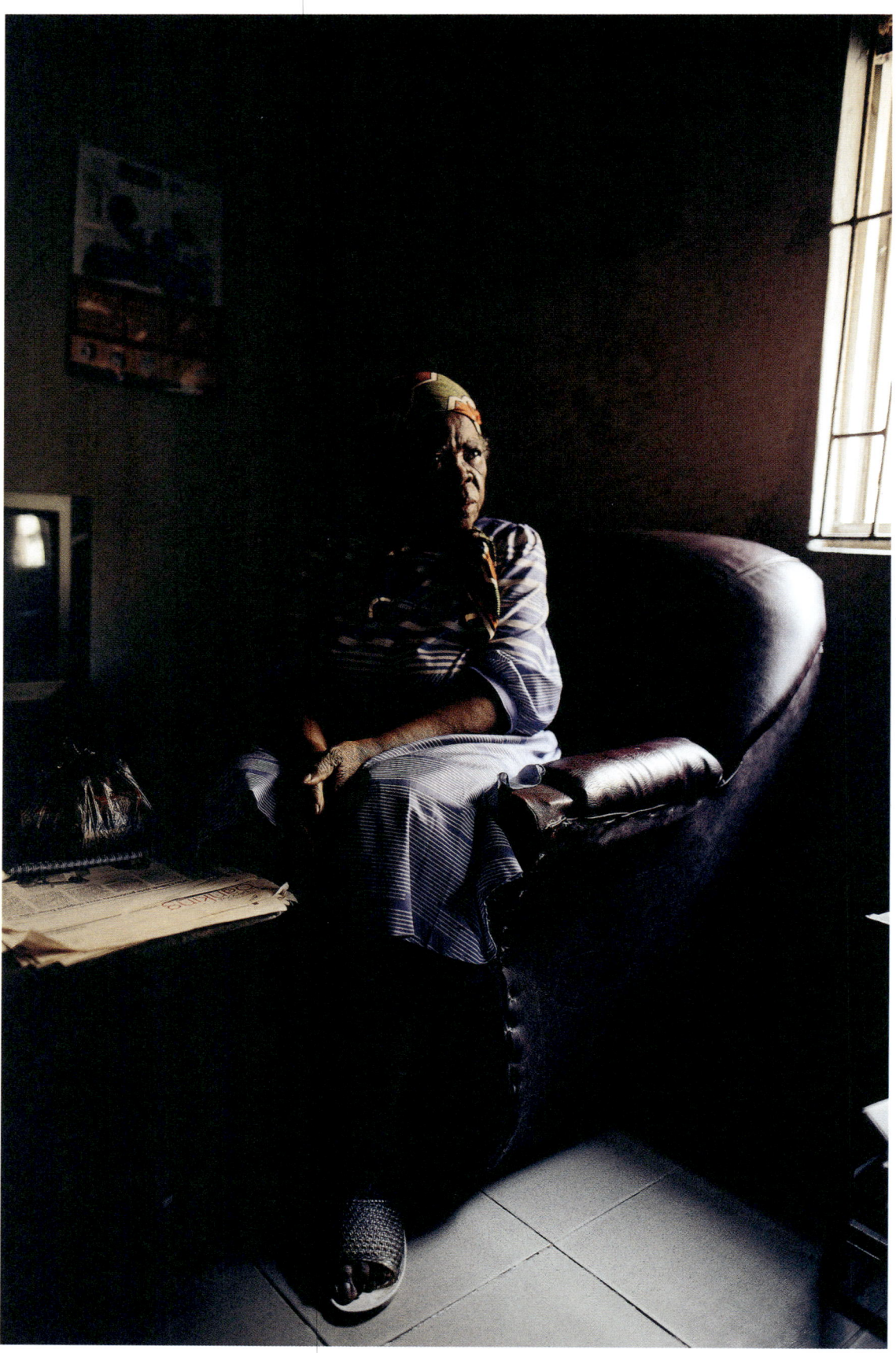

At peace, in her own home. I was struck by the way the light was shining on her, even in this dark corner.

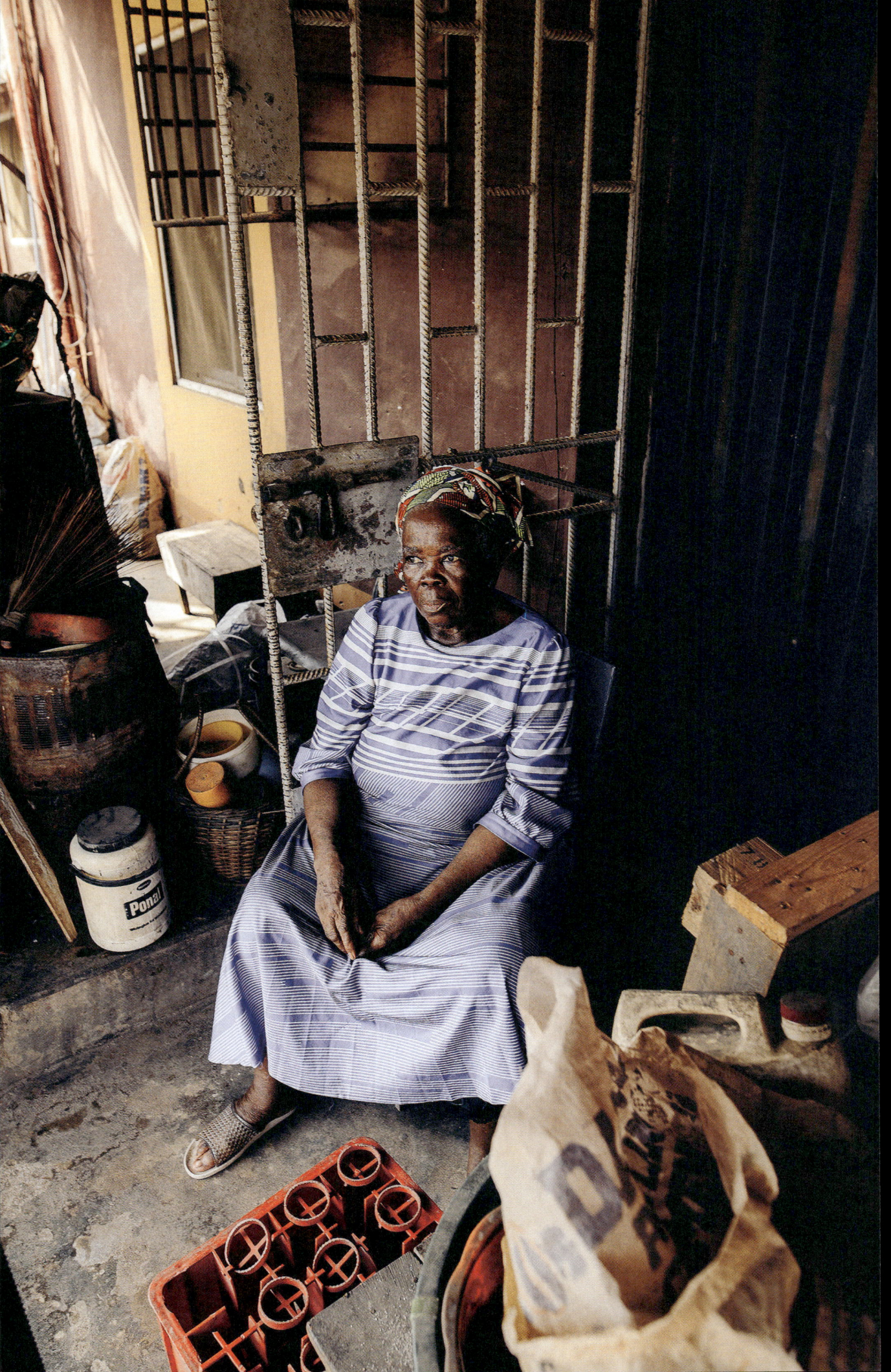

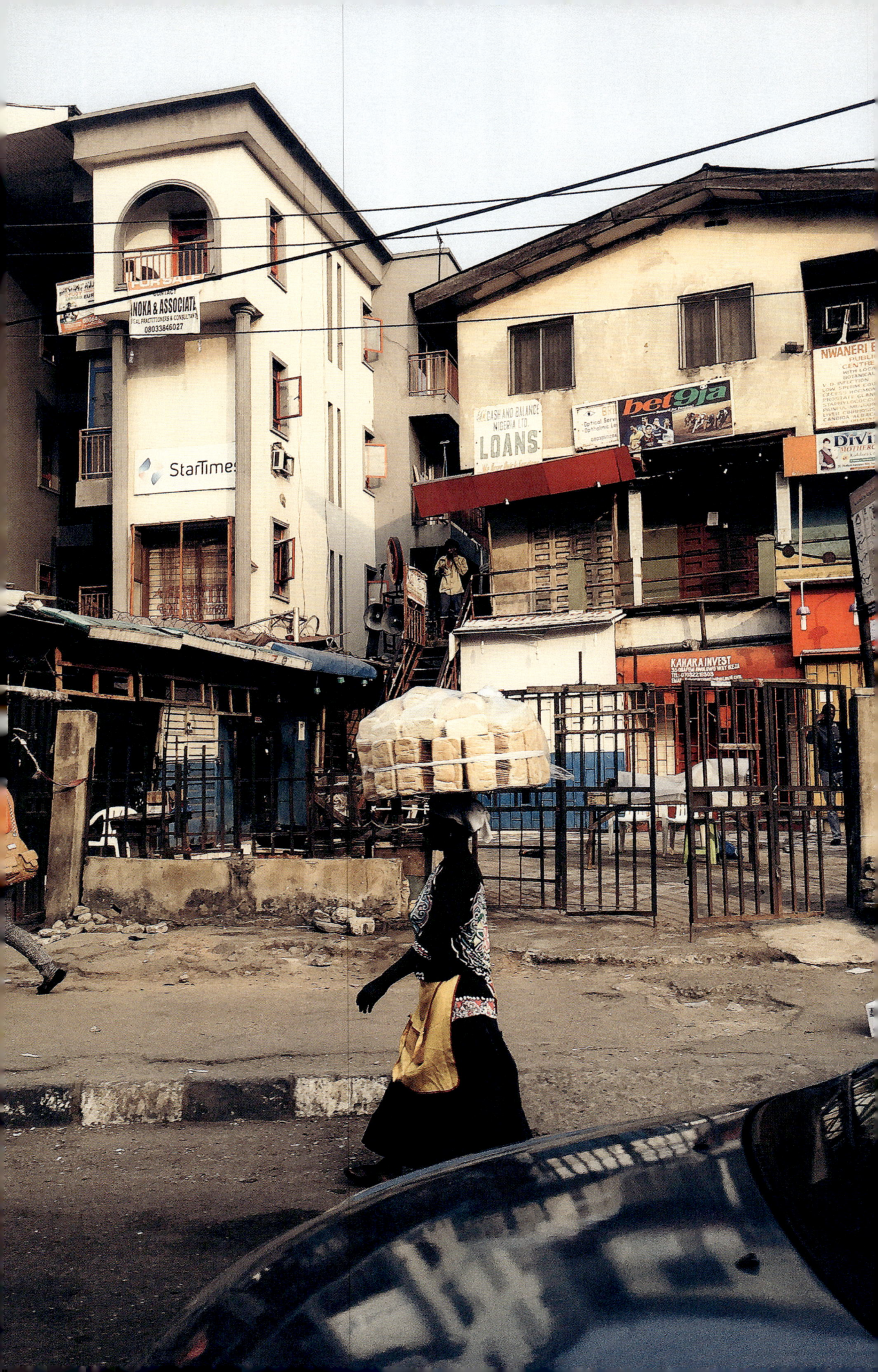

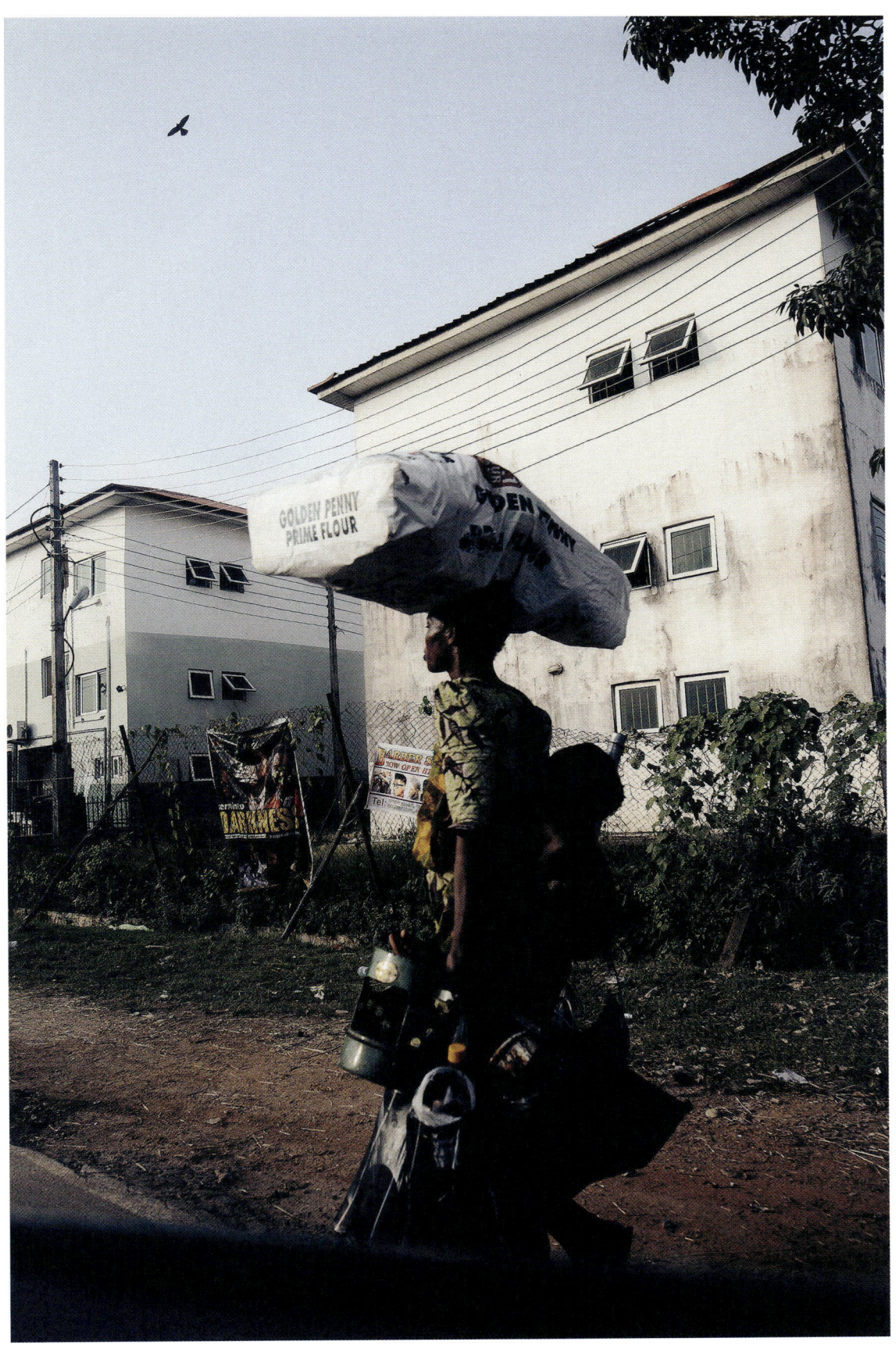

I spotted so many hardworking women walking the streets in conditions that couldn't have been easy. I respect and admire the strength and determination.

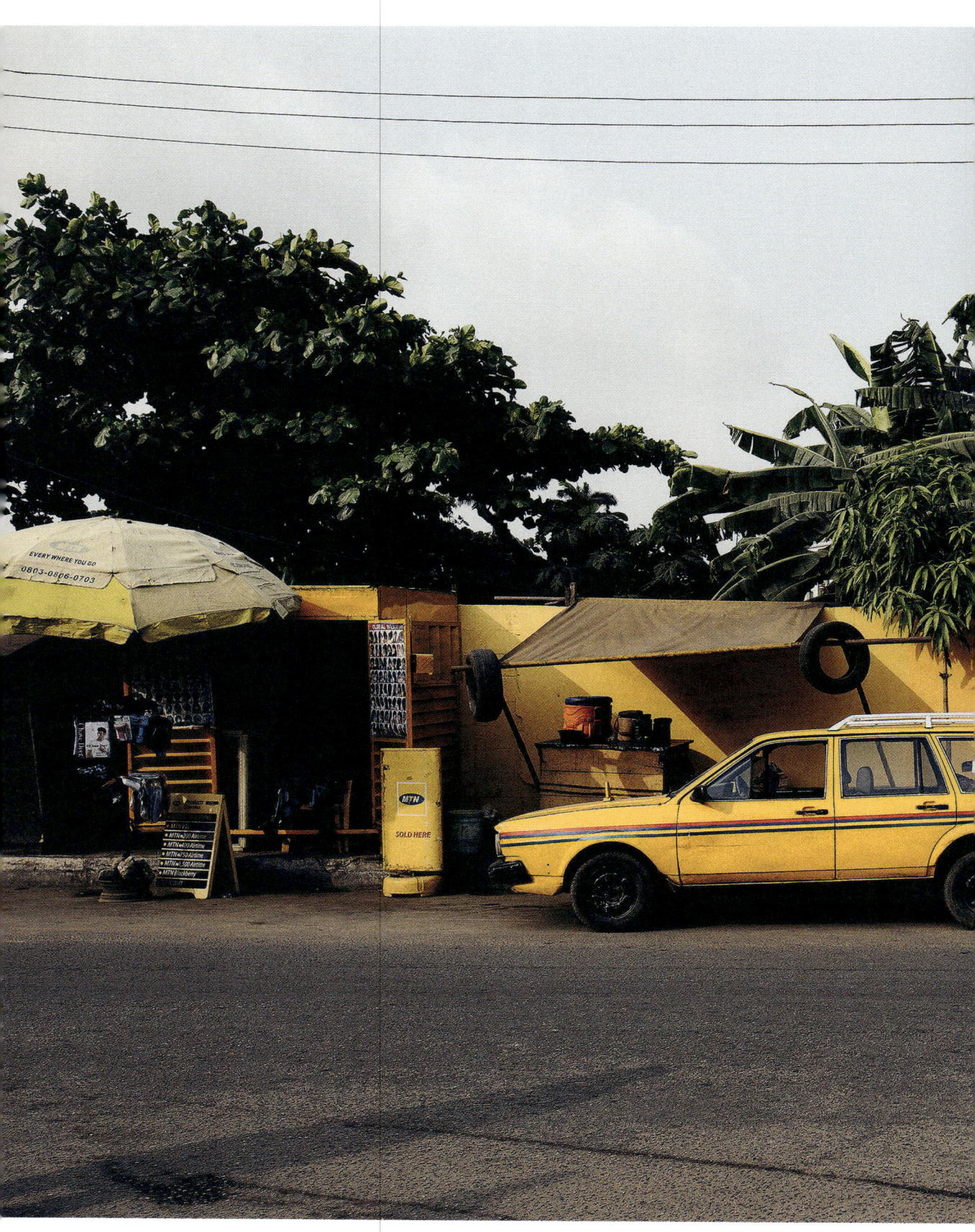

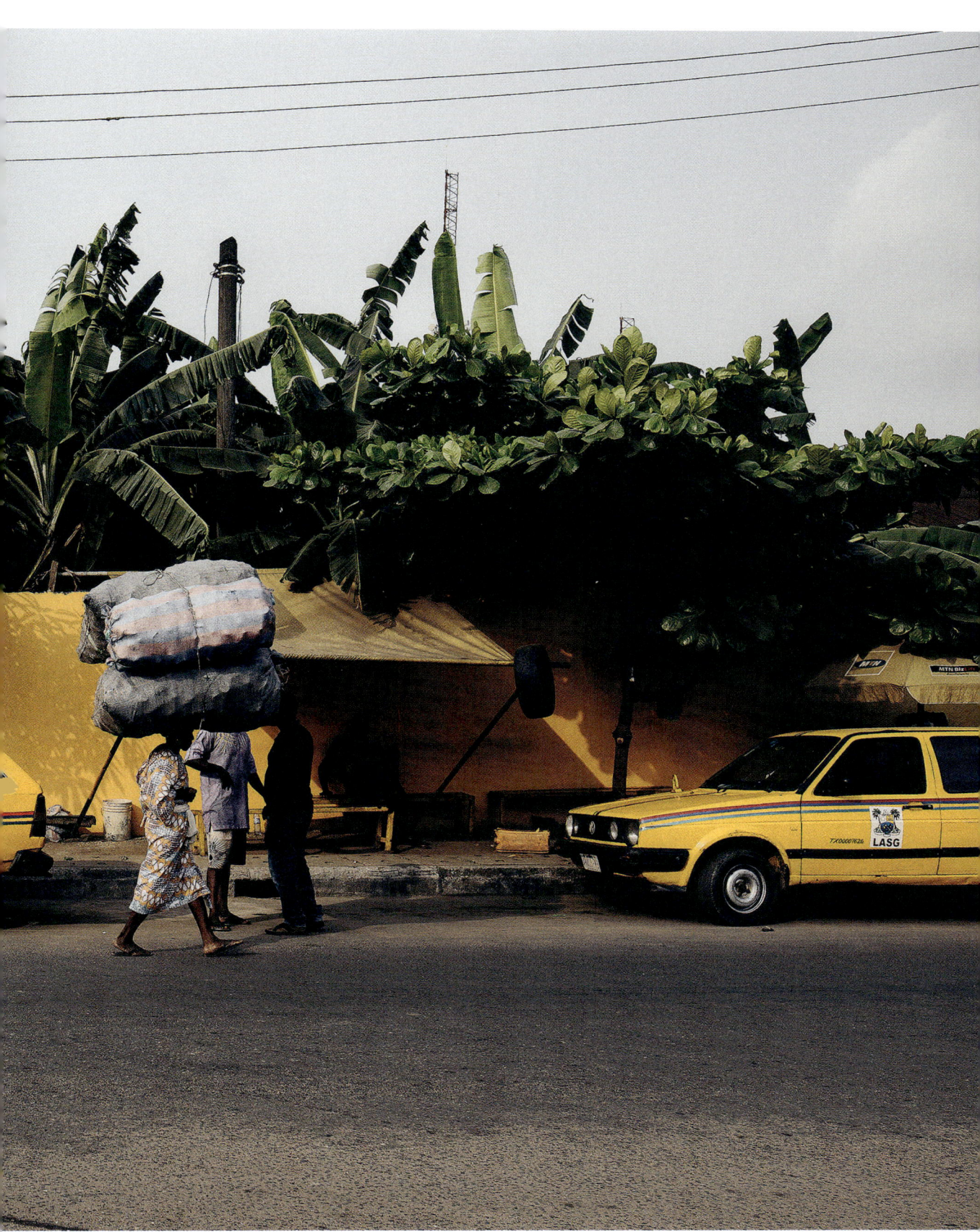

A little progress each day adds up to big results.

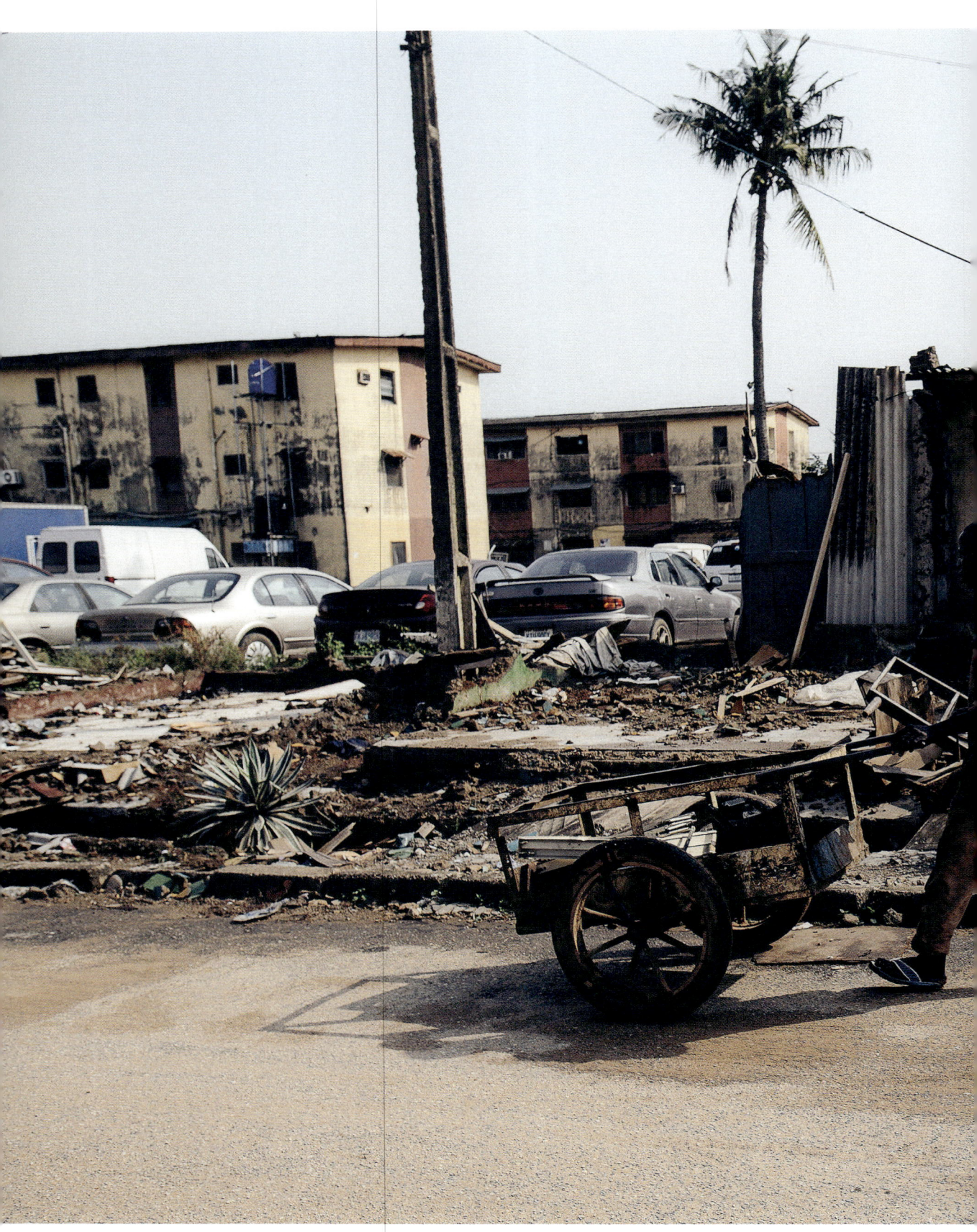

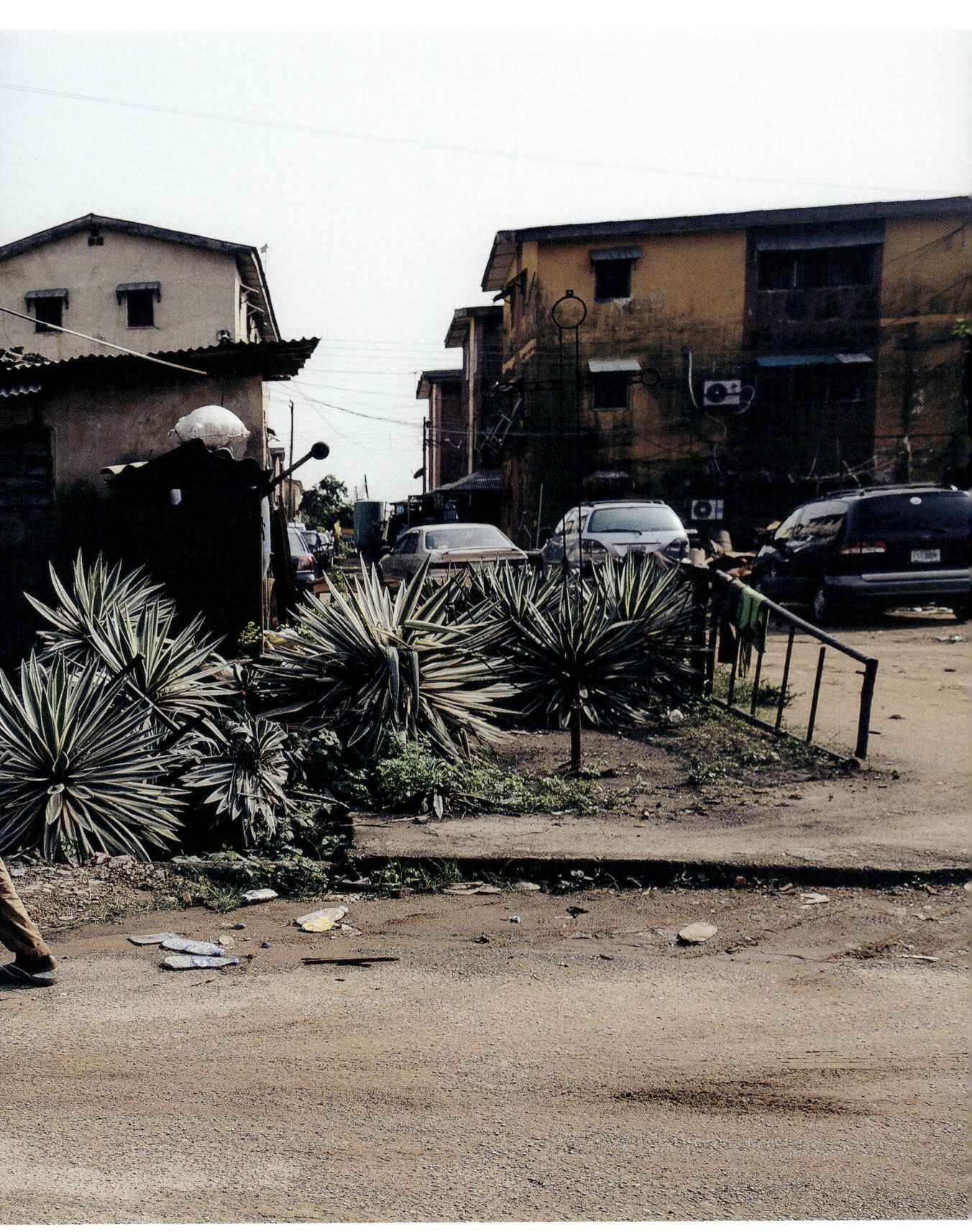

For every disciplined effort there are multiple rewards.

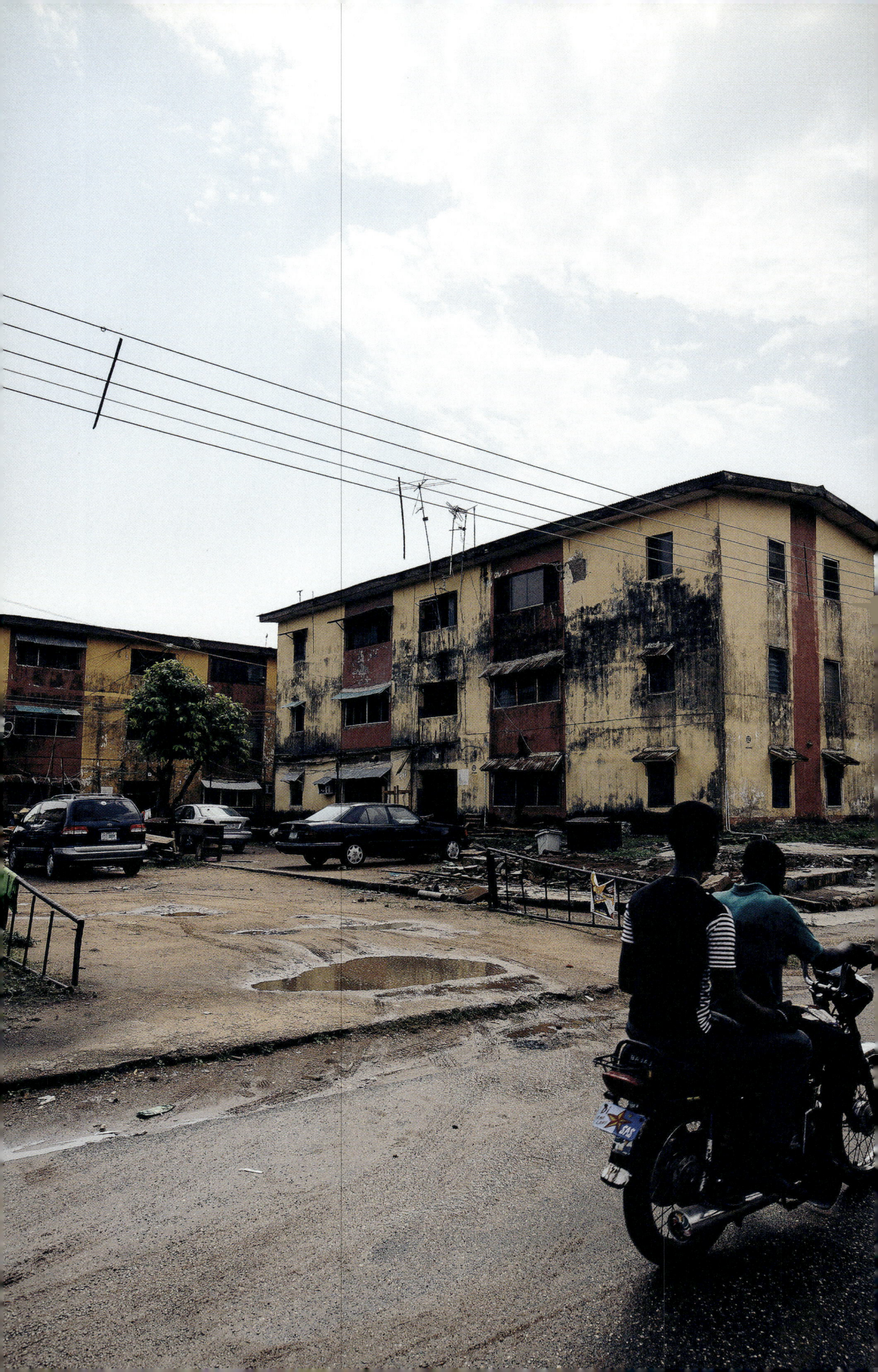

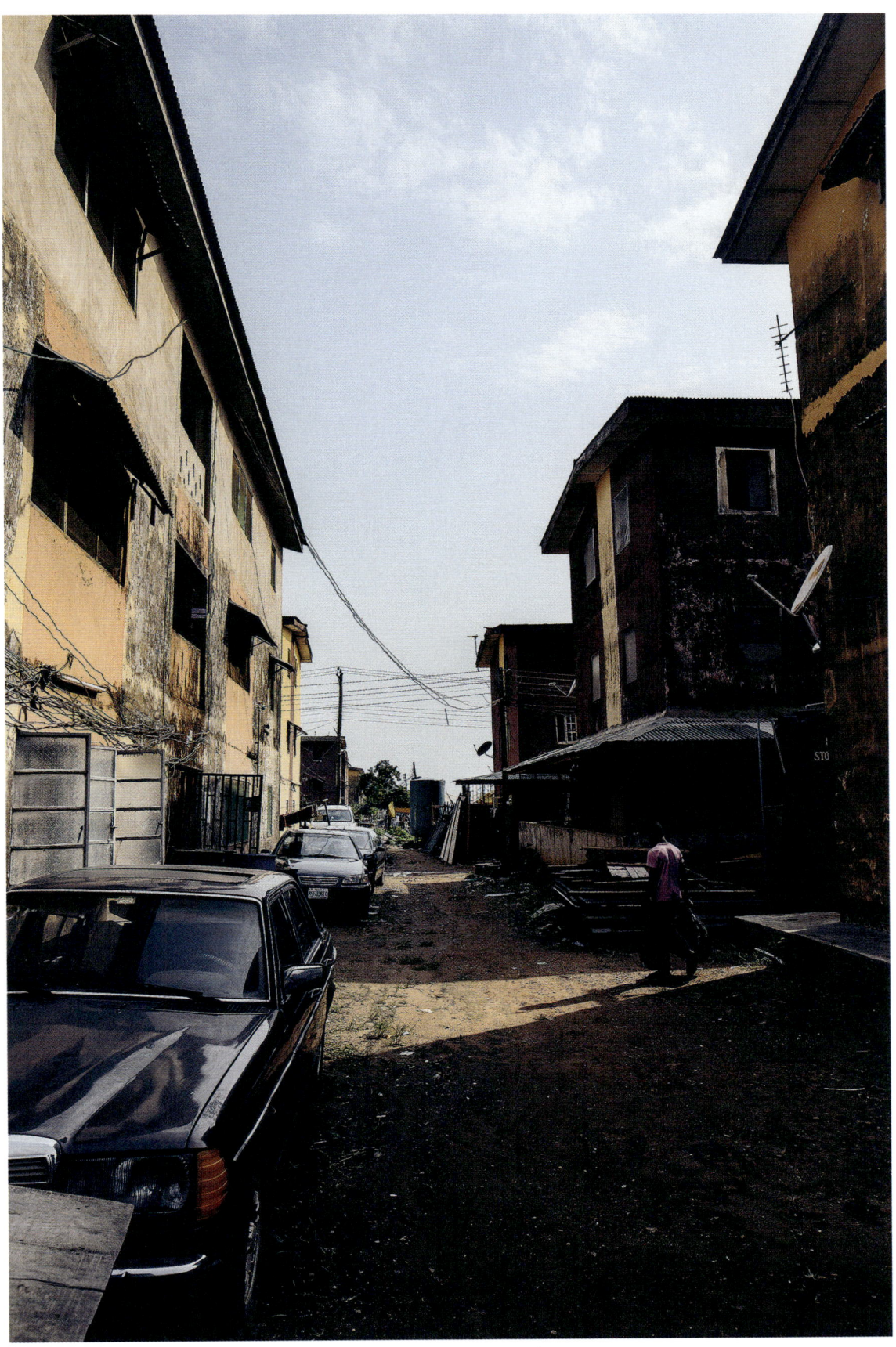

Just outside my grandmother's house, scoping out who's around. I loved the bit of light cast between the buildings, and waited for someone to walk through it for a more dynamic shot.

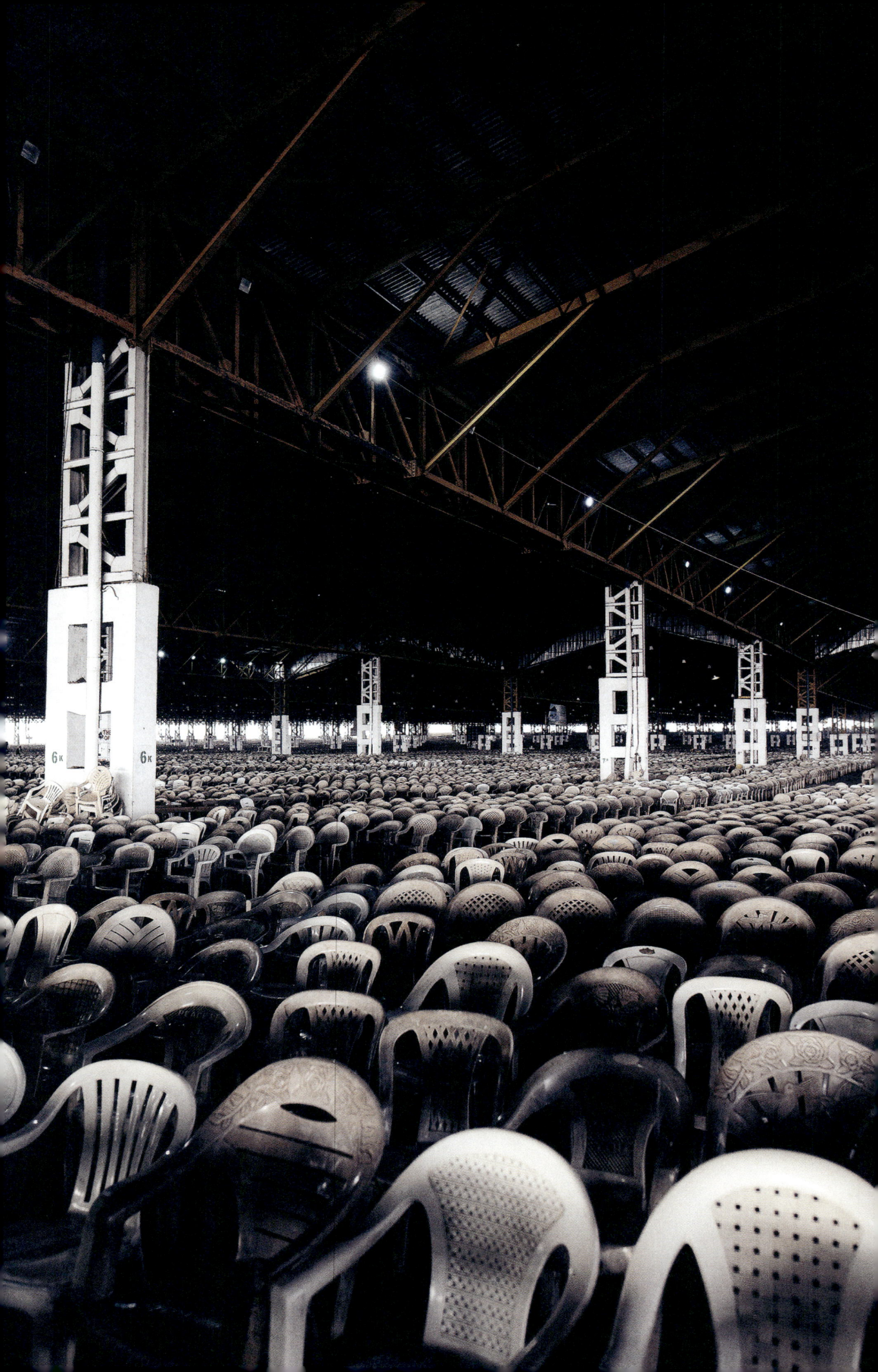

Exploring Redemption Camp, where the Redeemed Christian Church of God (RCCG) holds national services. It was a little weird walking through it empty; tens of thousands come for services every Sunday. I could only imagine how it feels when it's full of people worshipping.

A group of kids surrounded me as I was walking through the market. They were curious about my camera, so I start taking their pictures. I think it's fair to say they enjoyed posing. It's moments like these that give me joy, sharing my passion with others.

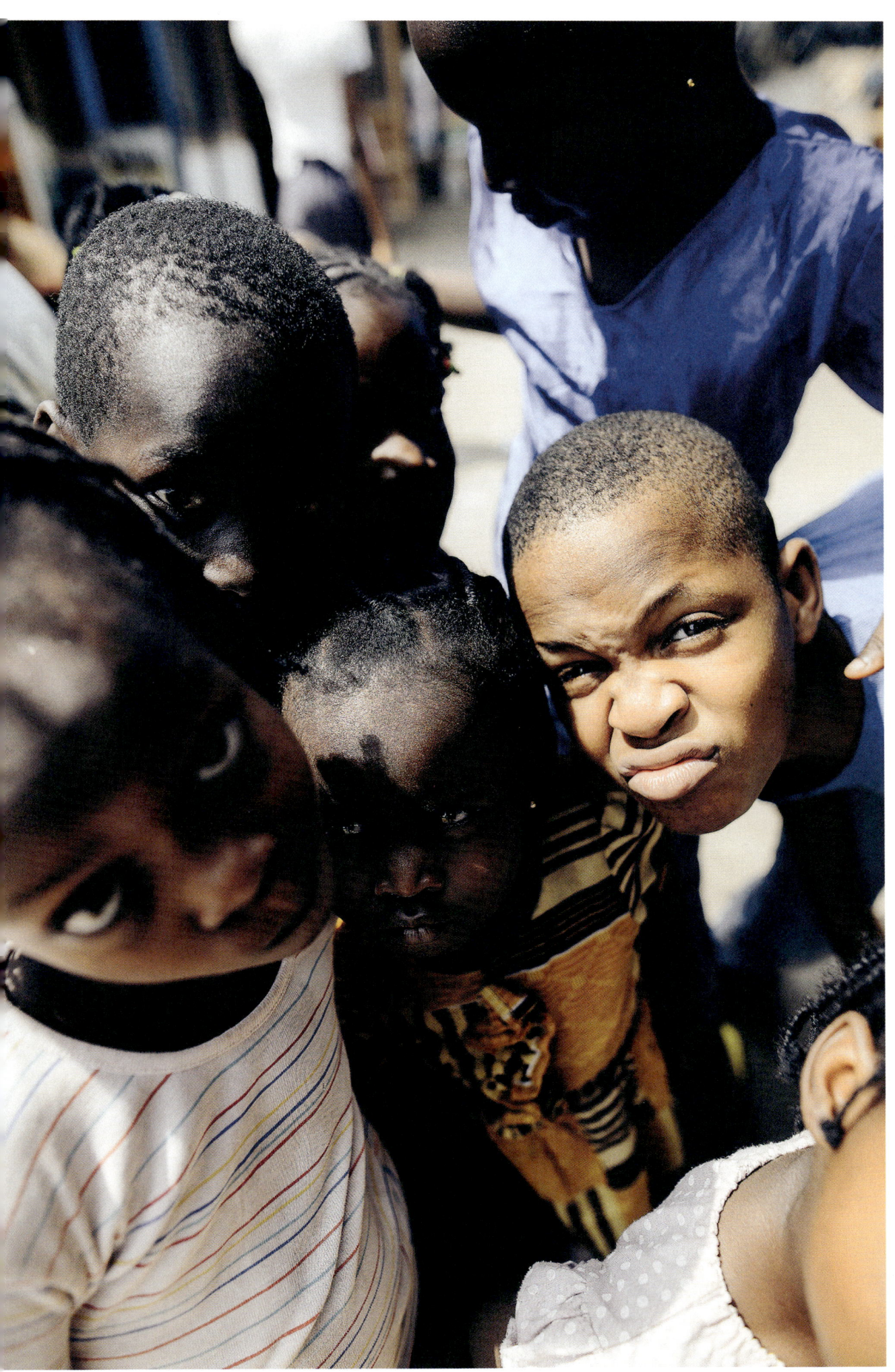

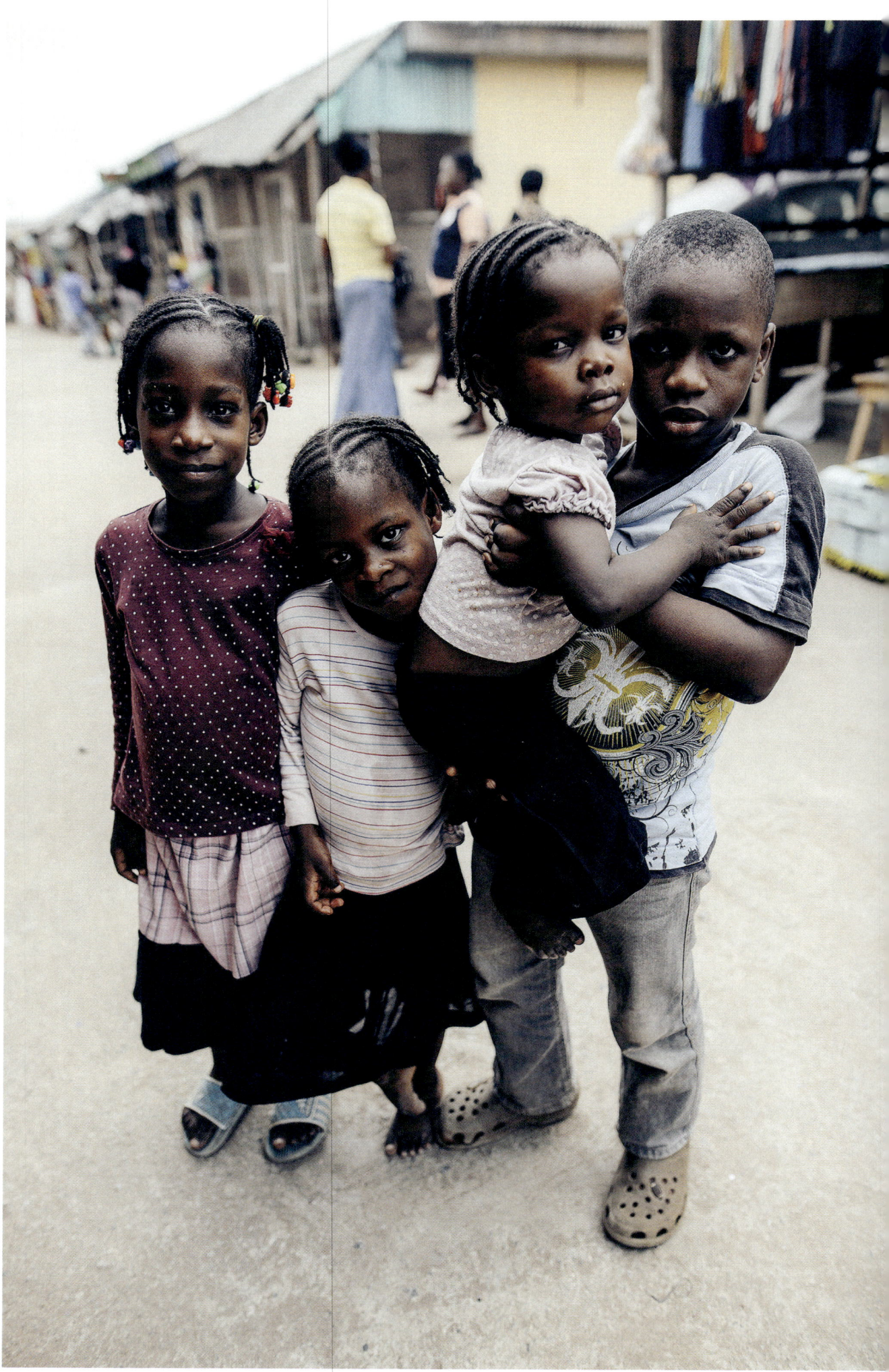

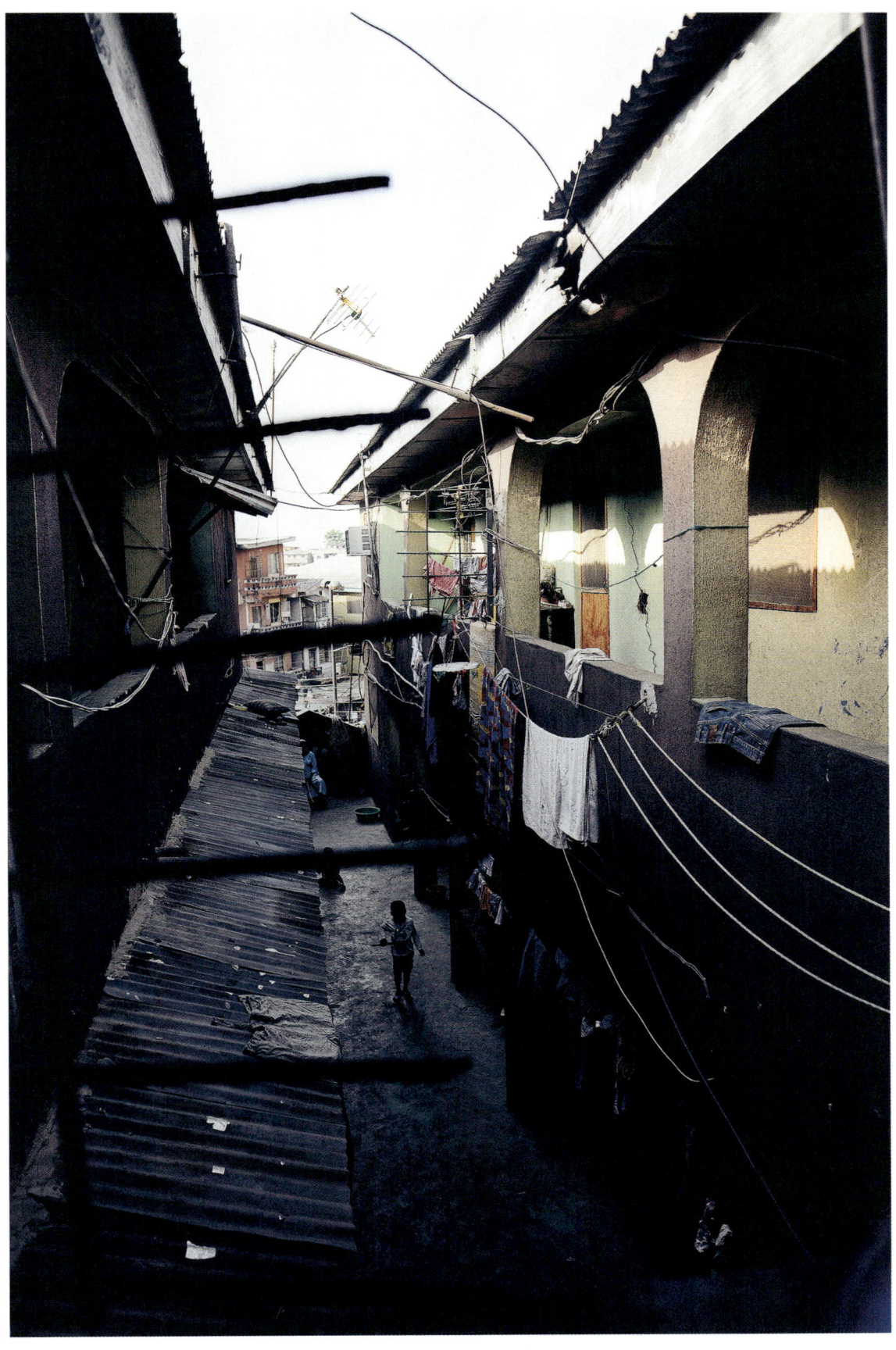

Every day is the opportunity for a better tomorrow.

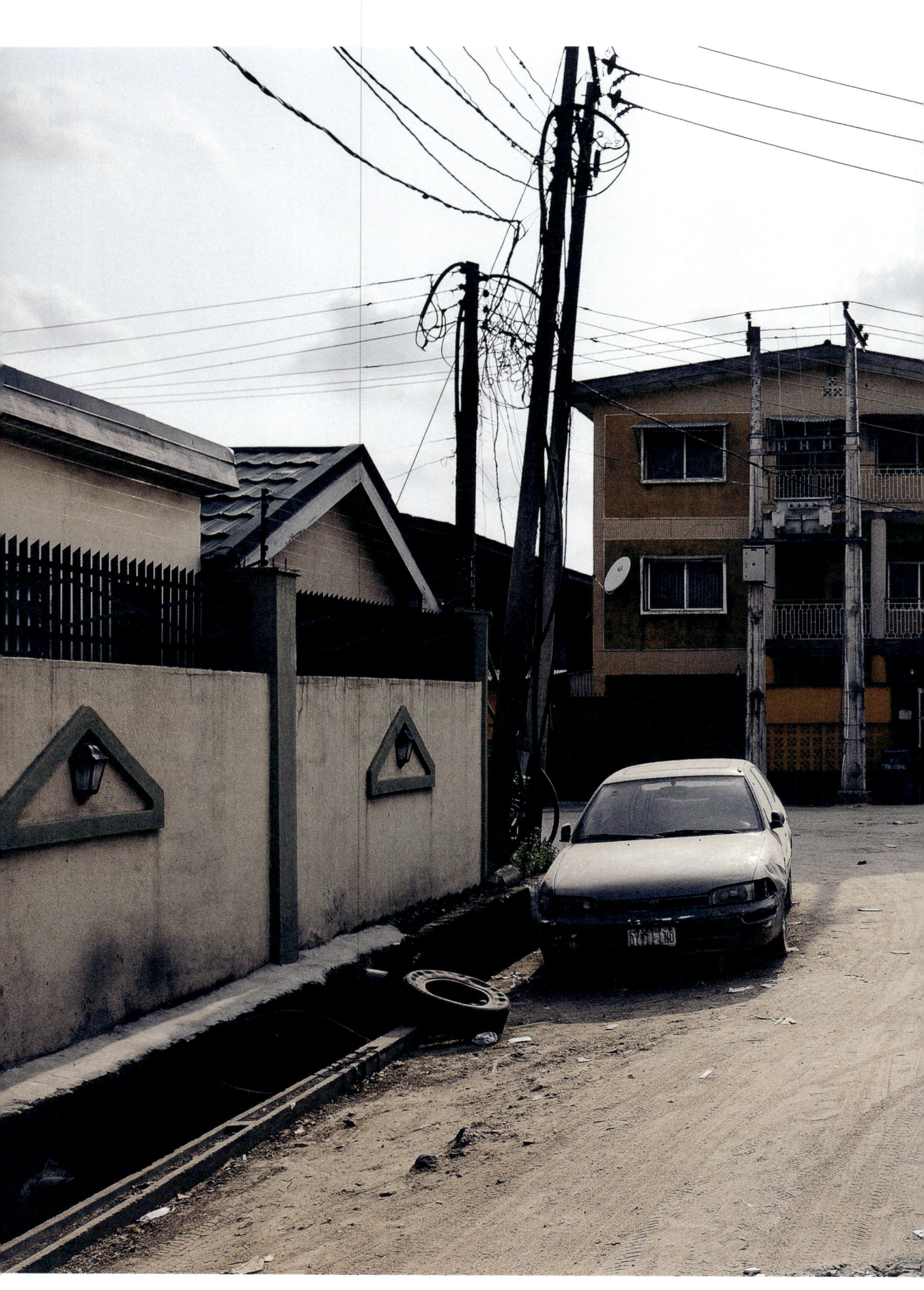

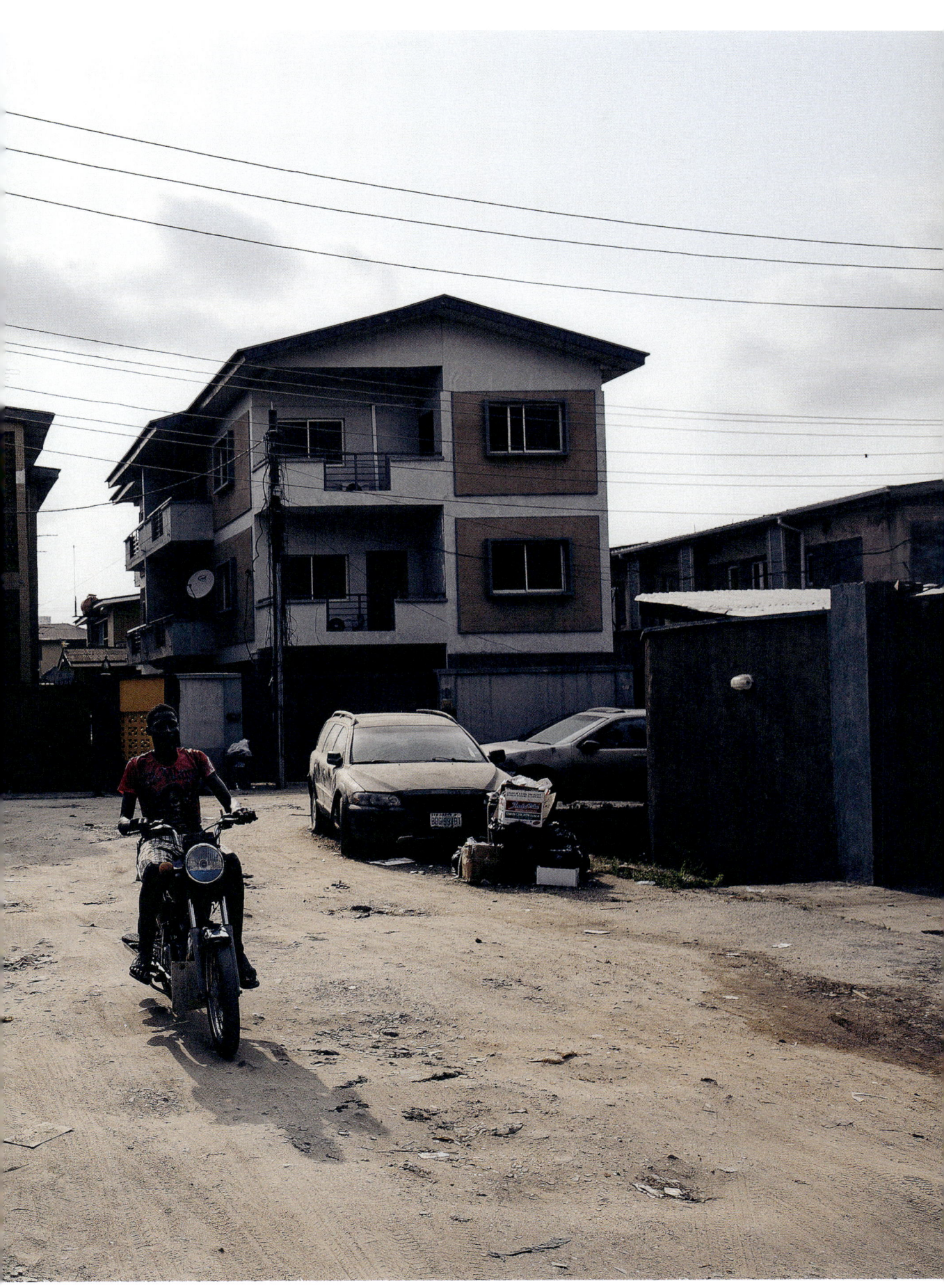

Just a couple of blocks away from my grandmother's house, there is a main street with traffic and noise. This calm, quiet spot was a bit of refuge from the hustle and bustle.

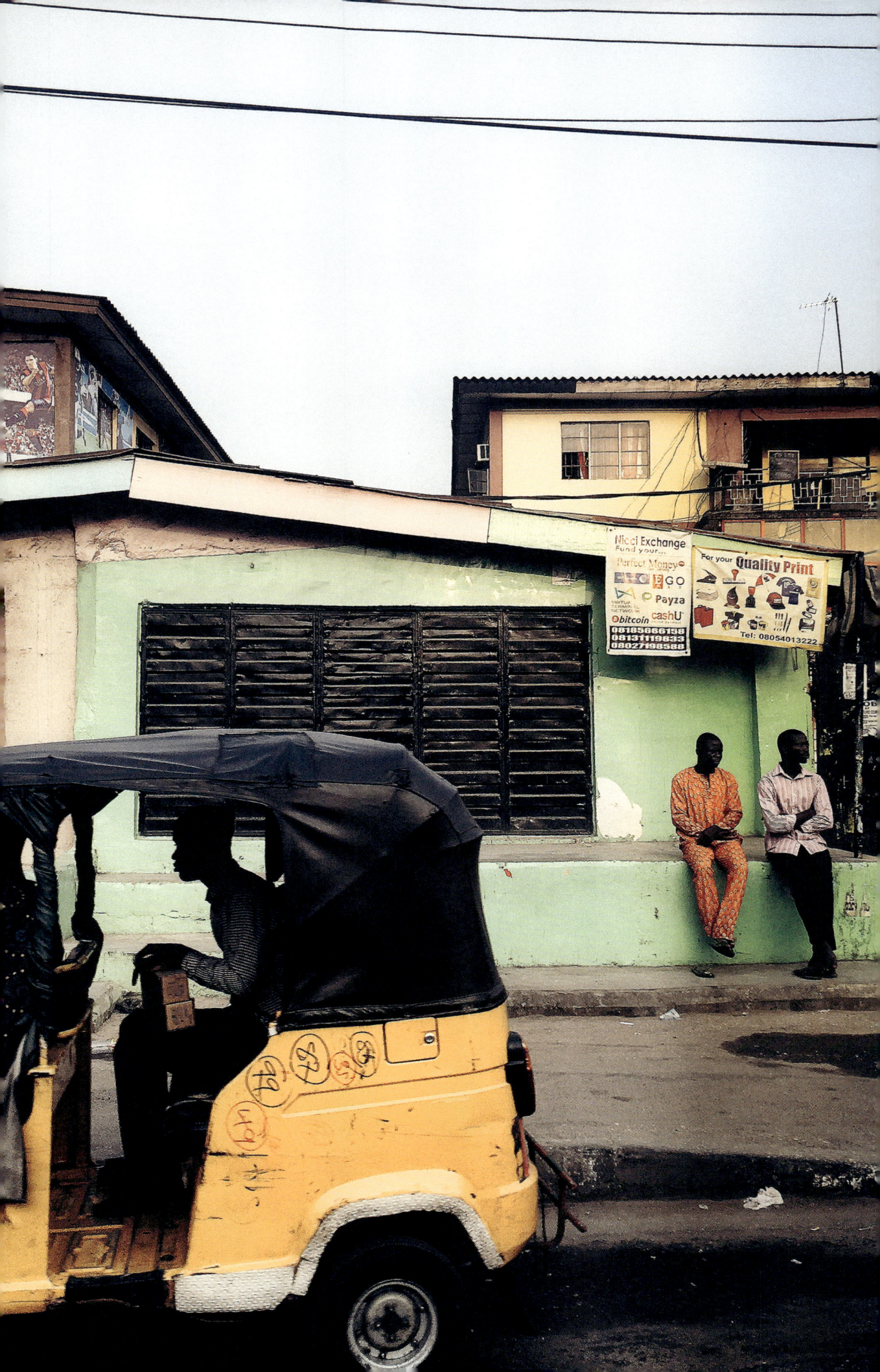

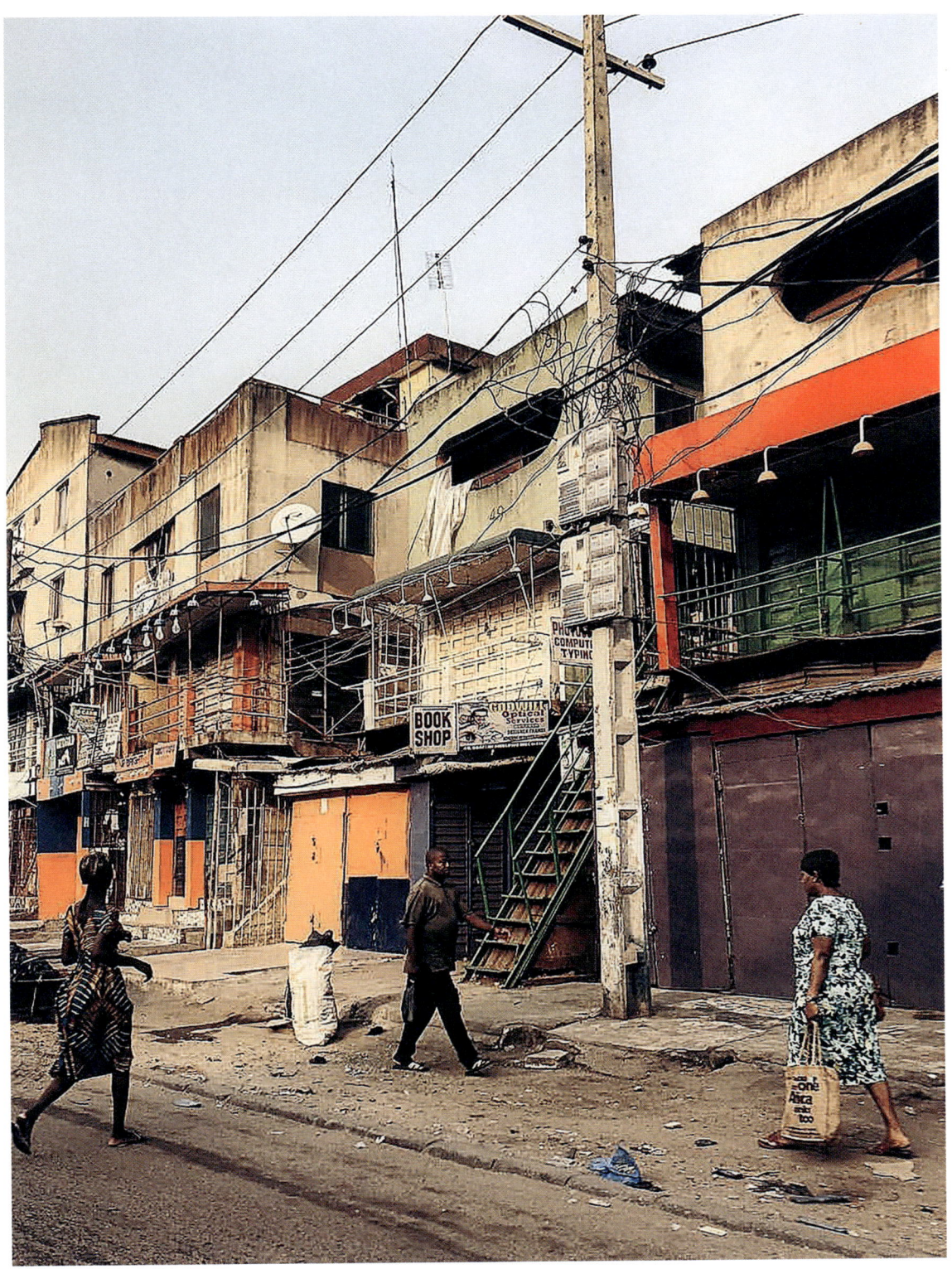

I just tried to take it all in, people going about their daily business in a place that was in some ways familiar, yet so very different than where I'm from.

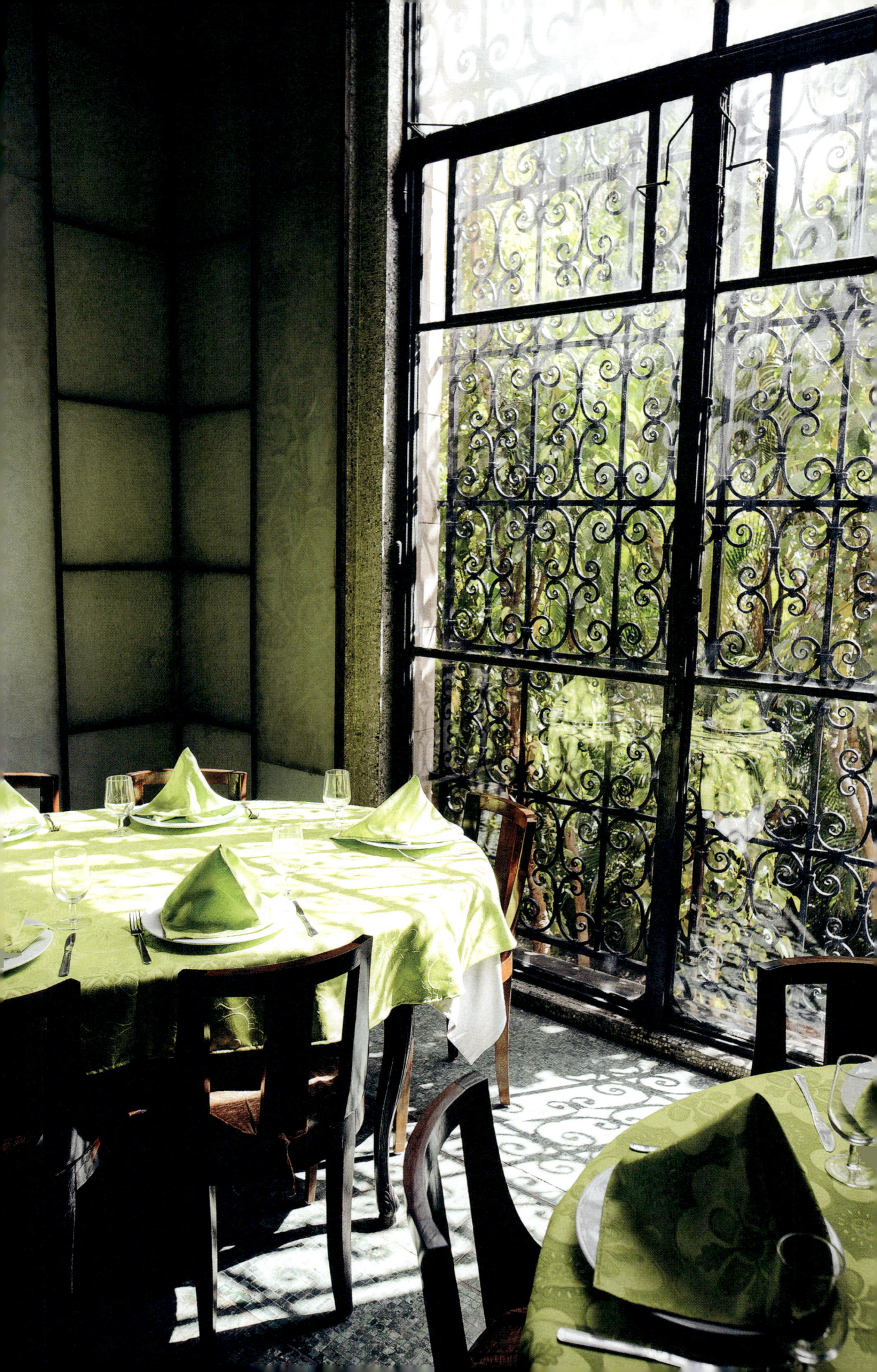

CHILLING IN CUBA

Cuba was definitely a place I never thought I'd visit, but I'm so glad I did. It was an eye-opening experience, a totally different world. I was there as a guest photographer for Havana Club, and after doing some research before my arrival I knew I wanted to document anything and everything. The locals were so welcoming, which really put me at ease – especially when taking the portrait shots.

After exploring its vibrant streets, my first impression of Havana was that everything is so chilled. Everywhere you look there are people hanging out and having a good time, just enjoying the company of others. For me, the people are what make the country so special; you can really see the love they have for their homeland. I was privileged to experience so much of their culture in the form of art, food and music, and wasn't disappointed. There's not a bad word I can say about my experience – other than how unlikely it is you'll get a decent internet connection.

I would love to go back; it's such a photogenic city filled with so many good vibes. When you go to a different country you can feel unanchored or lost, but this was not the case with Cuba. I felt so welcomed and was surprised at the number of people who allowed me, or even invited me, to take their photograph.

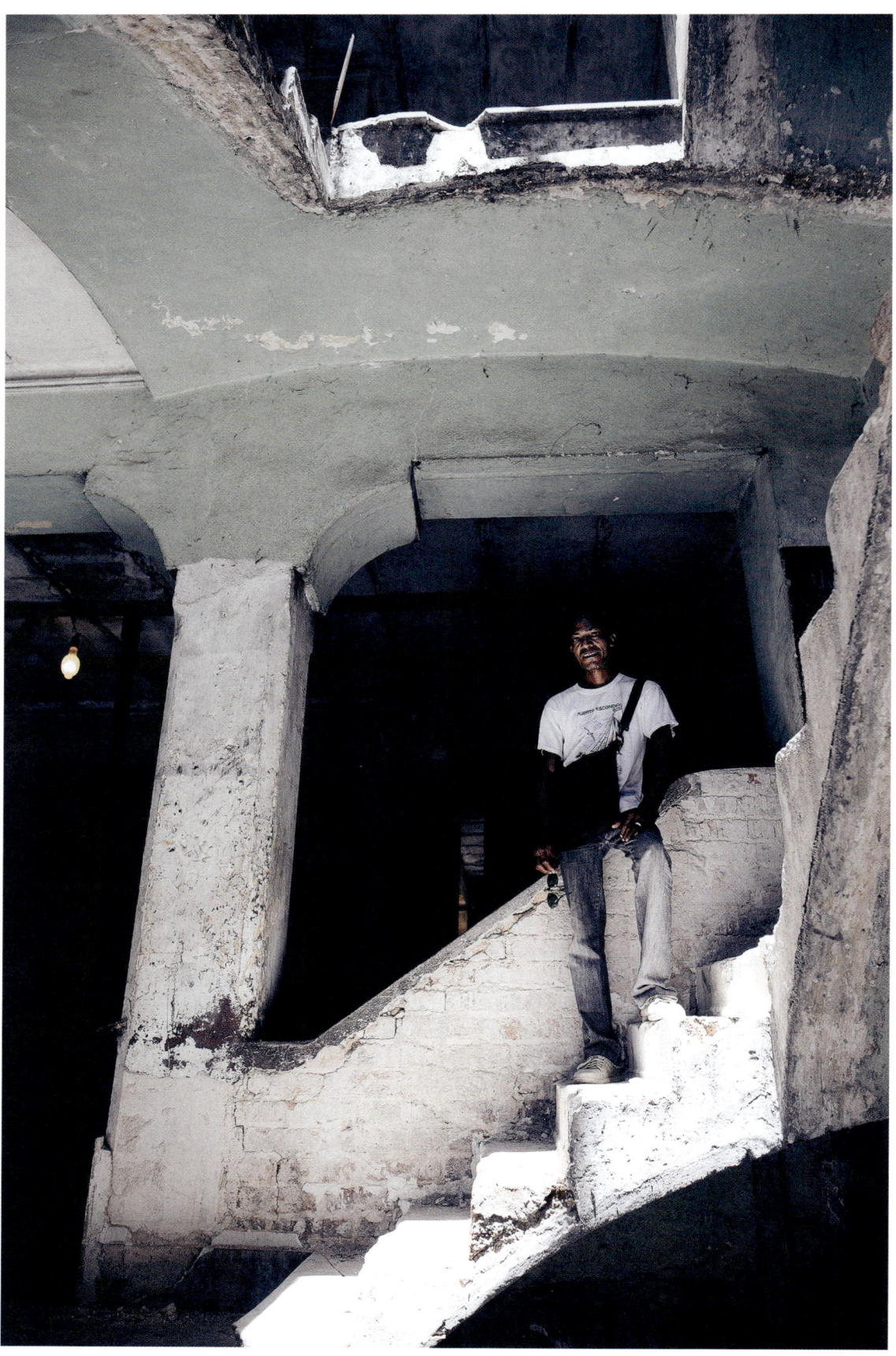

I met a man inside the house he's building for himself. His drive and pride of place was written on his face.

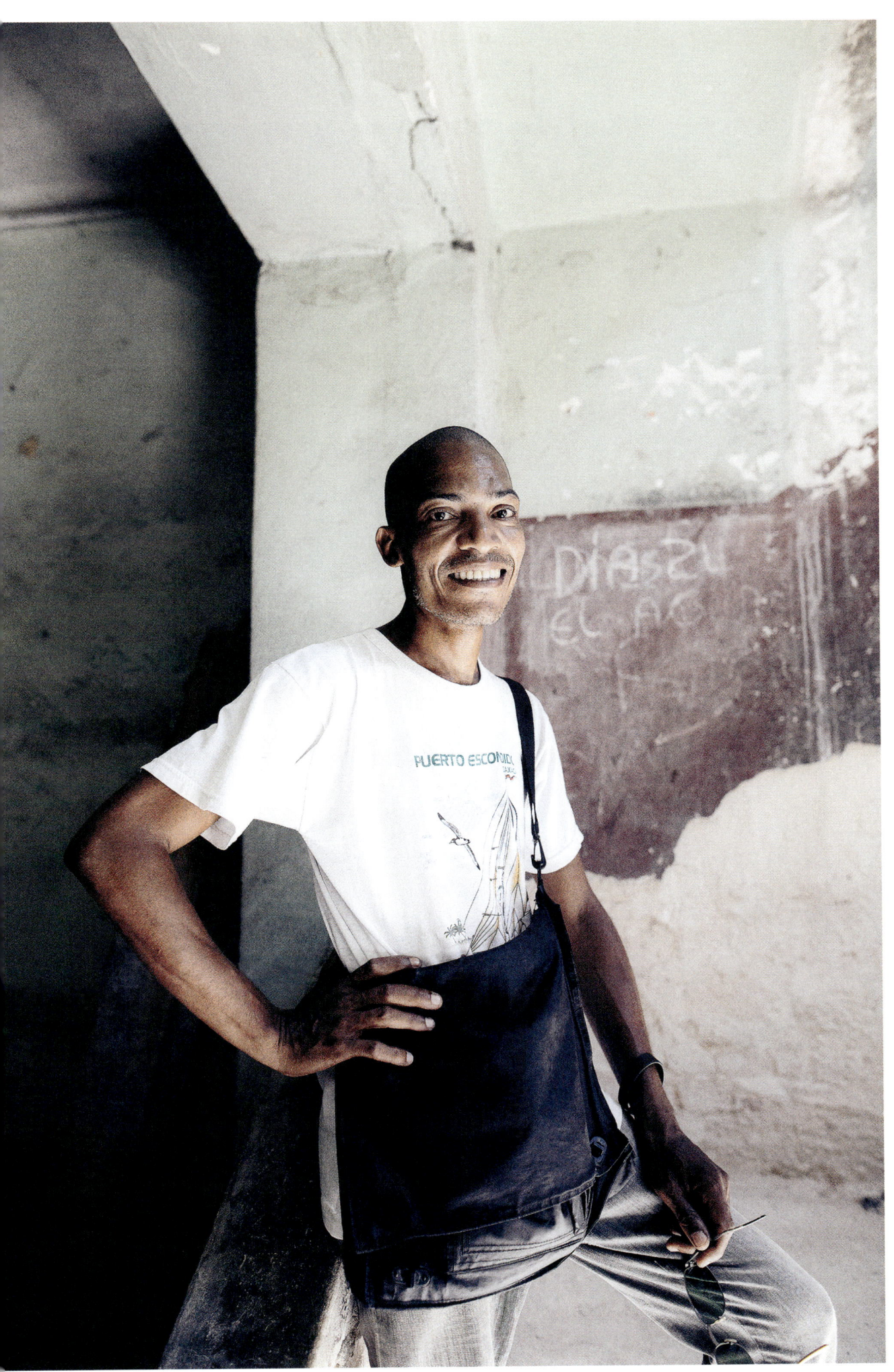

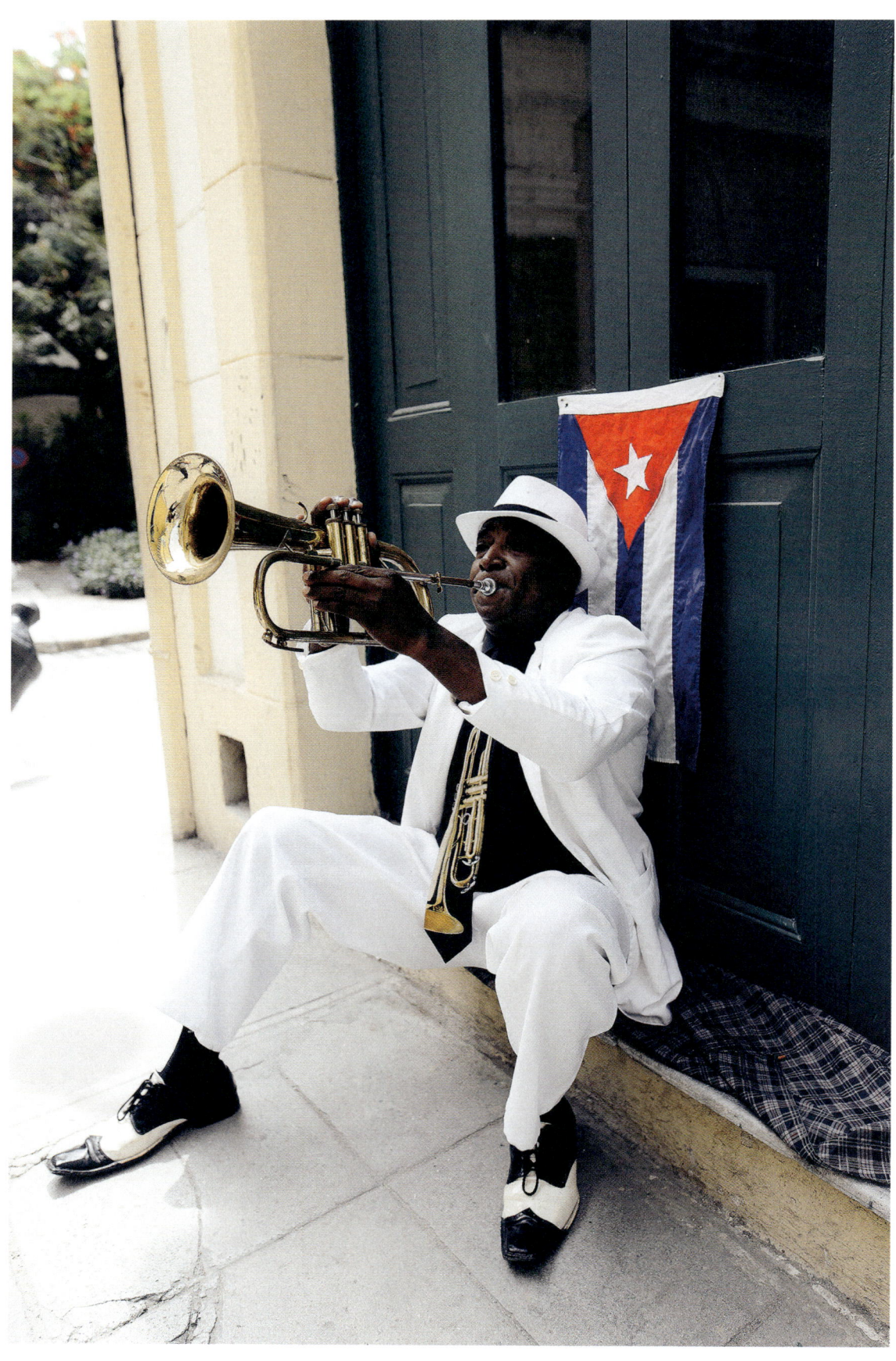

The people are what make Cuba so special; you can really see the love they have for their homeland. There's a sense of togetherness.

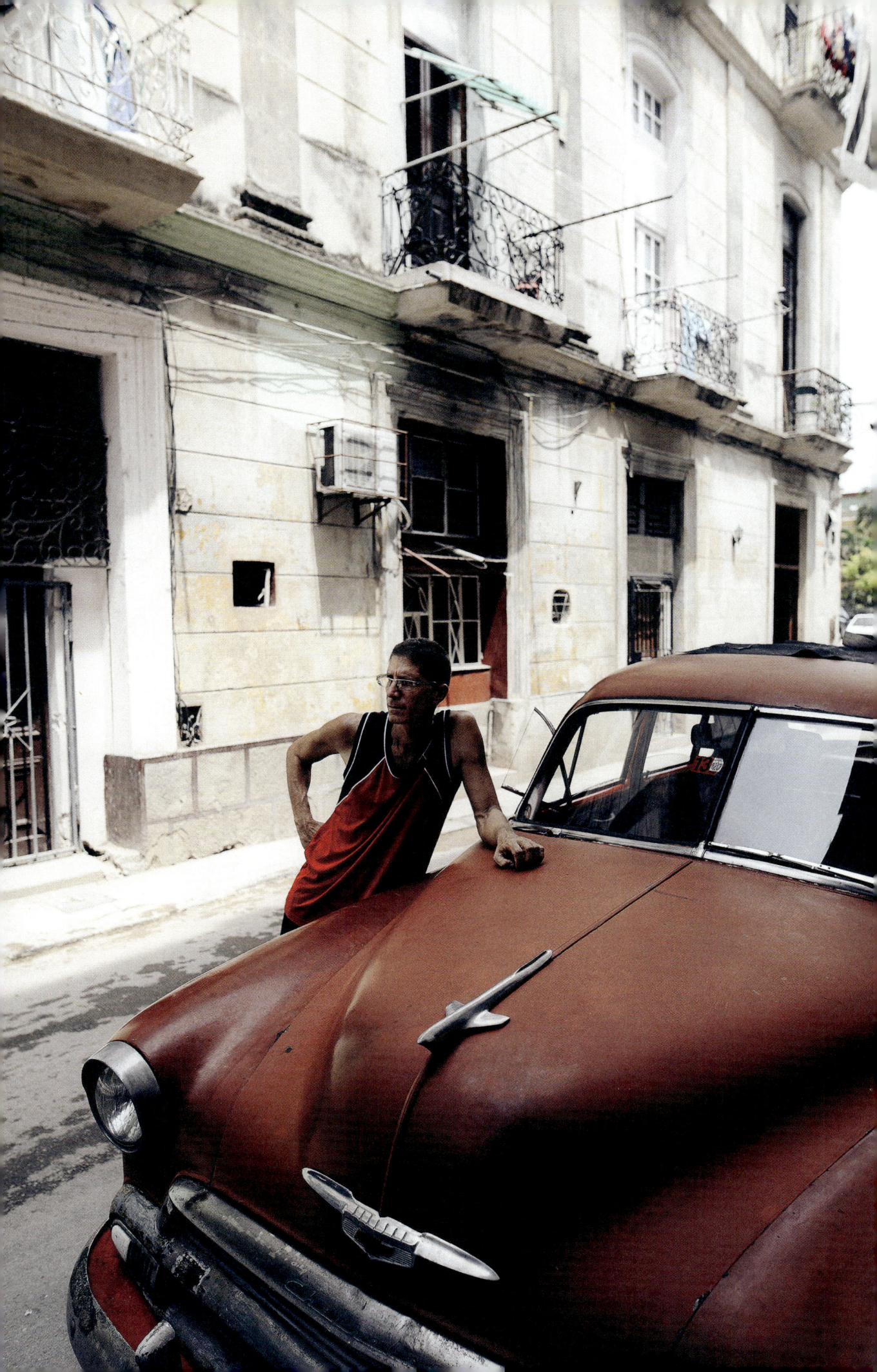

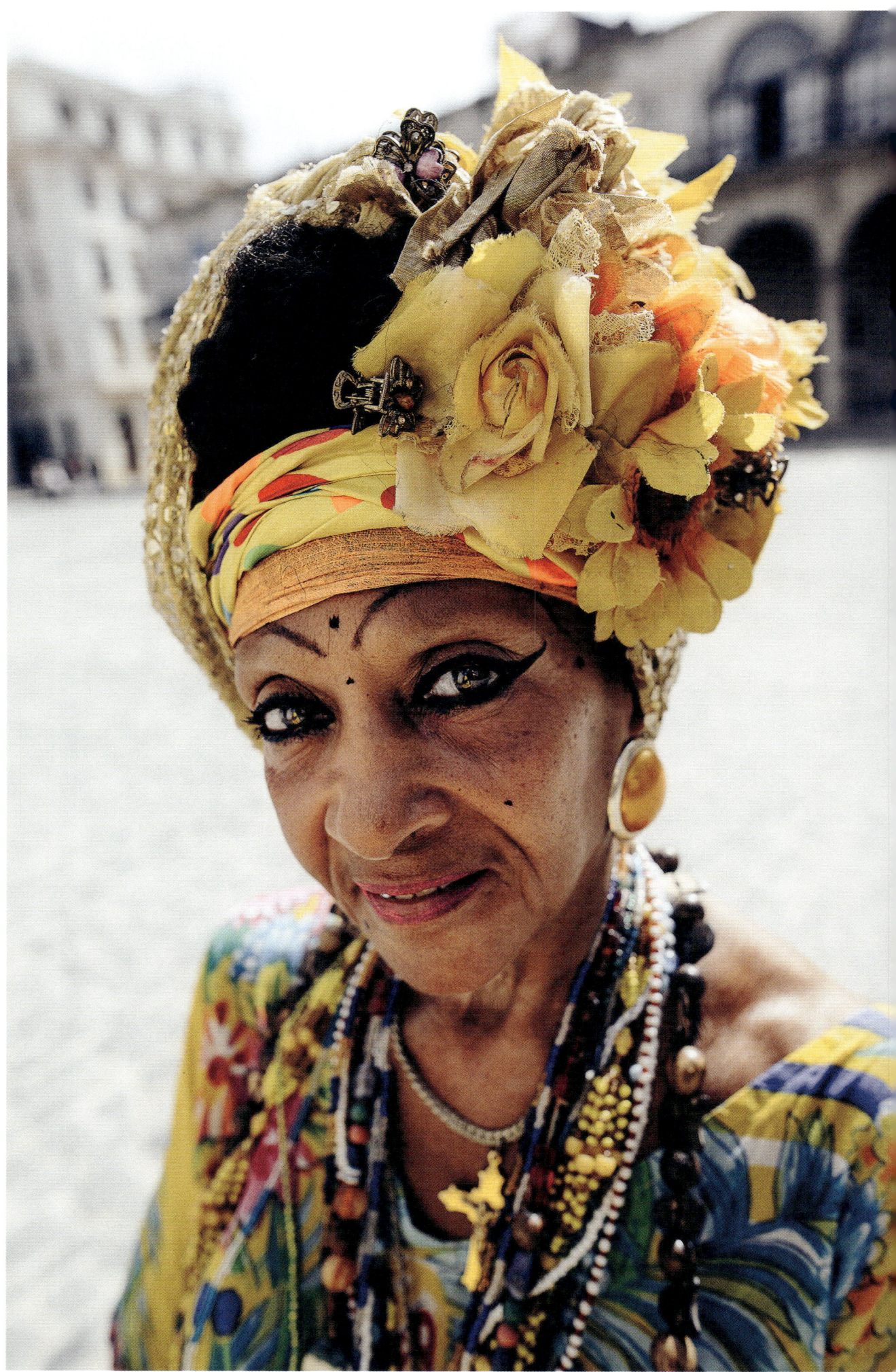

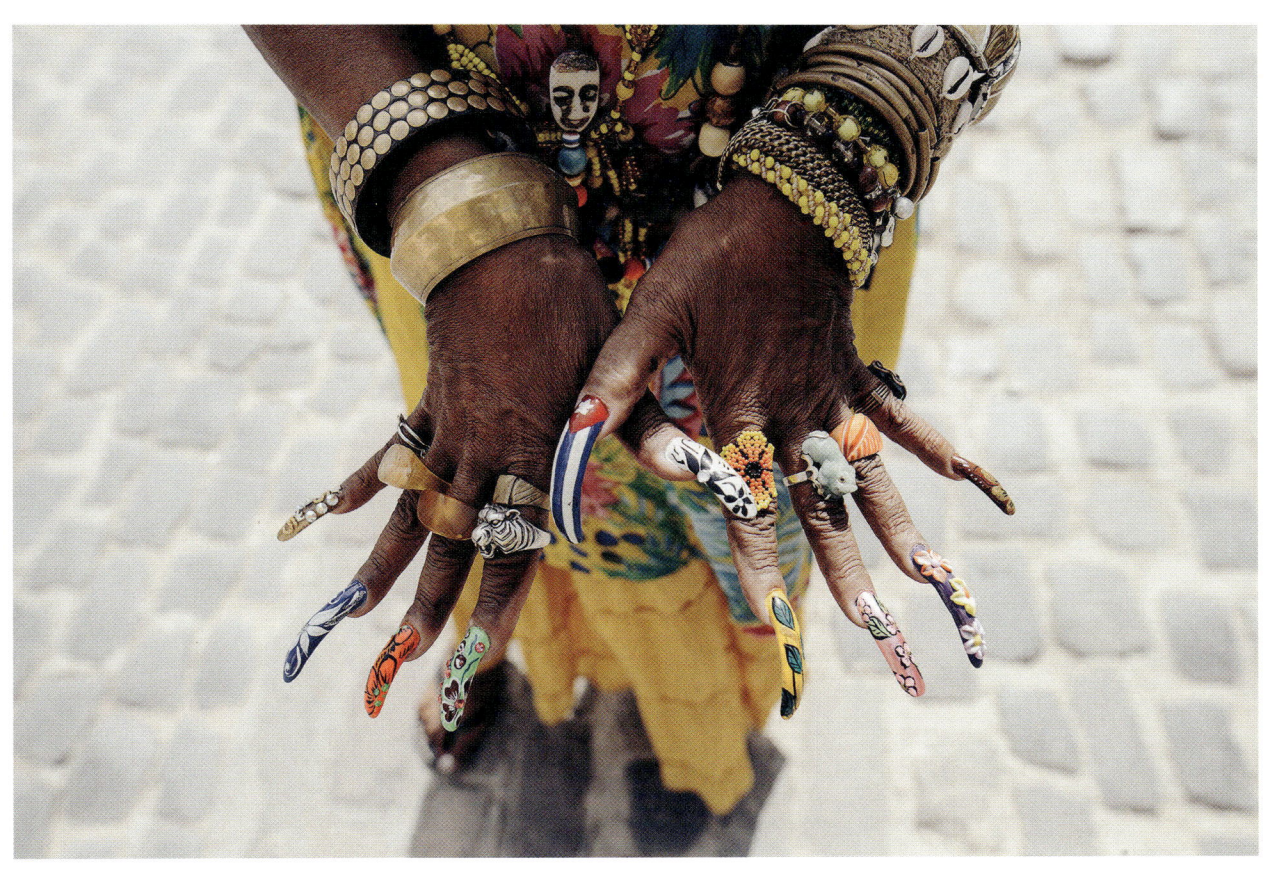

I saw this lady and I just had to photograph her, full of vibrancy she represents exactly what Cuba's about. She insisted I pay her for taking the photos, but it was worth it!

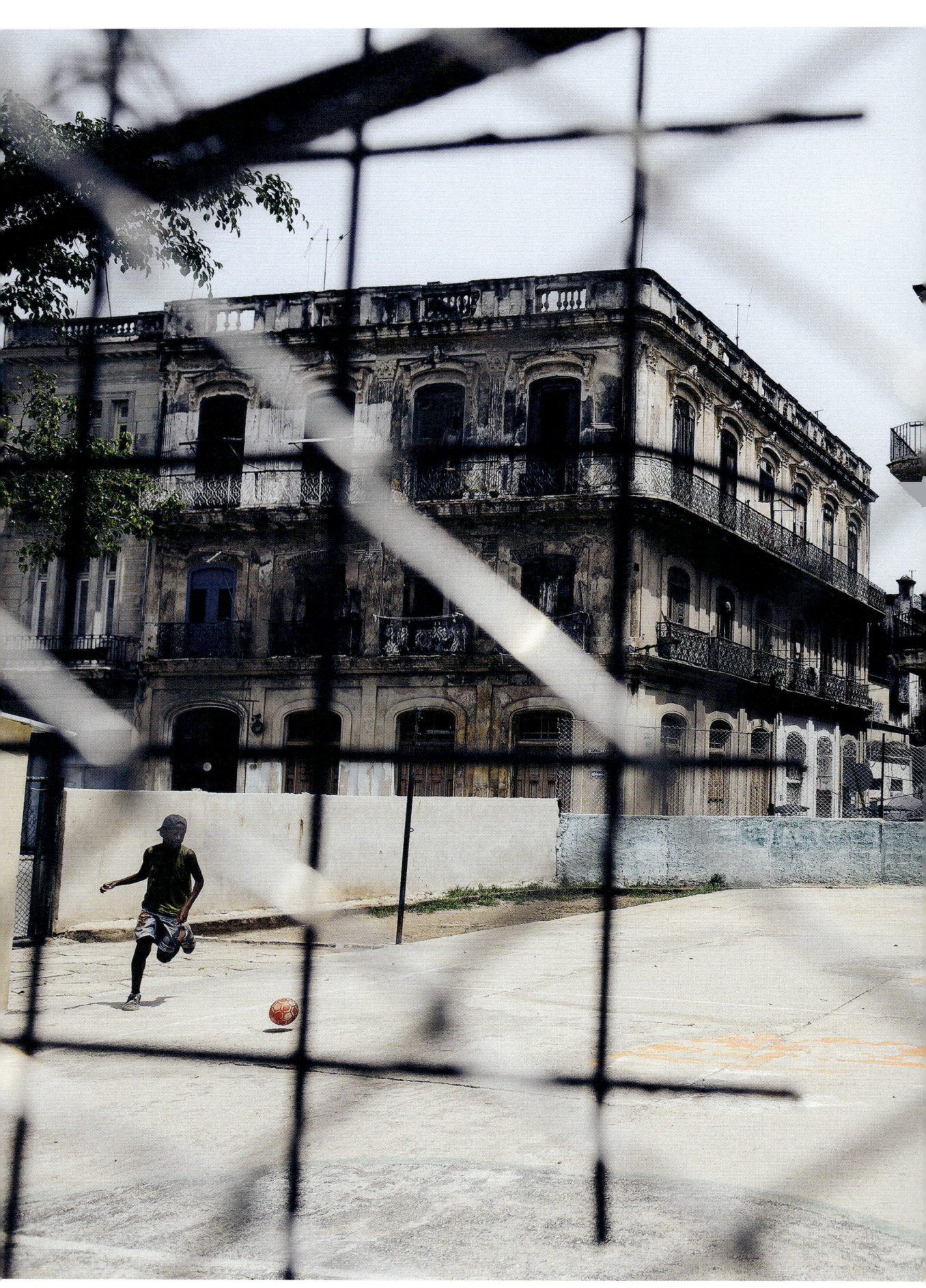

In London, kids spend so much time on screens. The kids I saw in Havana were all about adventure, playtime, getting out there. There was a joy, a contentment in their activity that I wanted to capture.

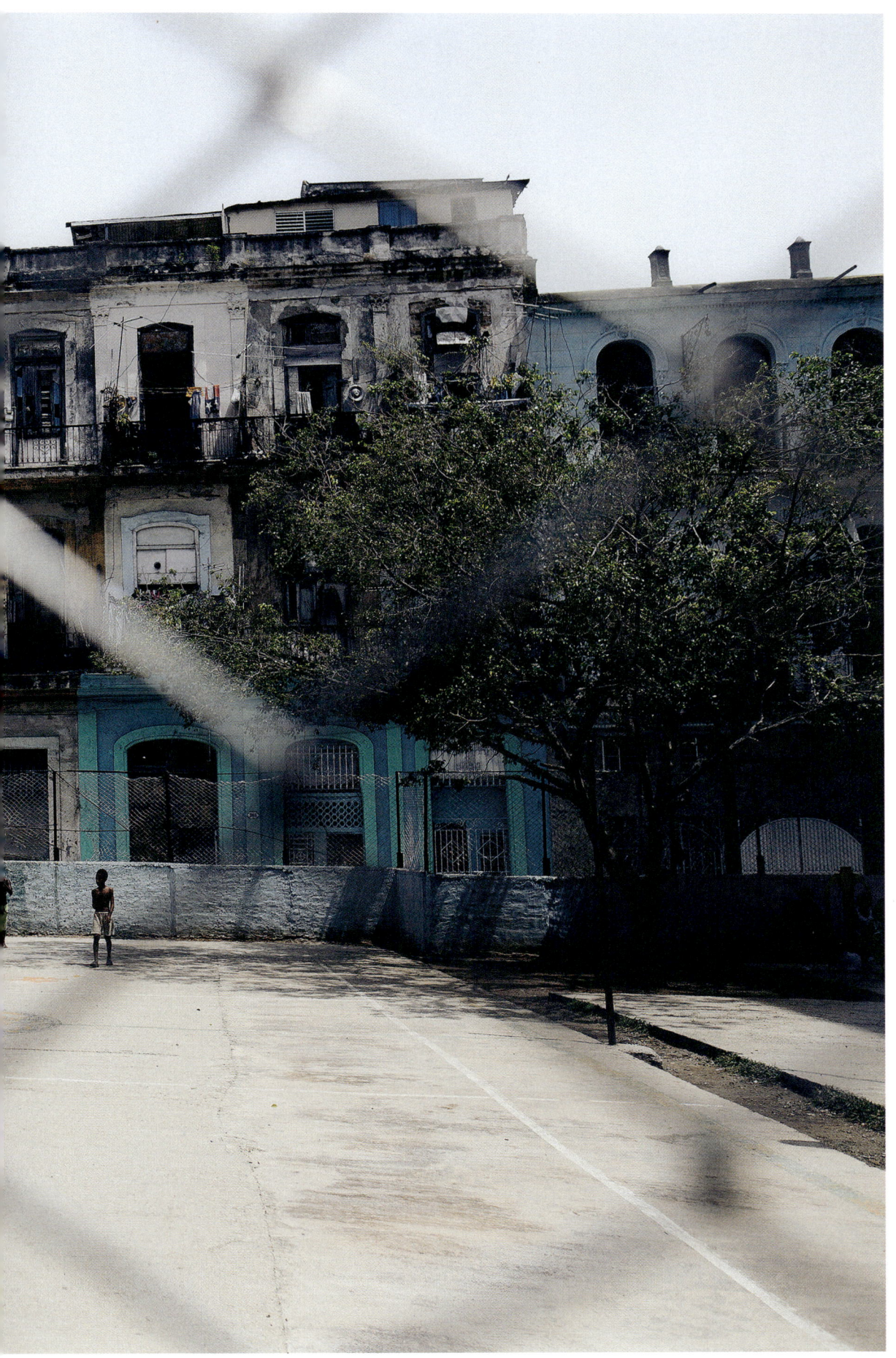

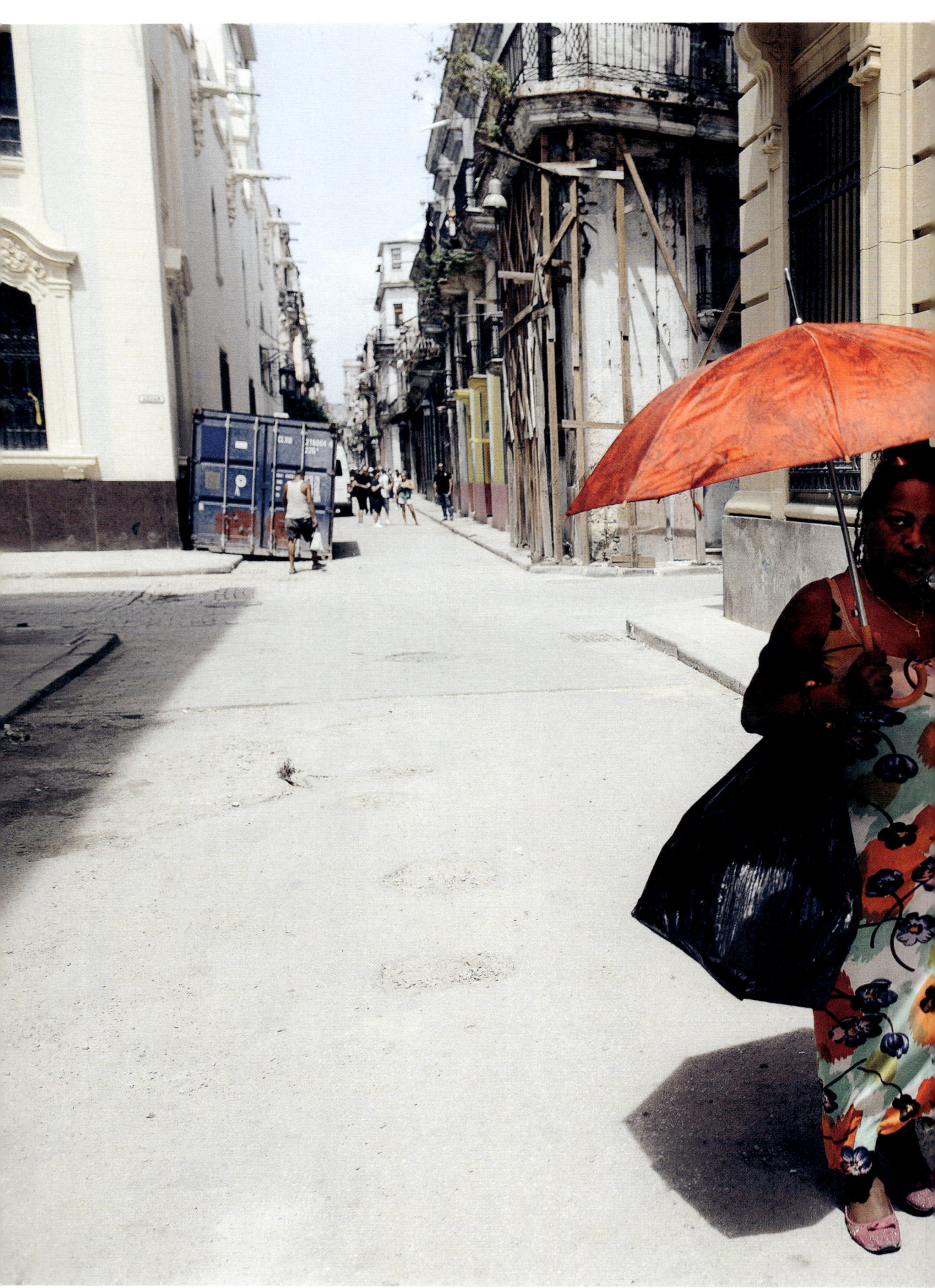

Not the look I expected to receive after complimenting her floral dress.

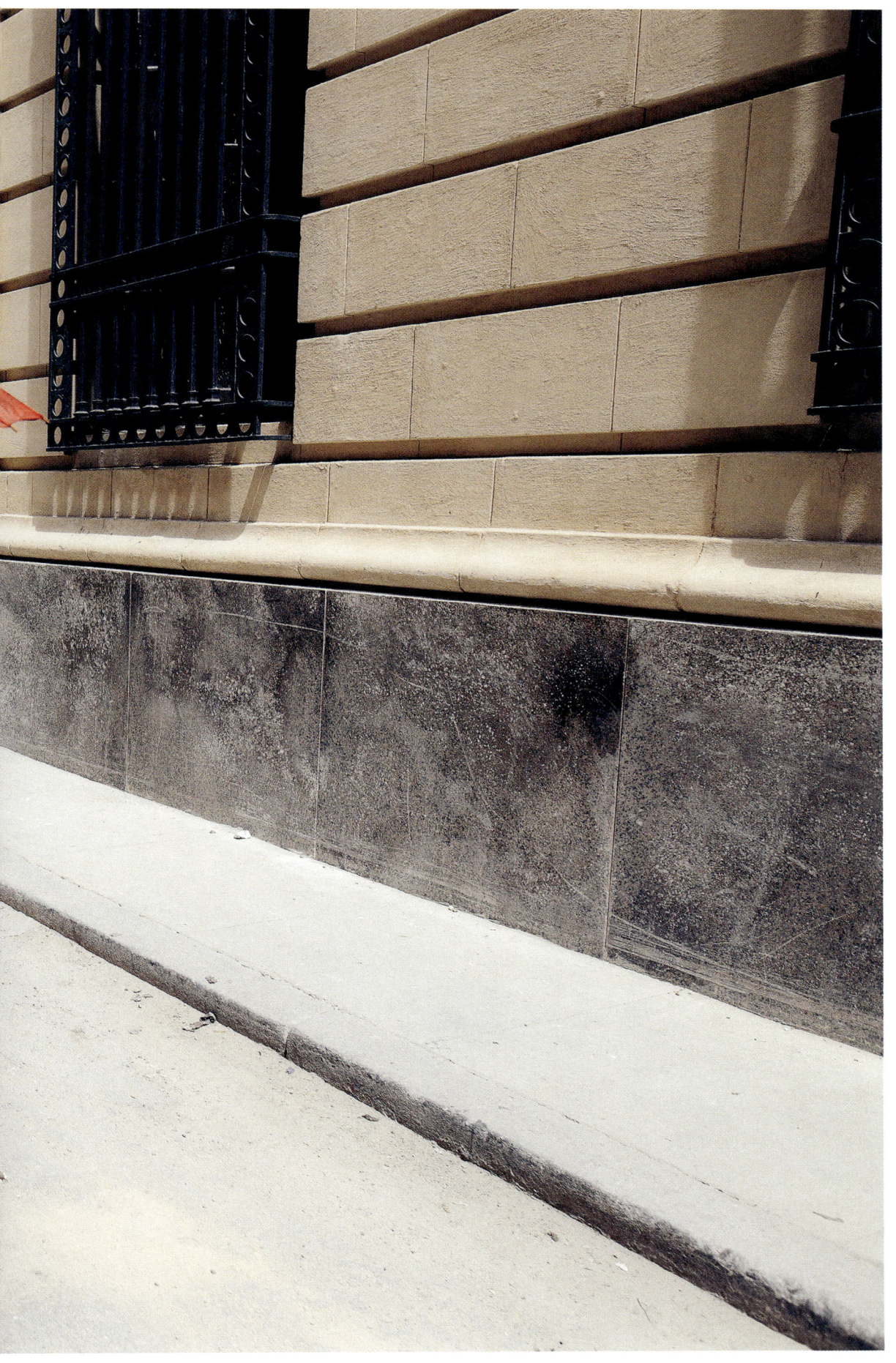

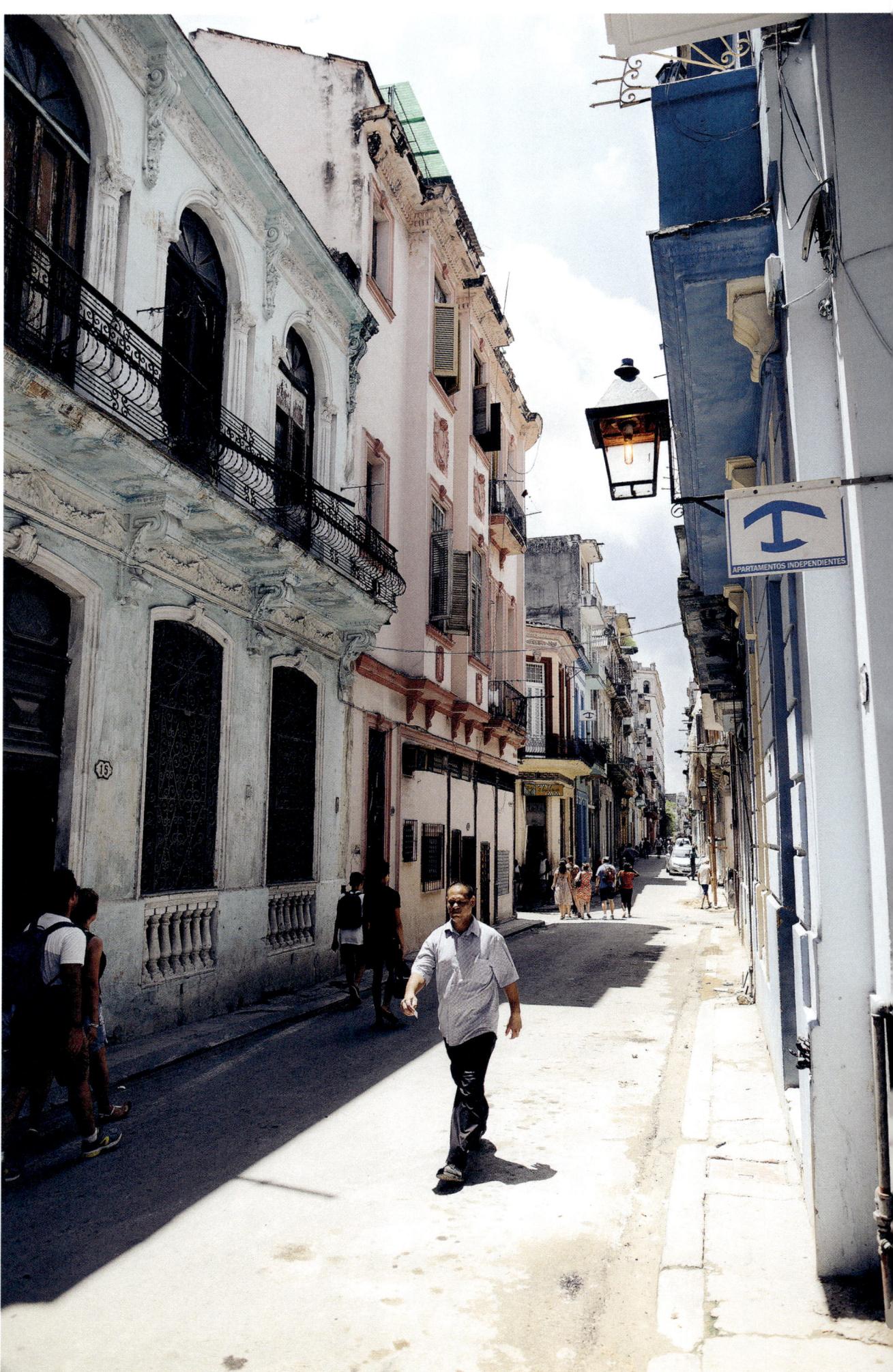

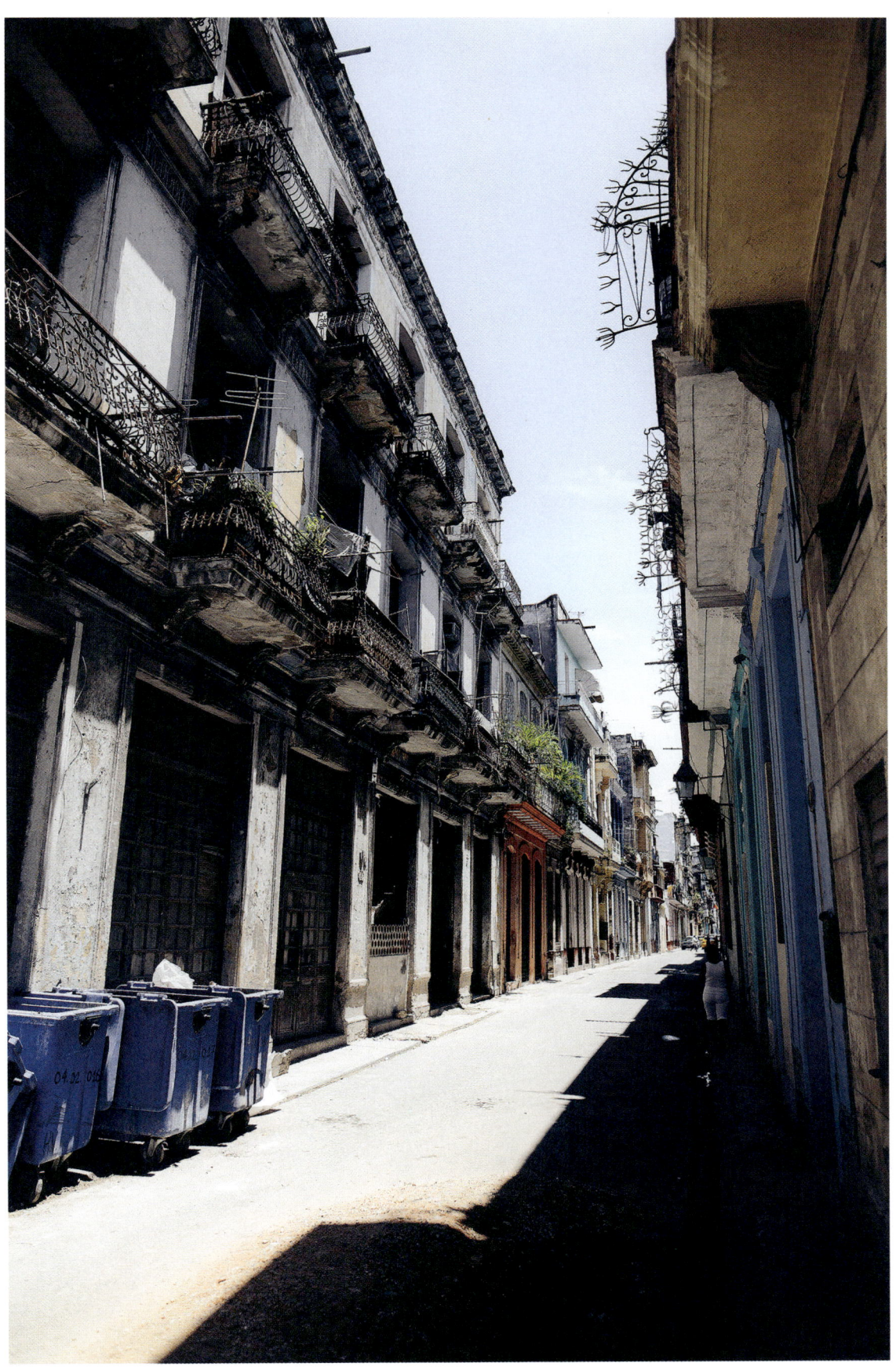

These streets stood out among so many similar ones; the buildings are quite old, but they've retained so much of their colour.

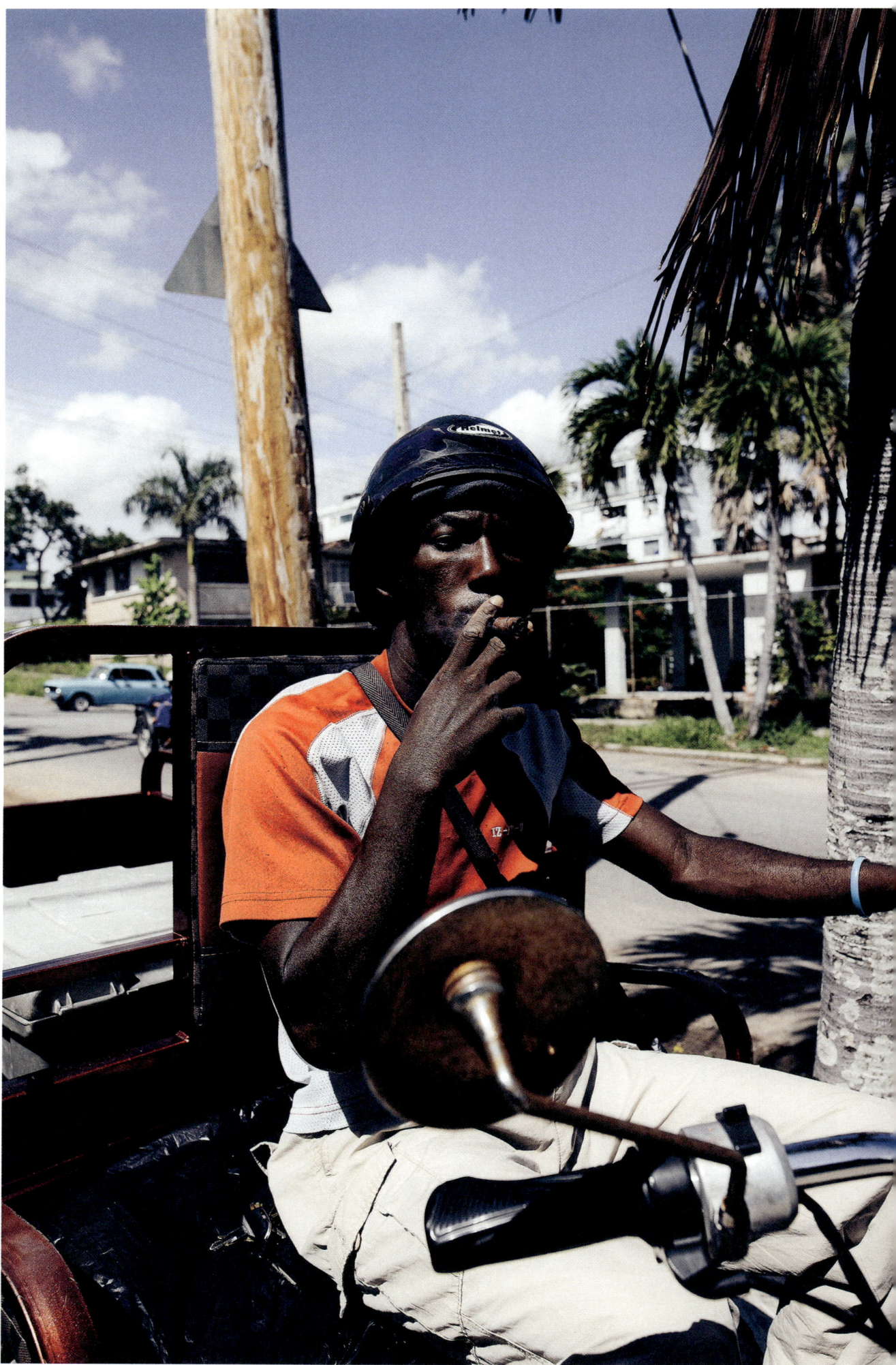

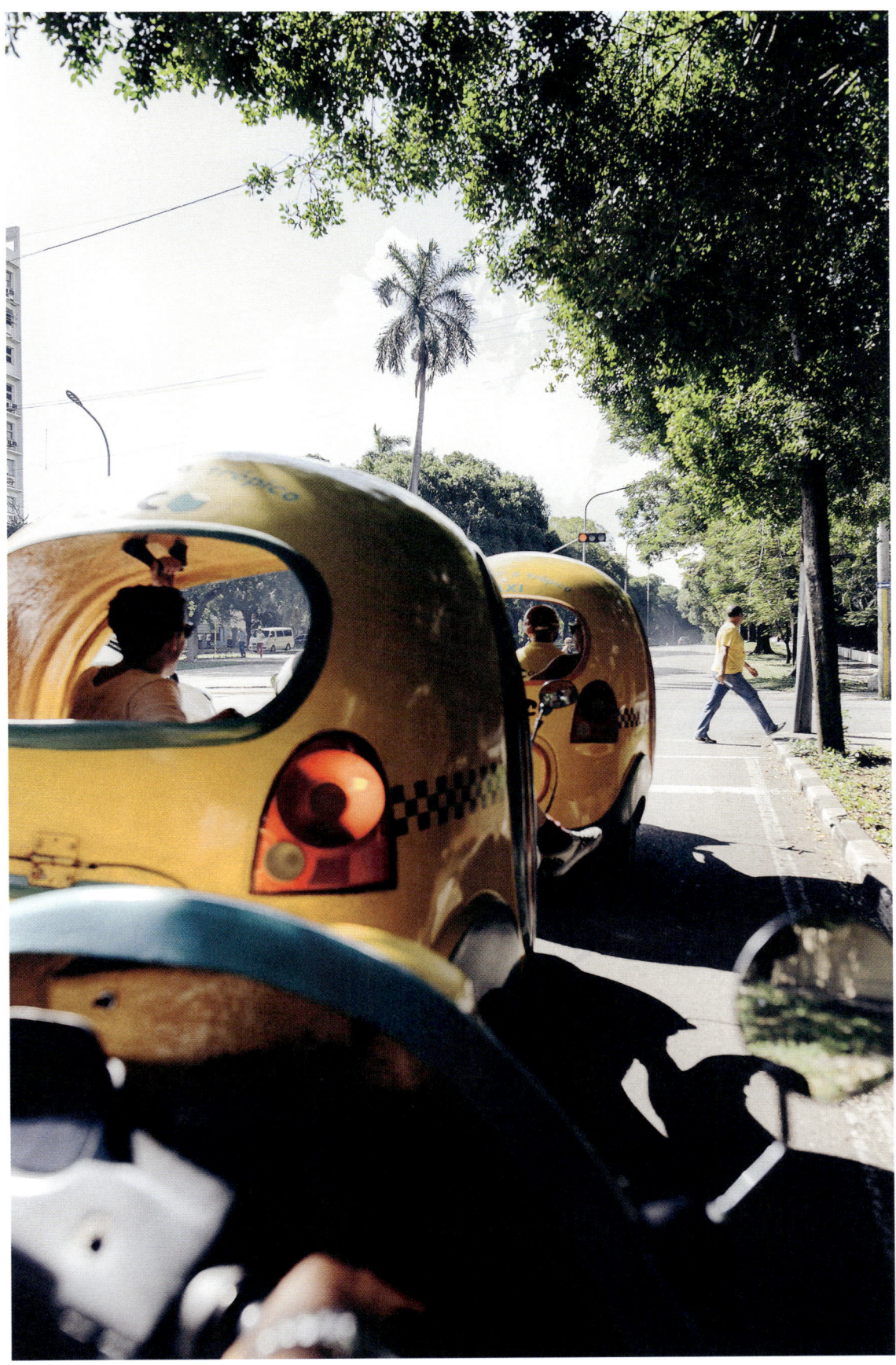

Left: Cigars are of course a big thing in Cuba. I really wanted to take this man's photo, but I was hesitant to approach. I took out my camera to show him, since I speak no Spanish, and got an entirely different reaction than I expected. He smiled and motioned for me to take his photo, then wanted me to take more when I showed him the picture.

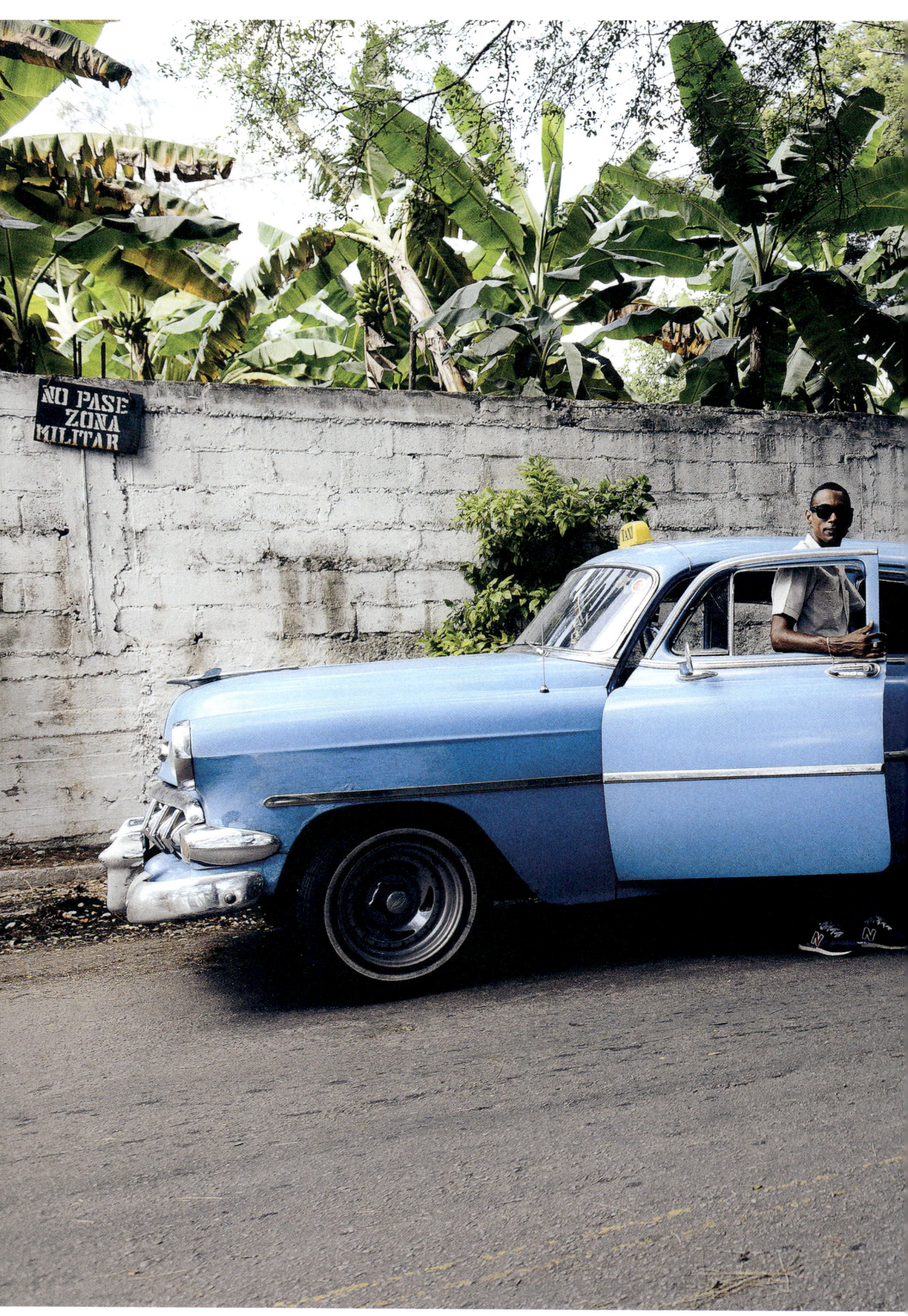

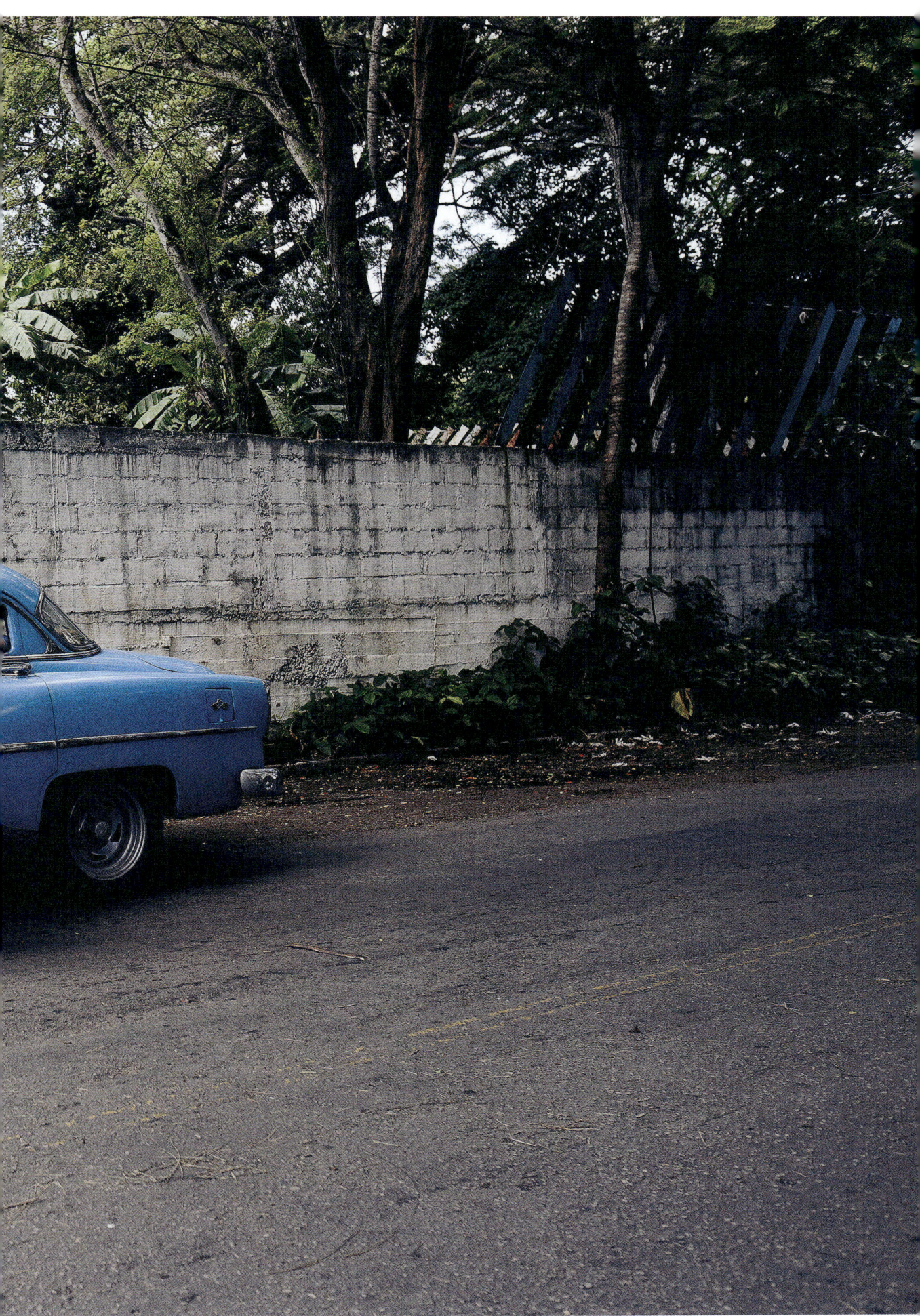

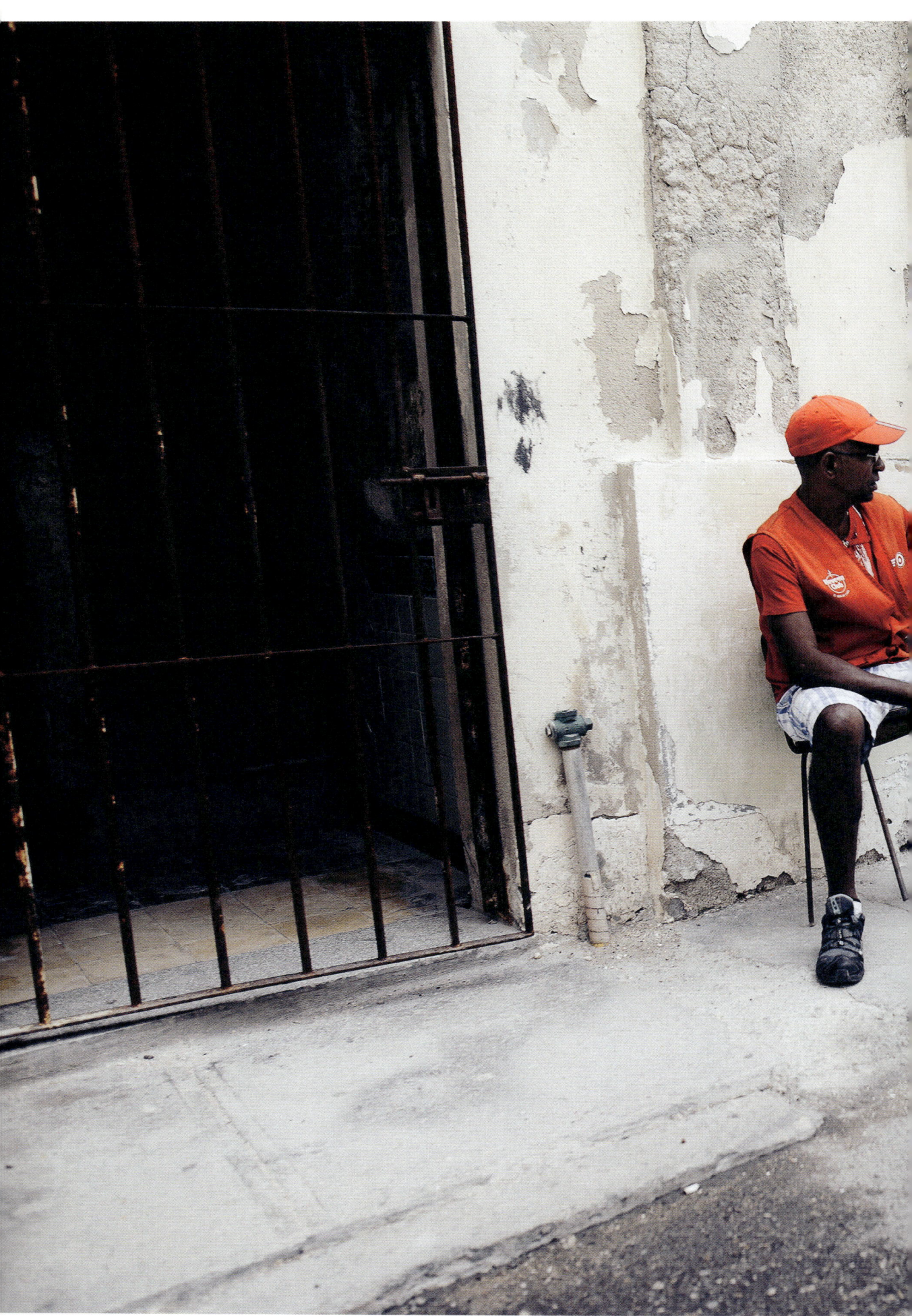

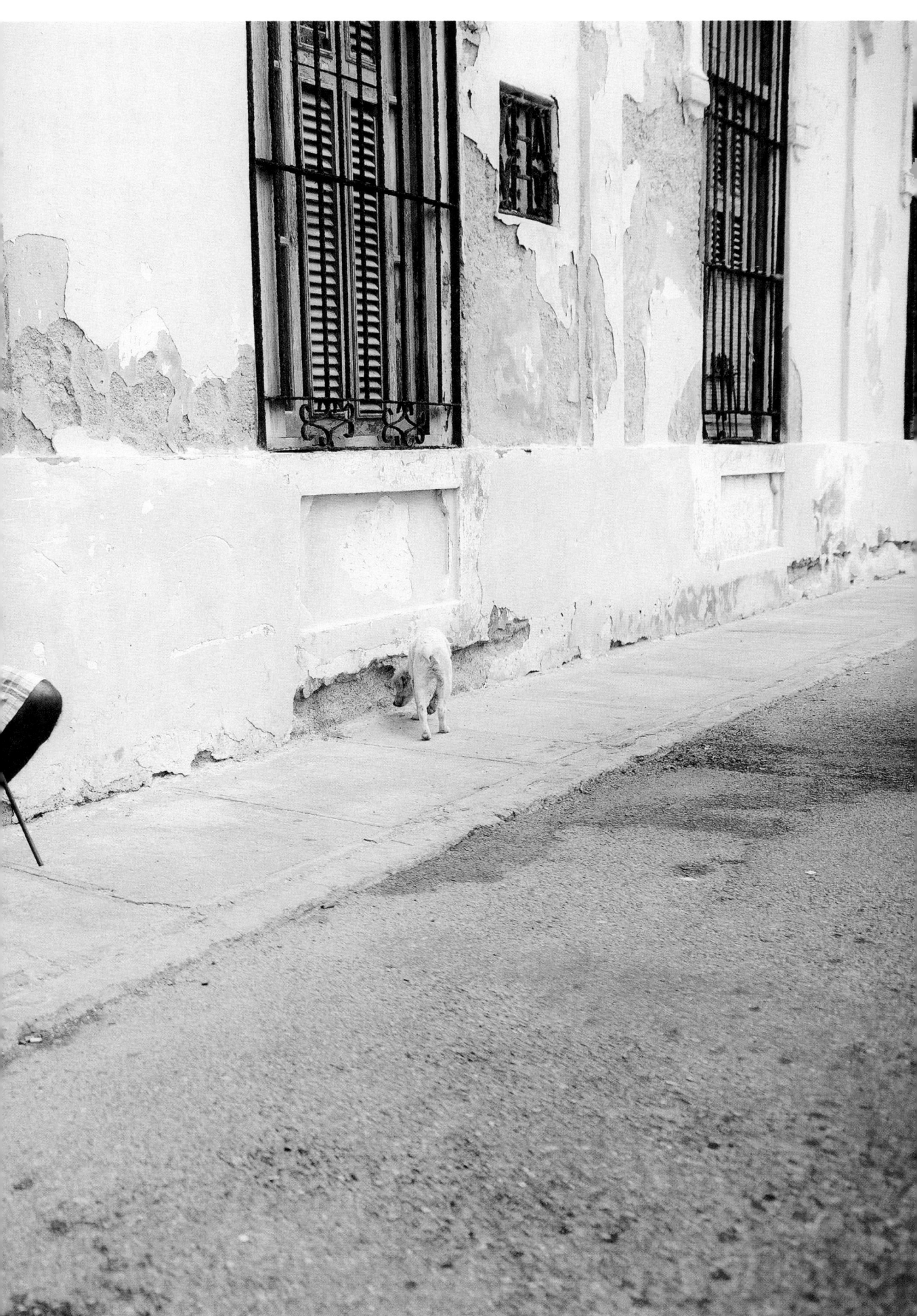

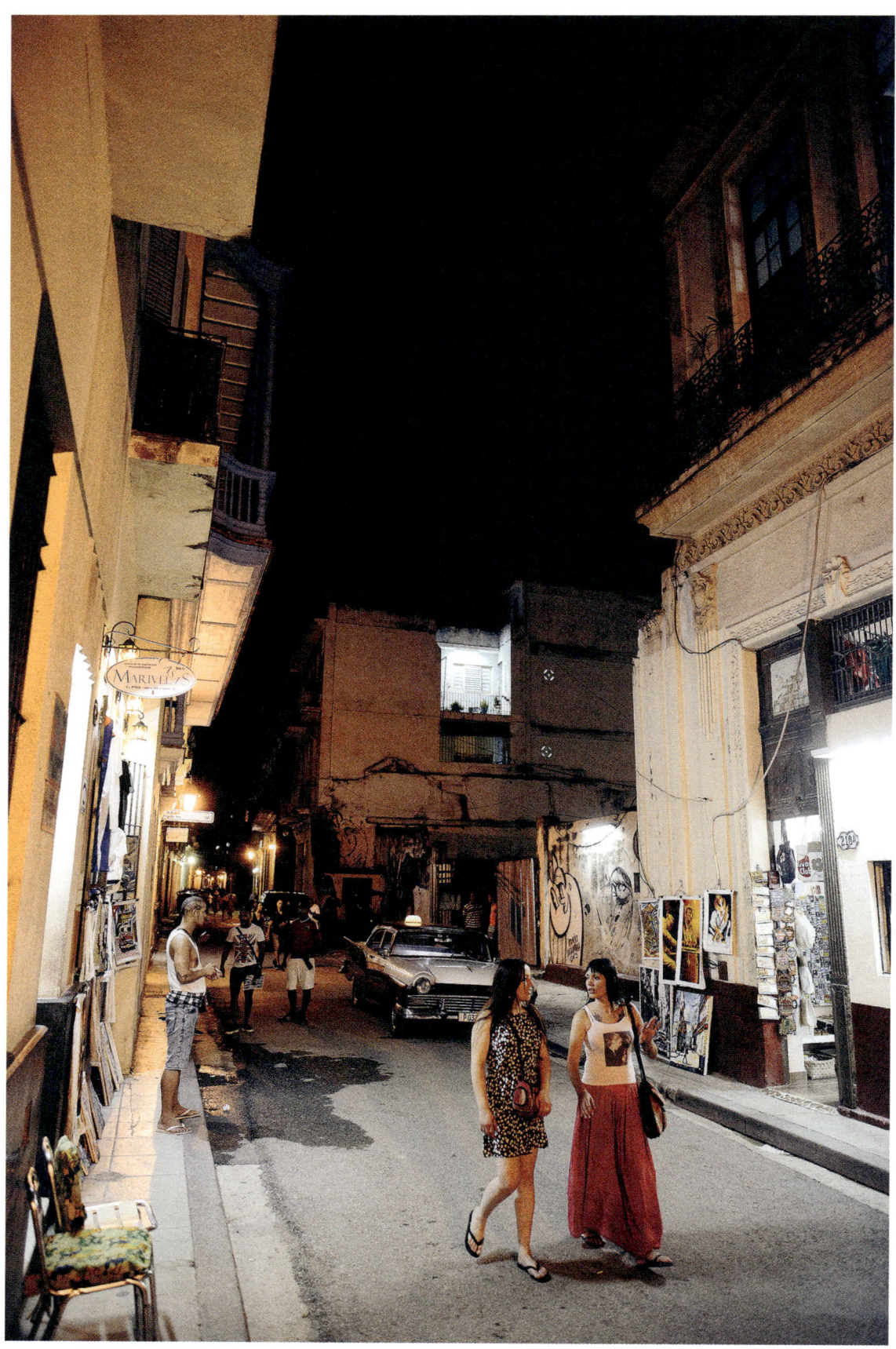

Seemed like no one wanted to sleep; people were out quite late, shops were open, there was just as much life and vibrancy at night.

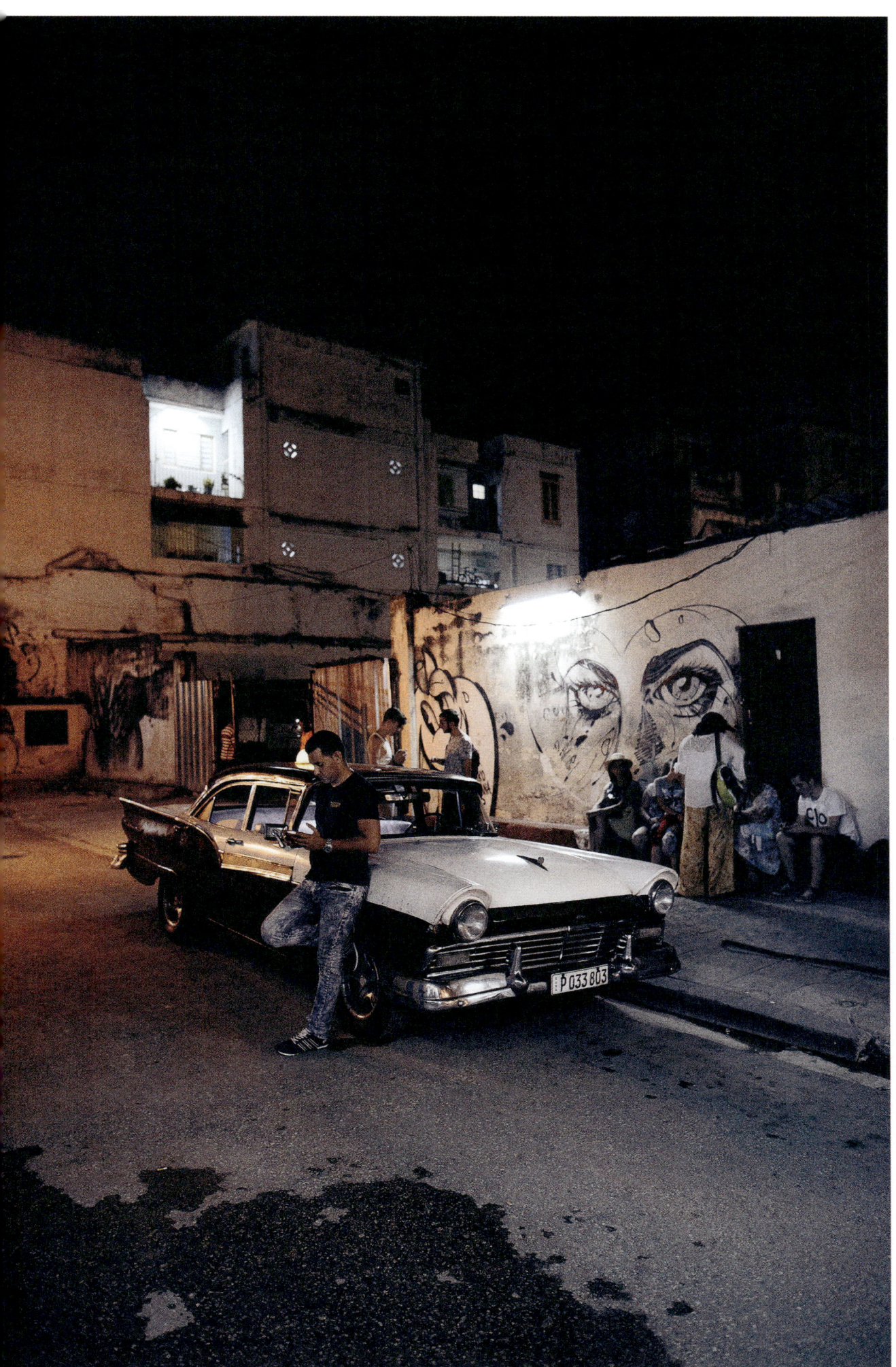

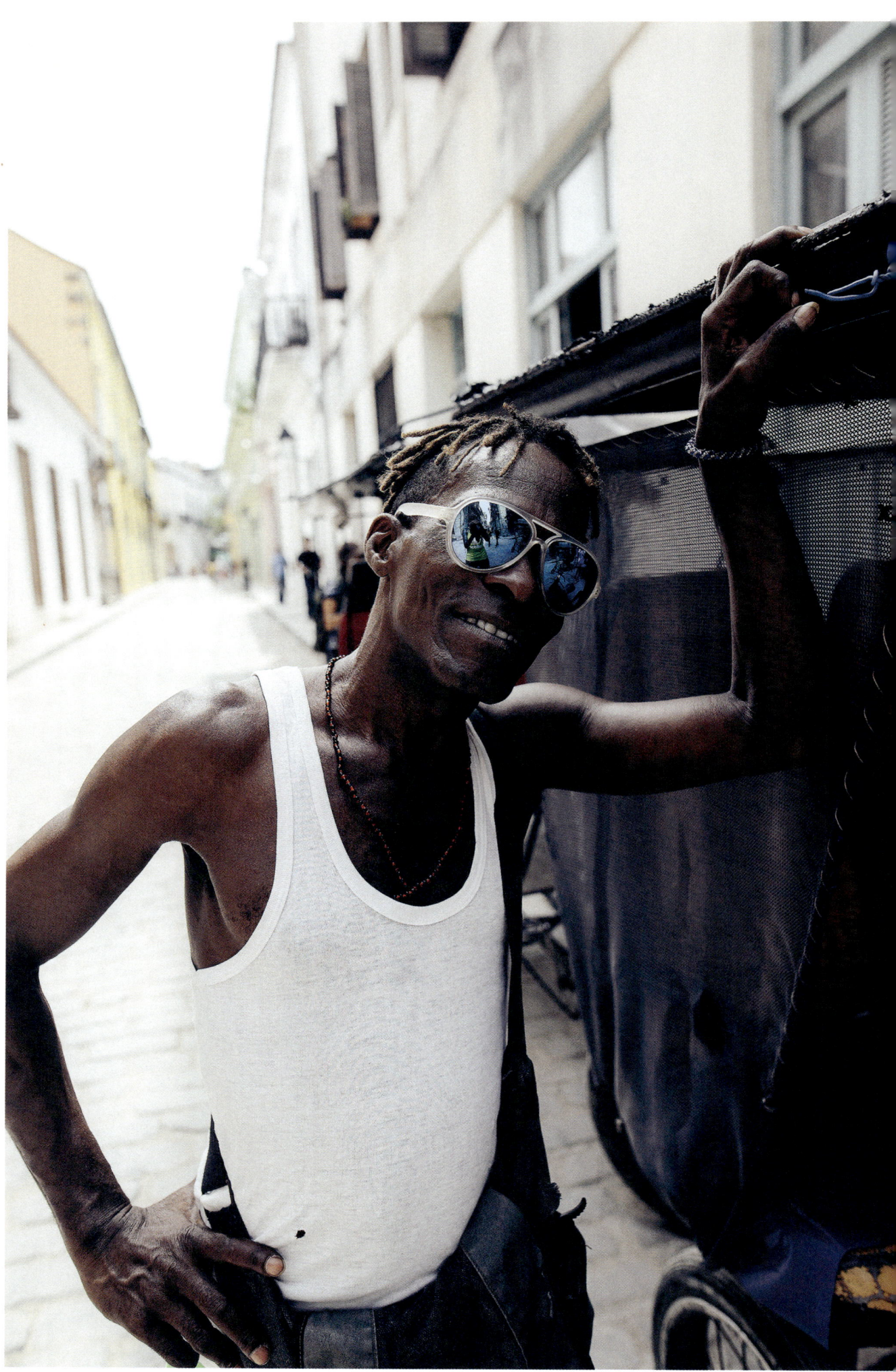

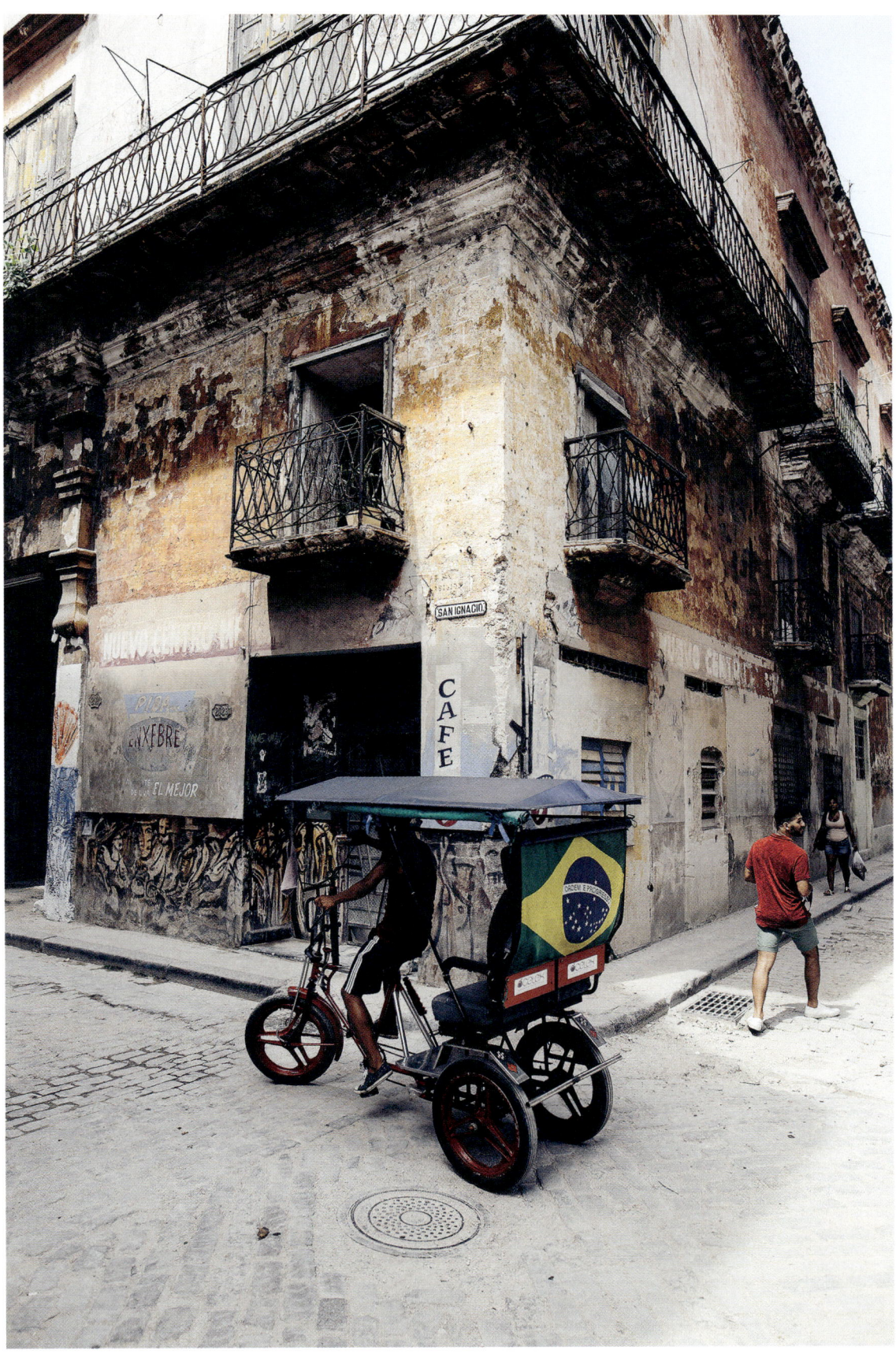

Everyone I saw seemed to have a sense of pride, something they were happy about.

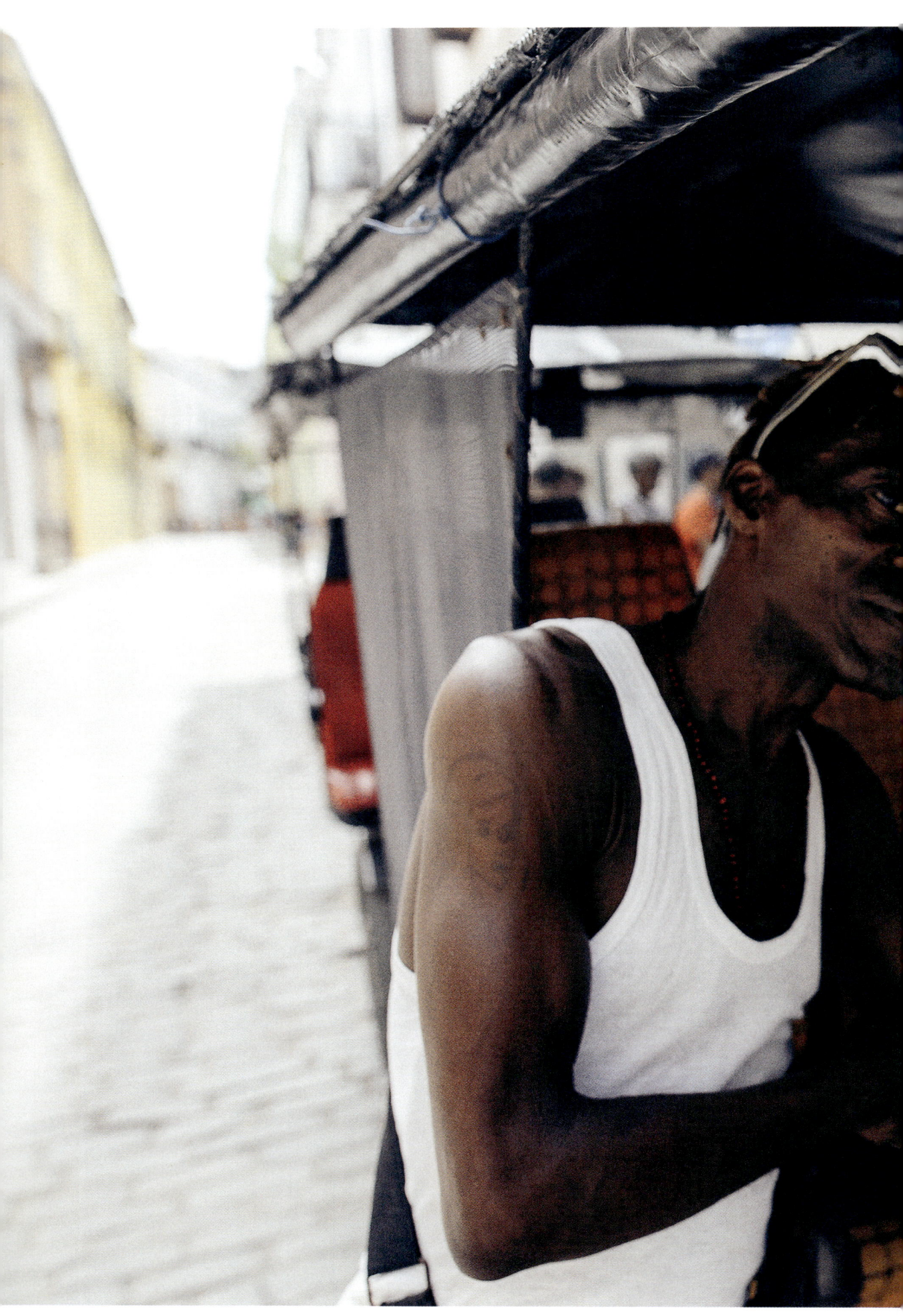

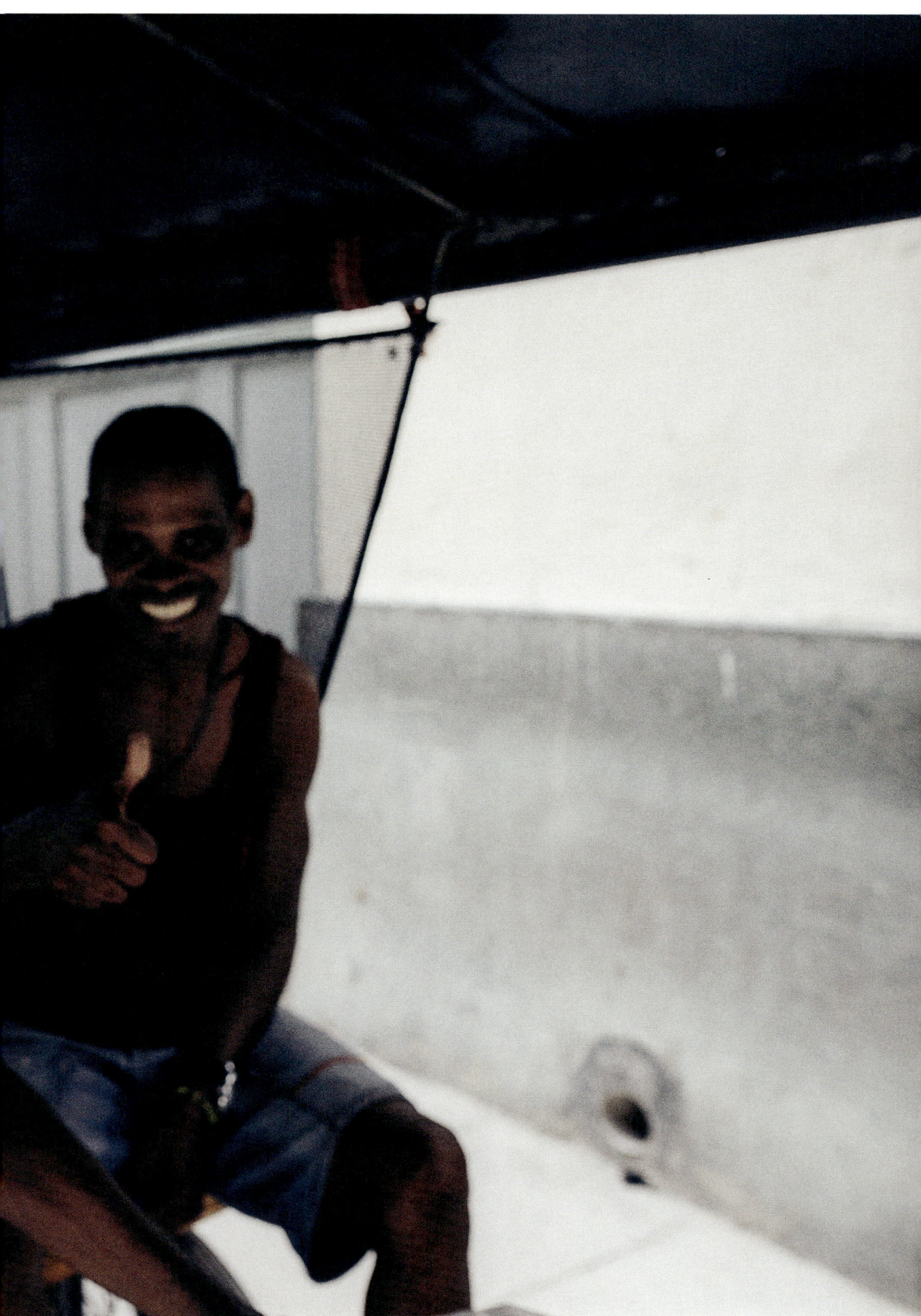

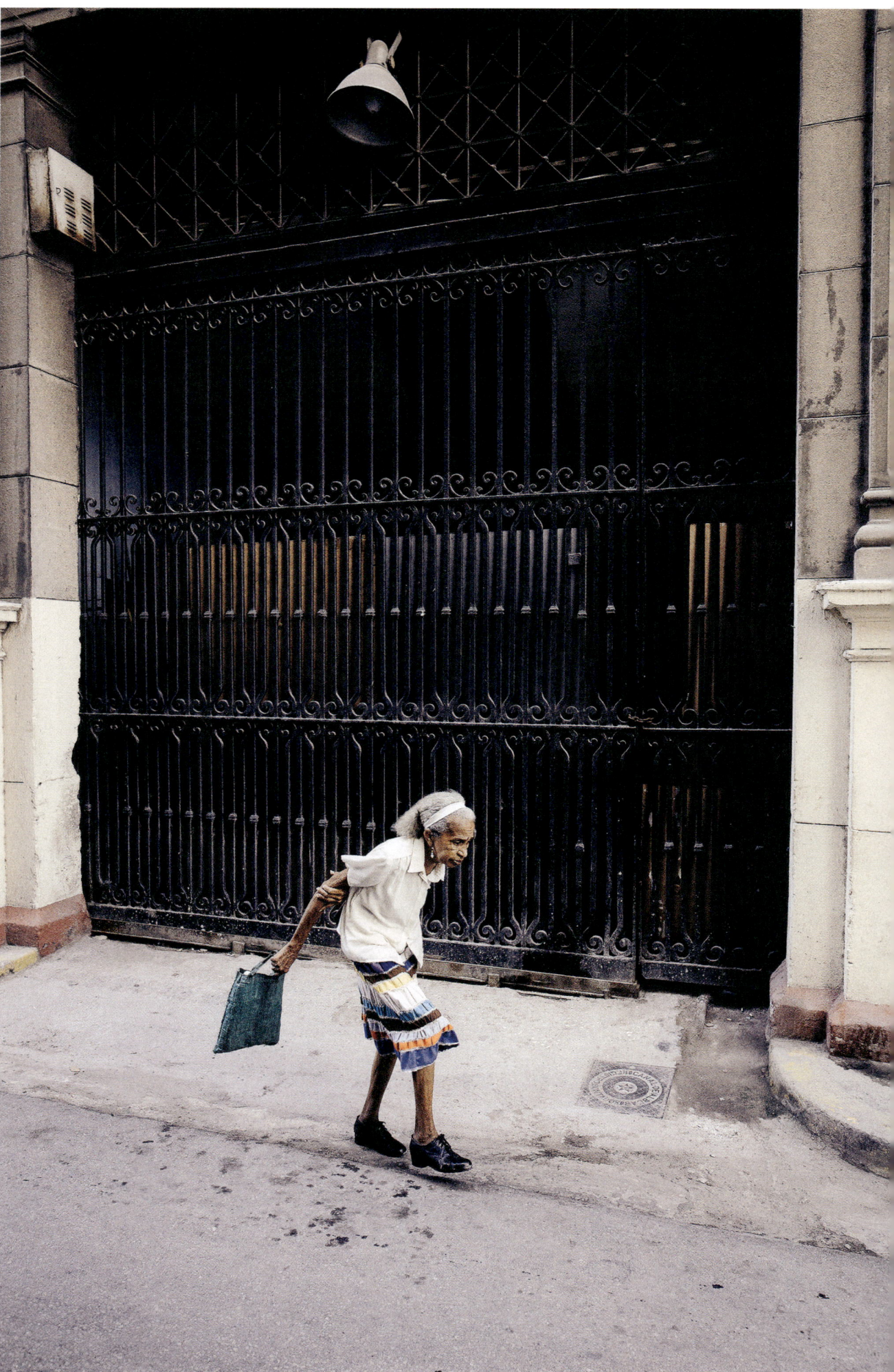

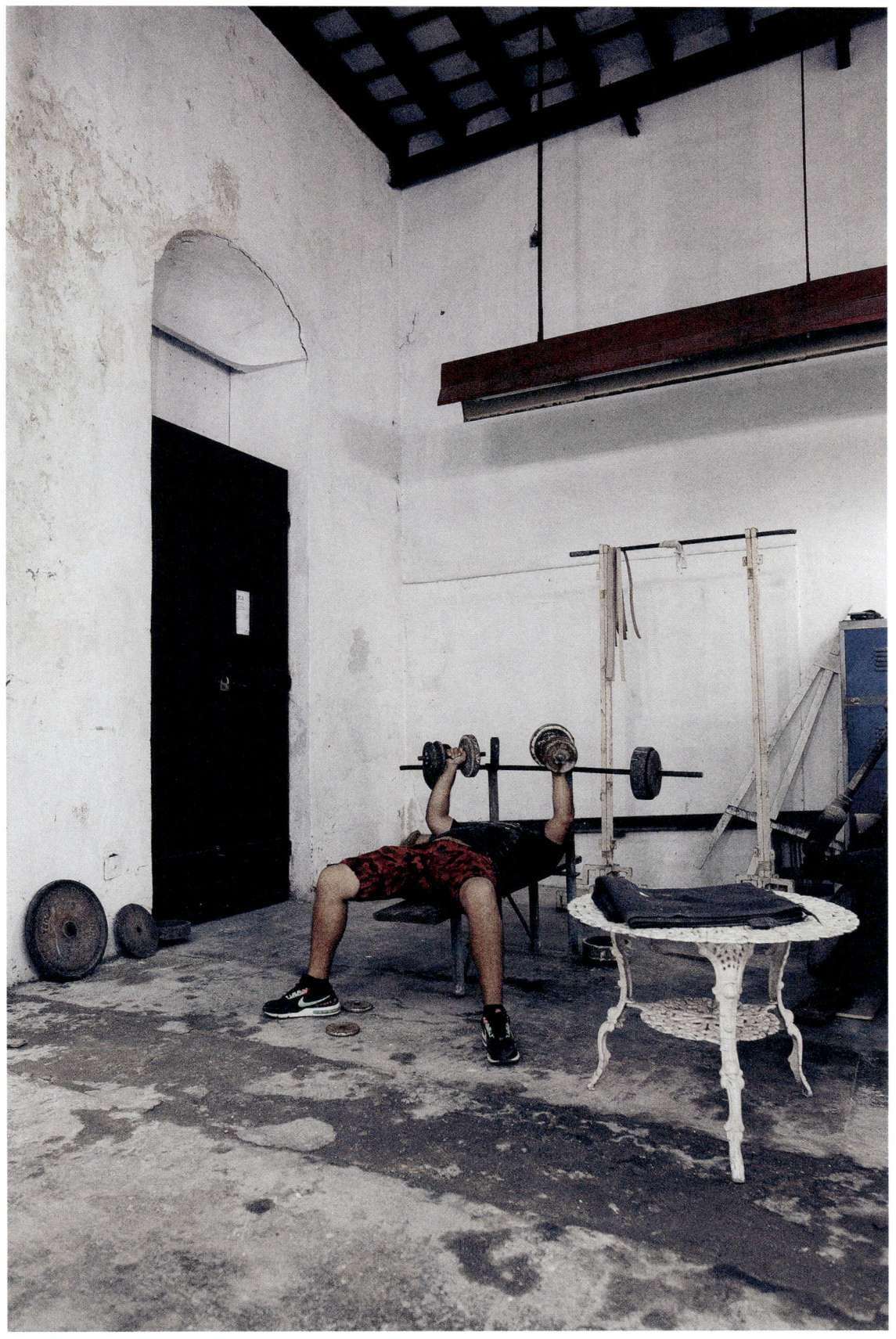

Whilst touring a print studio, it was a little unusual encountering this guy in his makeshift gym area.

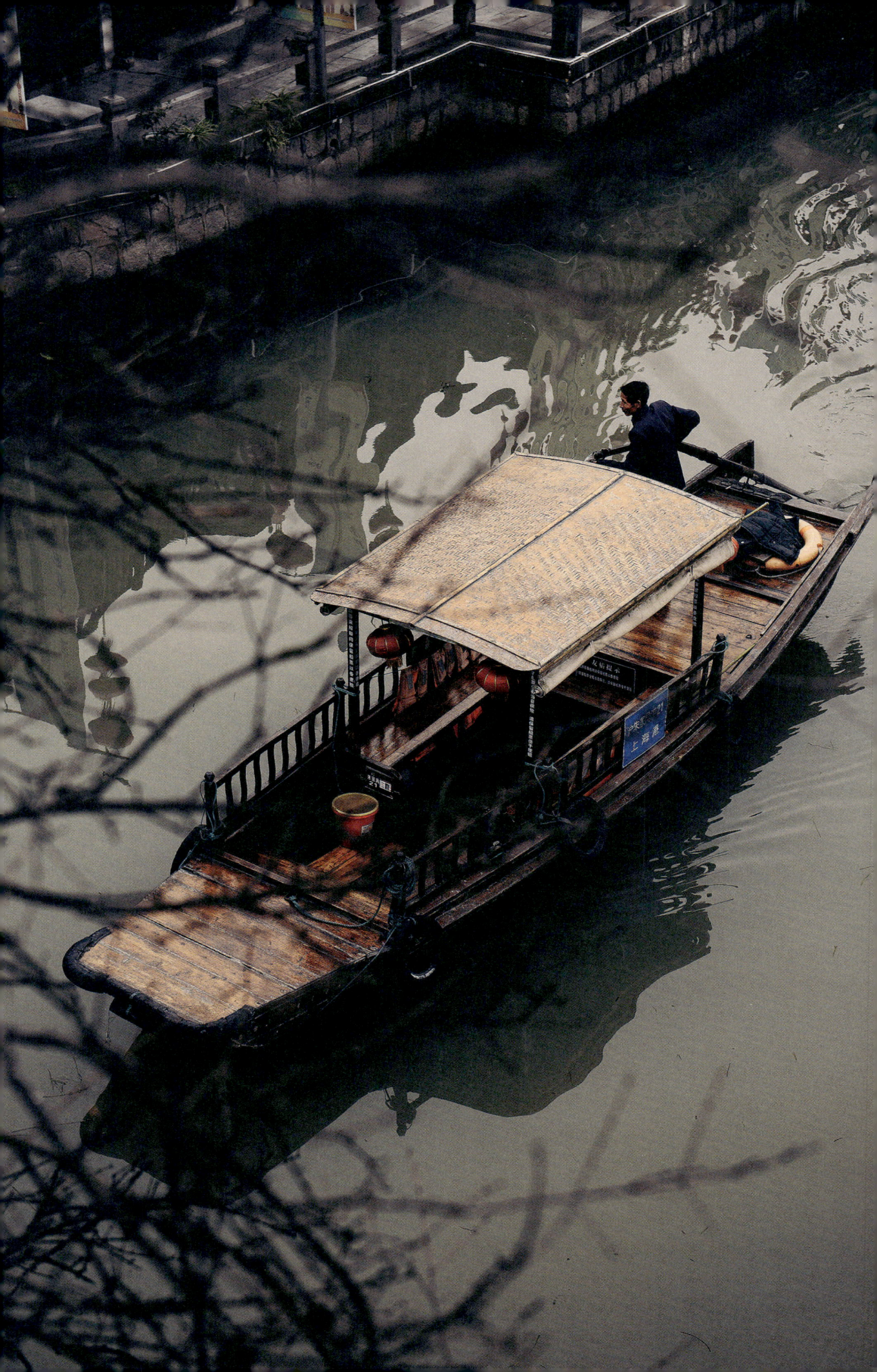

NOTES ON ASIA

I loved every minute of my experiences in Asia — Hong Kong, Shanghai & Japan for the stunning, ever-changing architecture, and Thailand for the embracing locals and addictive street food! Again, the people made me feel very welcome, and that's always a big plus when taking photographs in foreign countries, especially when not many speak any English. There was so much to explore and capture in each of these locations, so much that I feel I haven't done them justice with just one visit. I definitely would love to return someday, as I knew there were certain places I missed out on photographing.

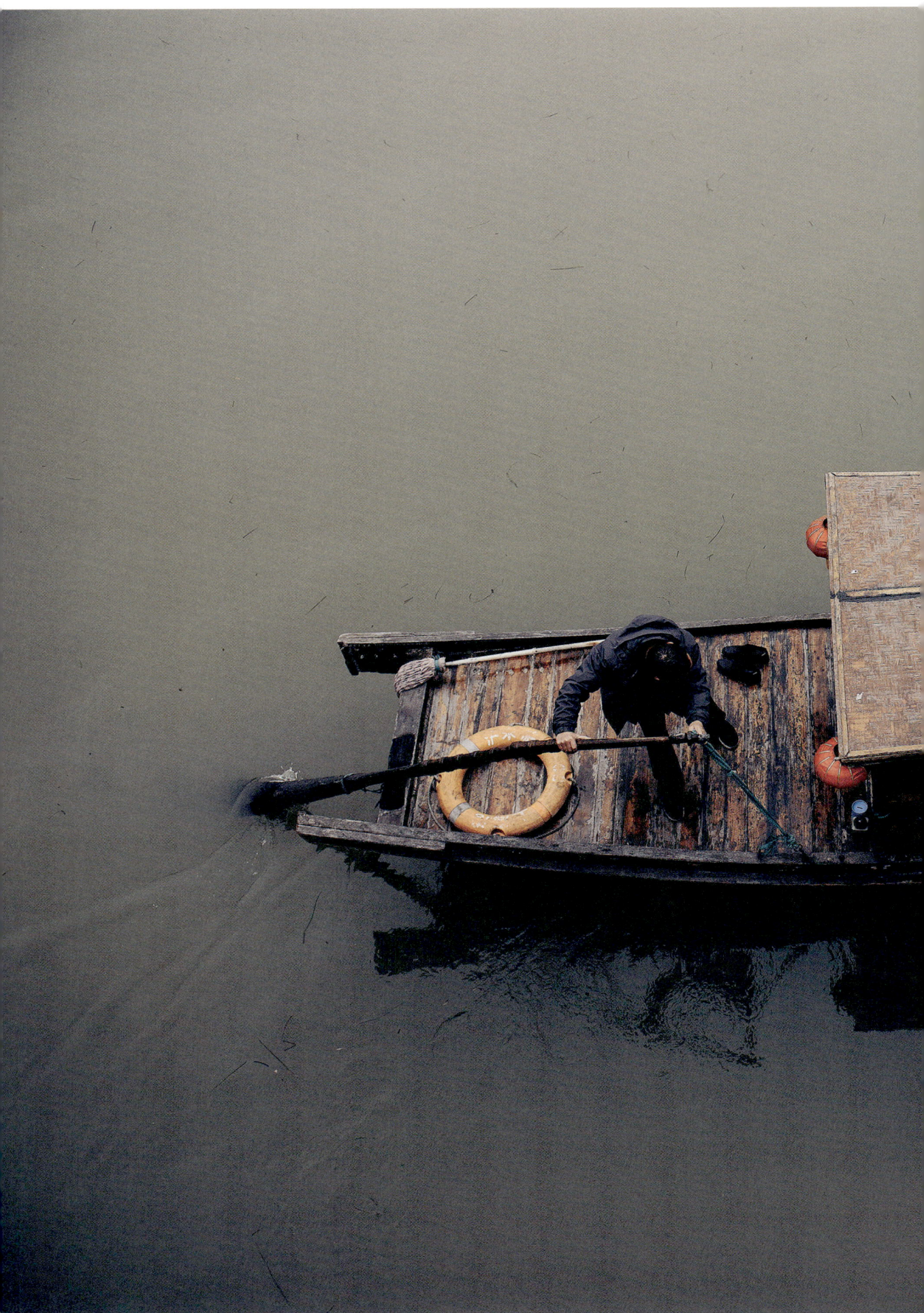

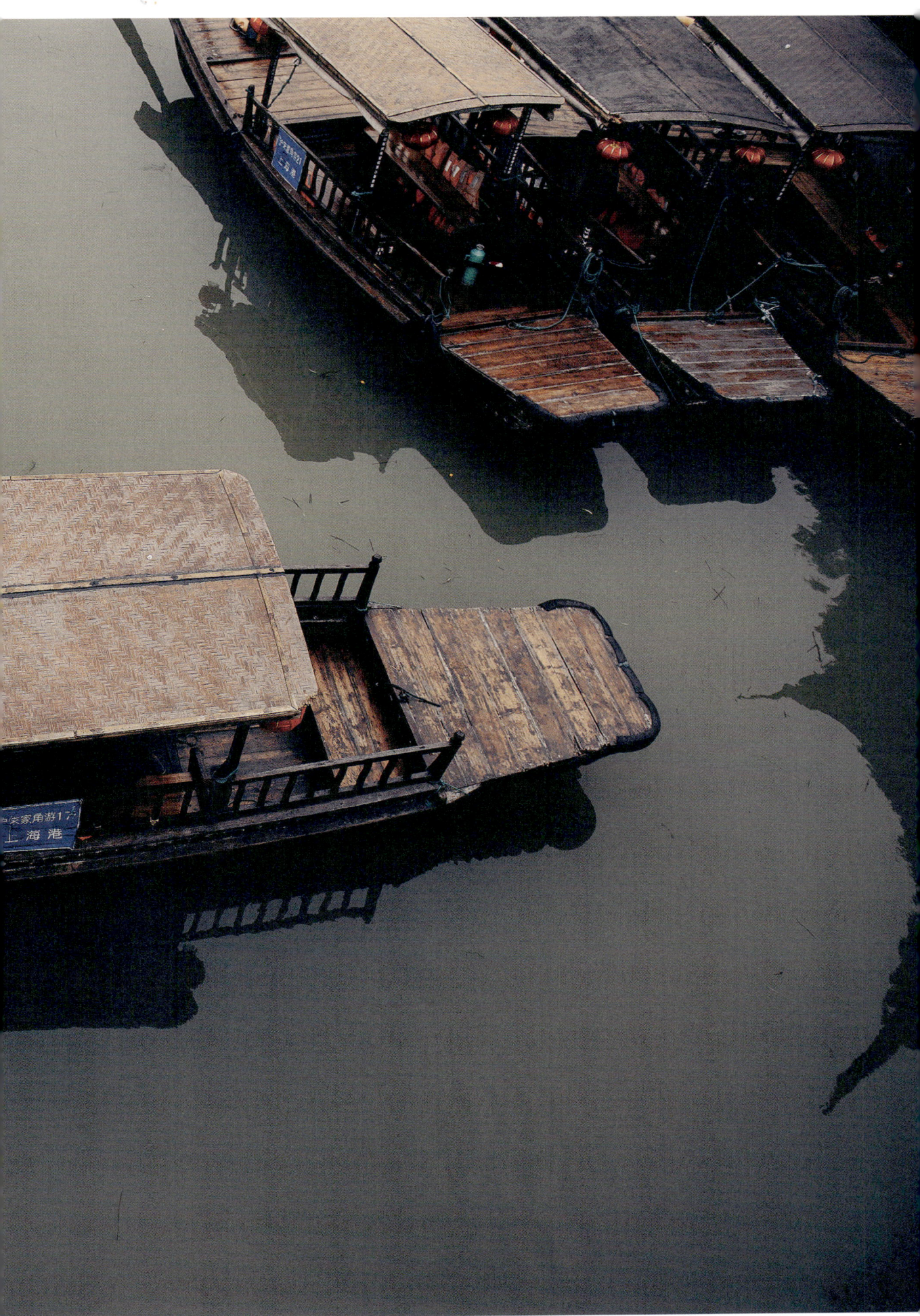

So much life happens on the water in Bangkok. Kitchens opening directly onto the river. Floating markets. There was a sense of going with the flow, of fulfilment, among the hardworking people I met and photographed.

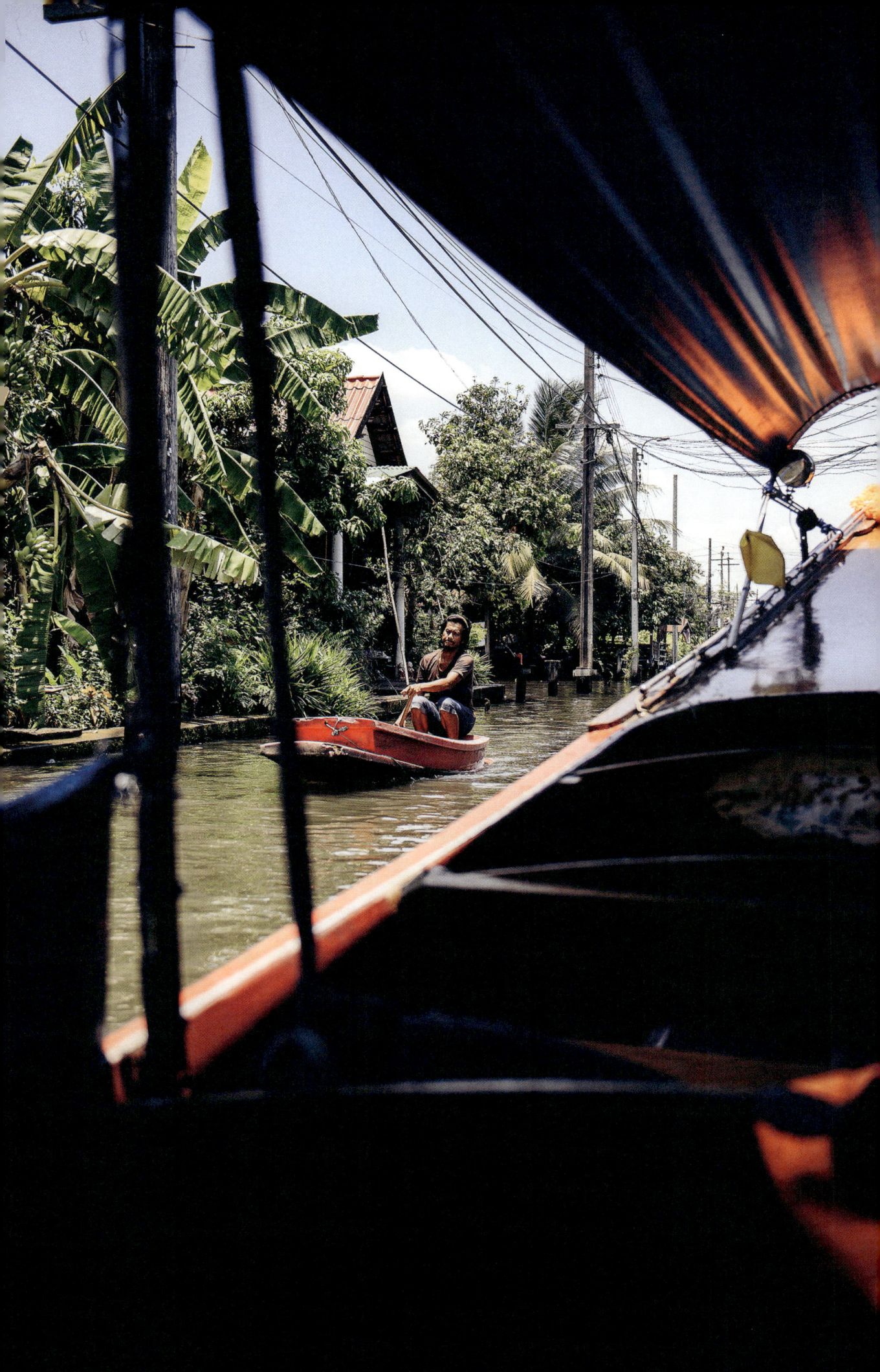

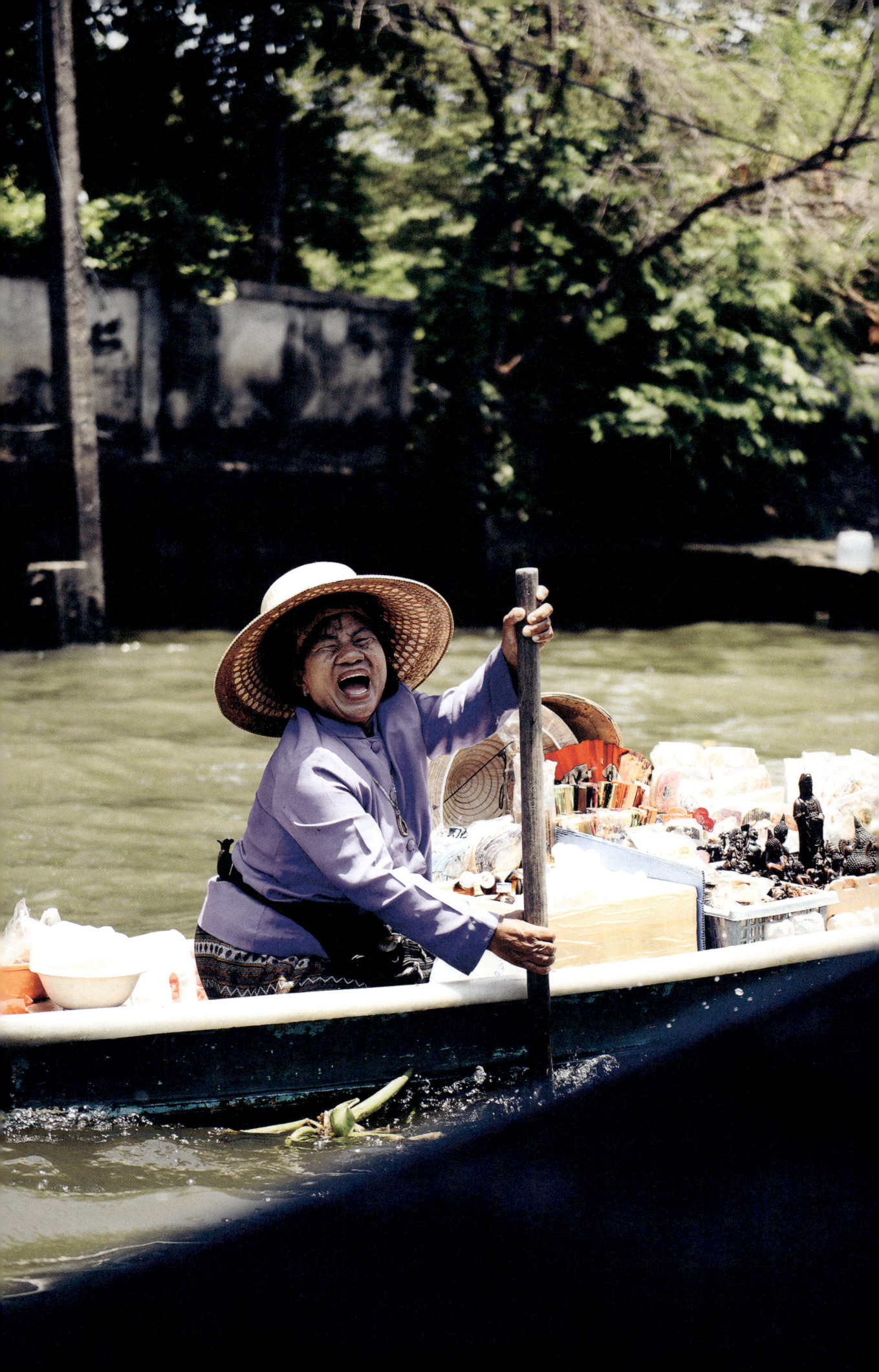

Respect the hustle. Doesn't matter how old you are. Never witnessed anyone row so fast as this lady right here, coming at our boat in Thailand. She was selling all sorts of tchotchkes – ornaments, keyrings, other tourist stuff. She was so enthusiastic, so cheerful, I had to buy something. I would have anyway, based on her sheer effort alone.

The train runs directly through Maeklong Railway Market. Vendors know the schedule; they pack up in seconds before the train pulls in, and unpack just as fast, with barely a pause.

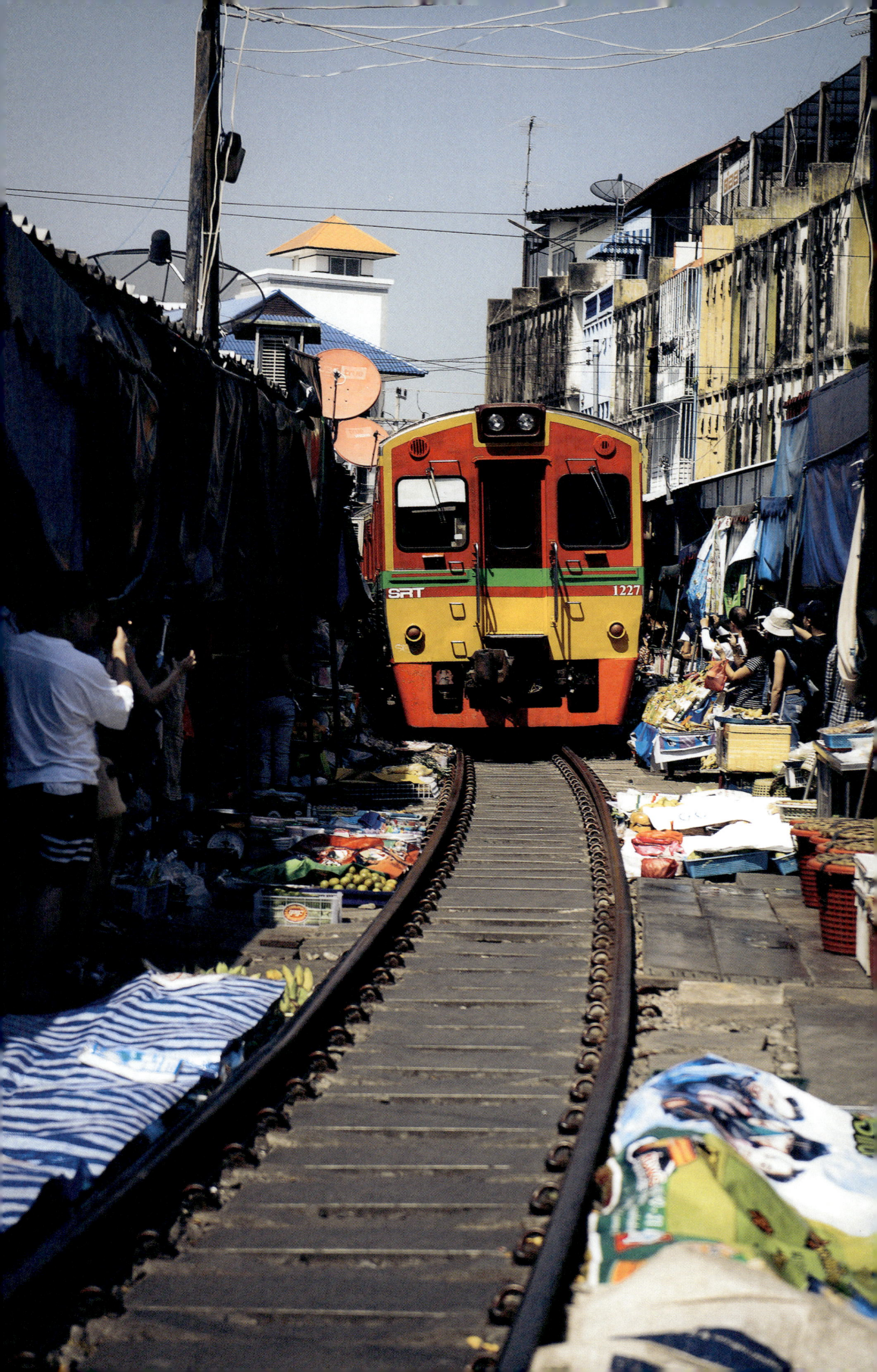

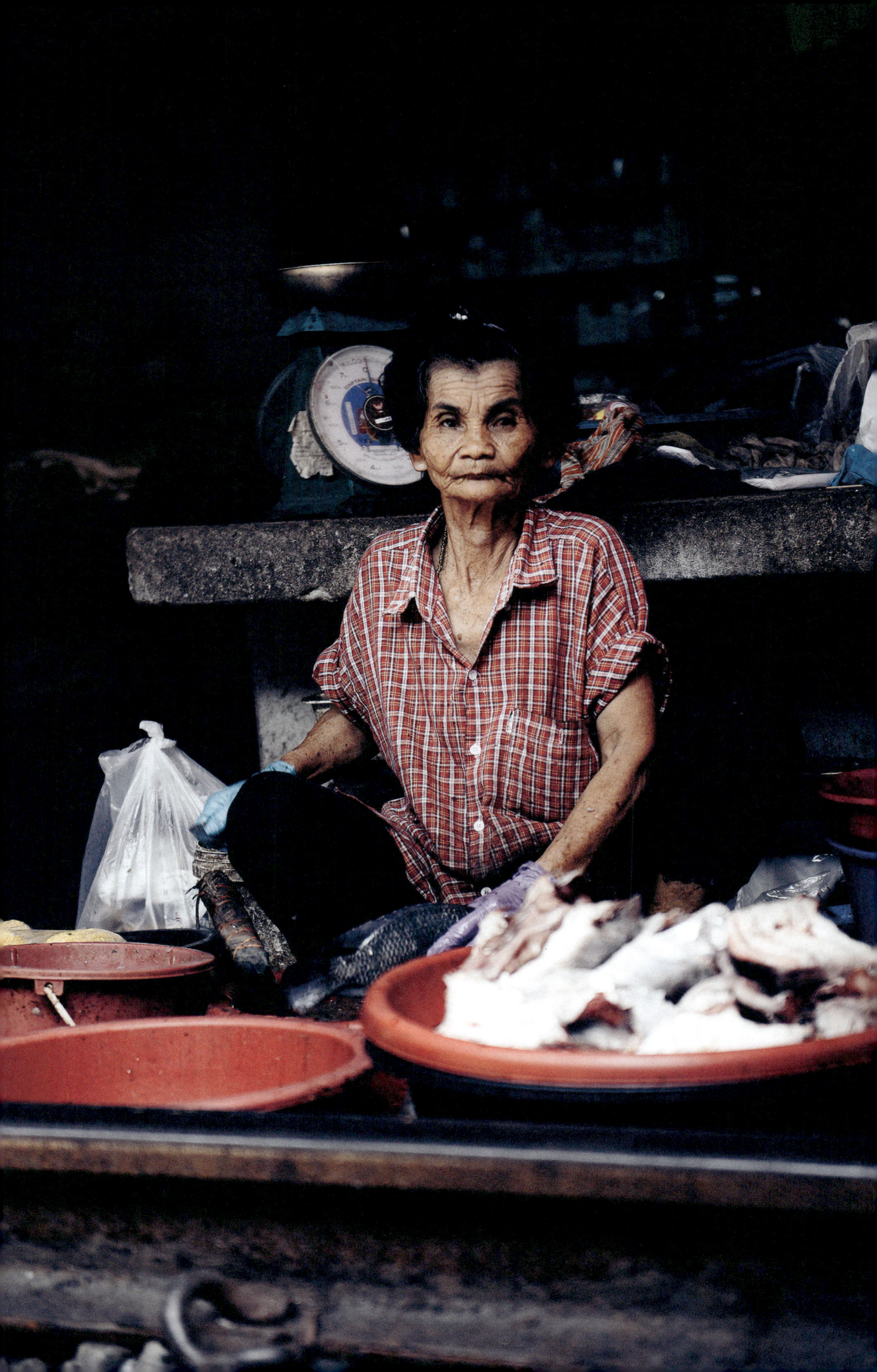

The moment after the train pulled through the railway market, this woman was back to her work. I was watching her from across the track and she knew I was taking her picture, but she didn't mind; she just got on with it. She seemed content in that moment, just absorbed in her work without worrying about anything going on around her.

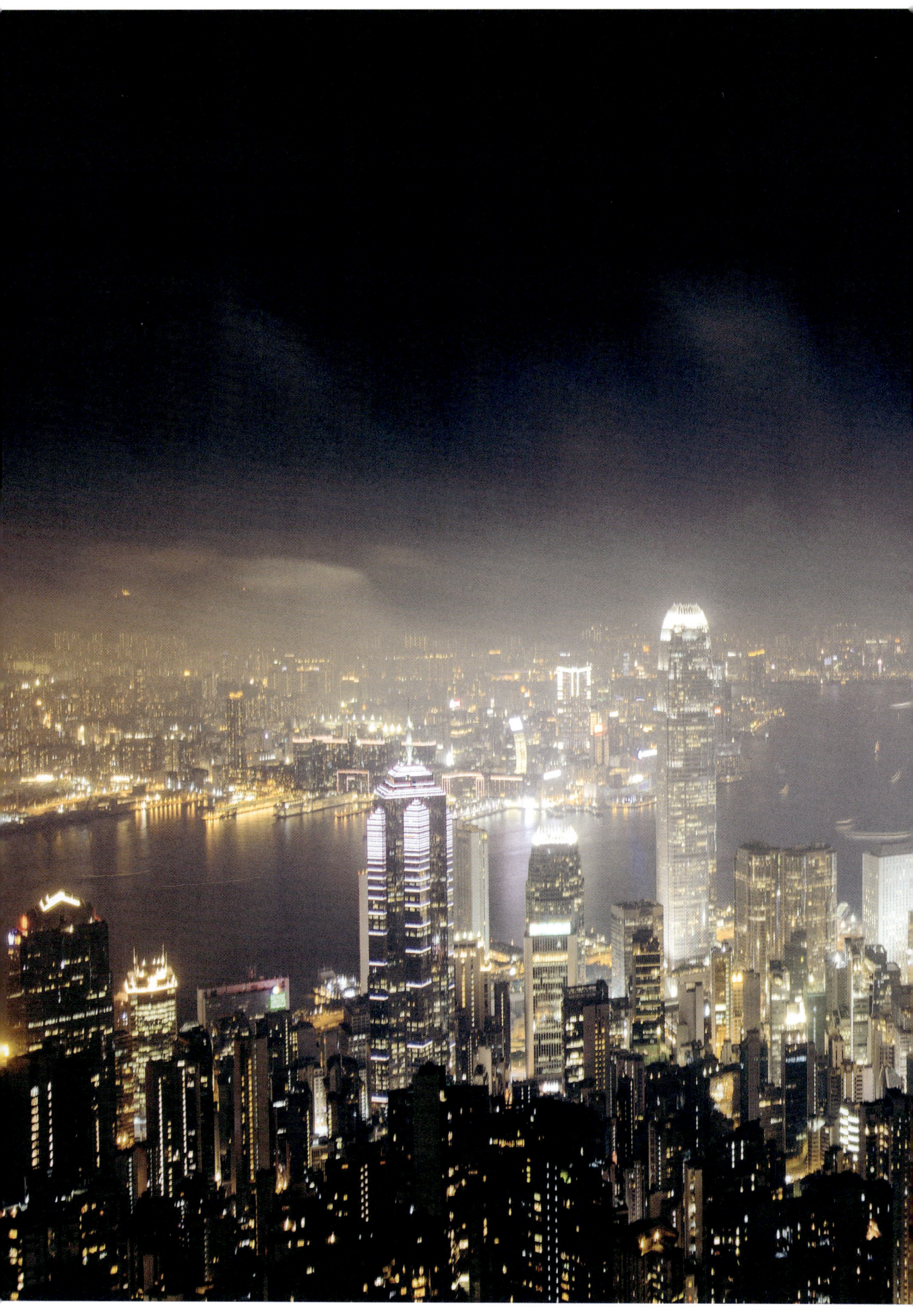

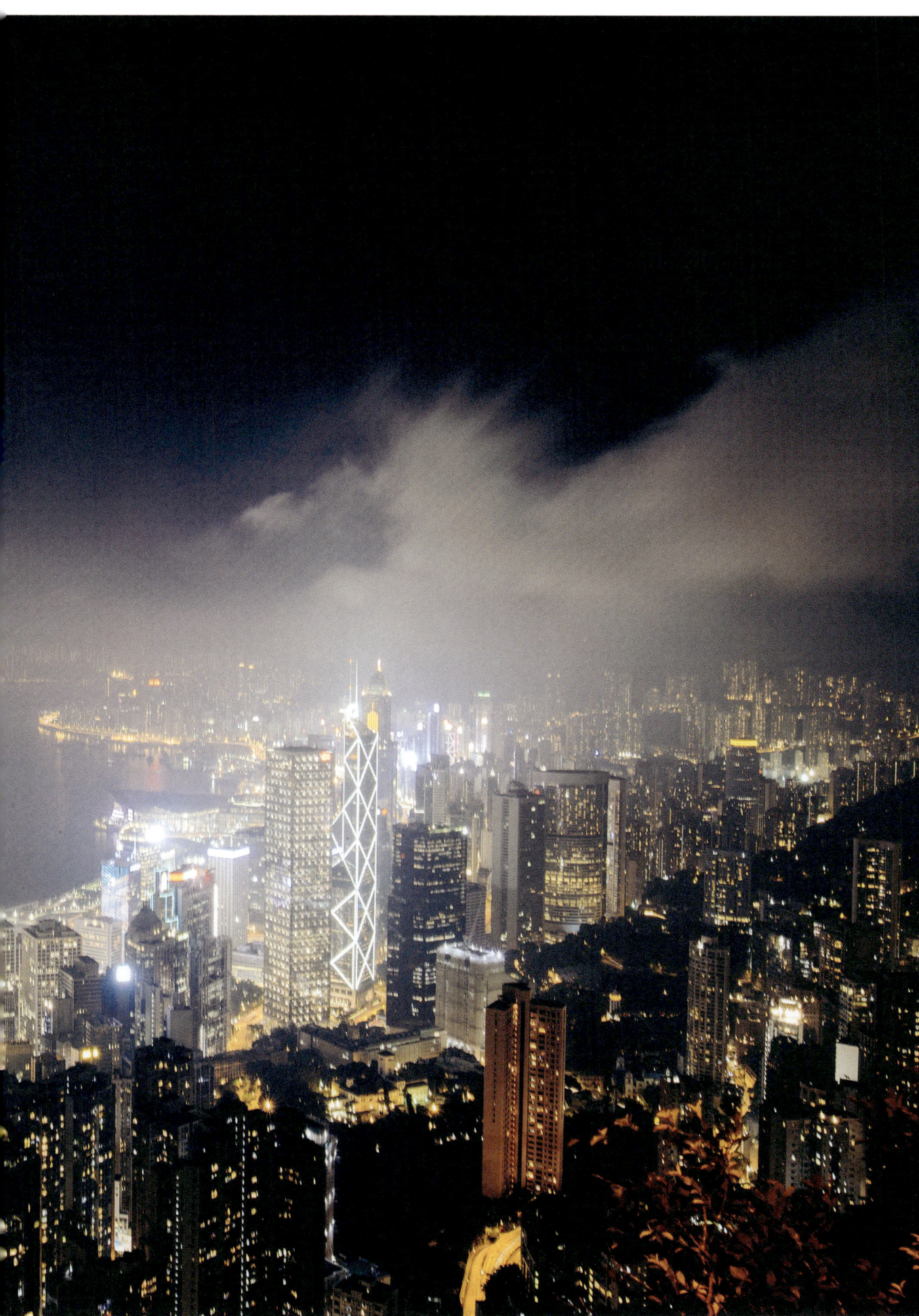

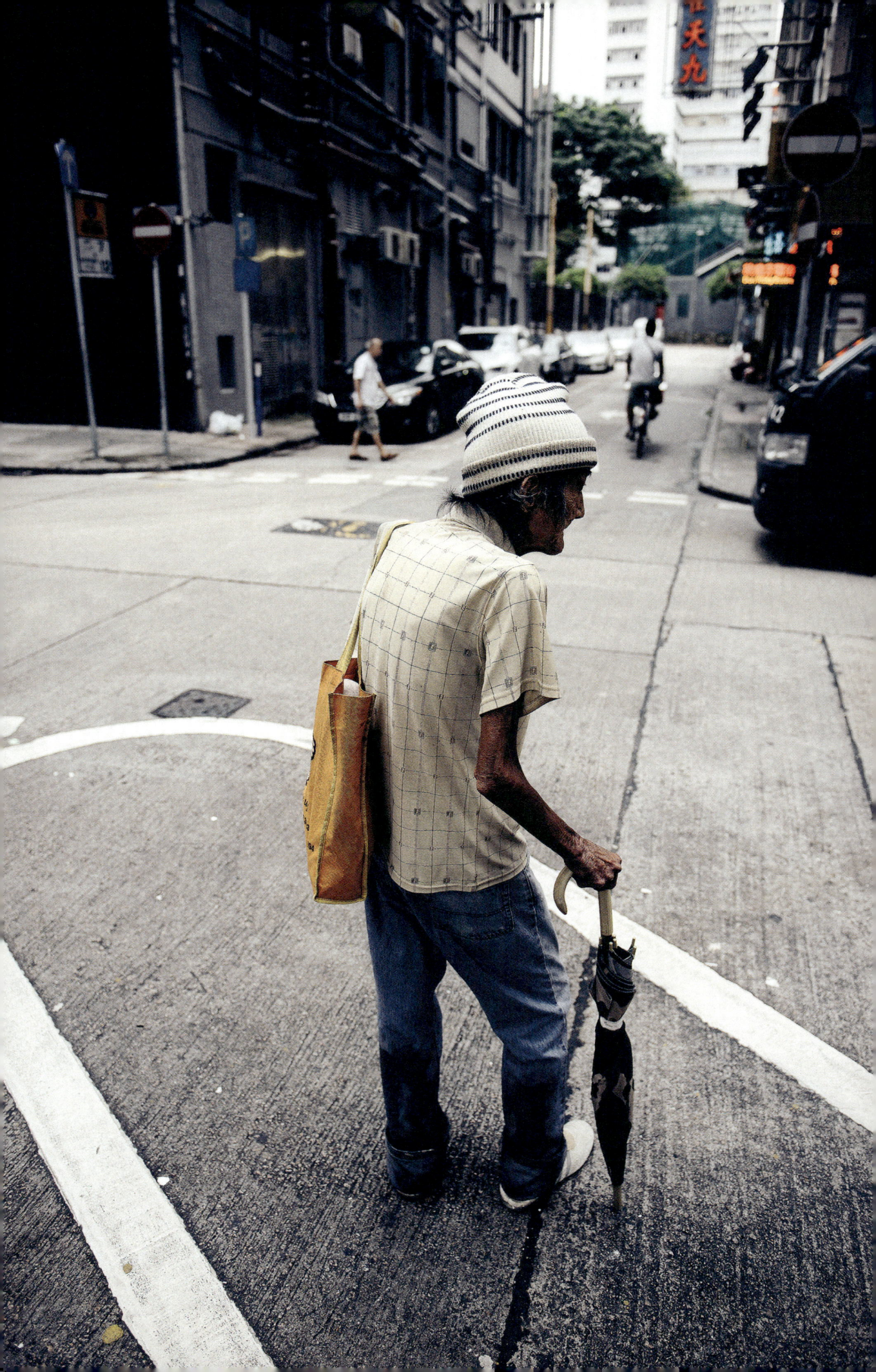

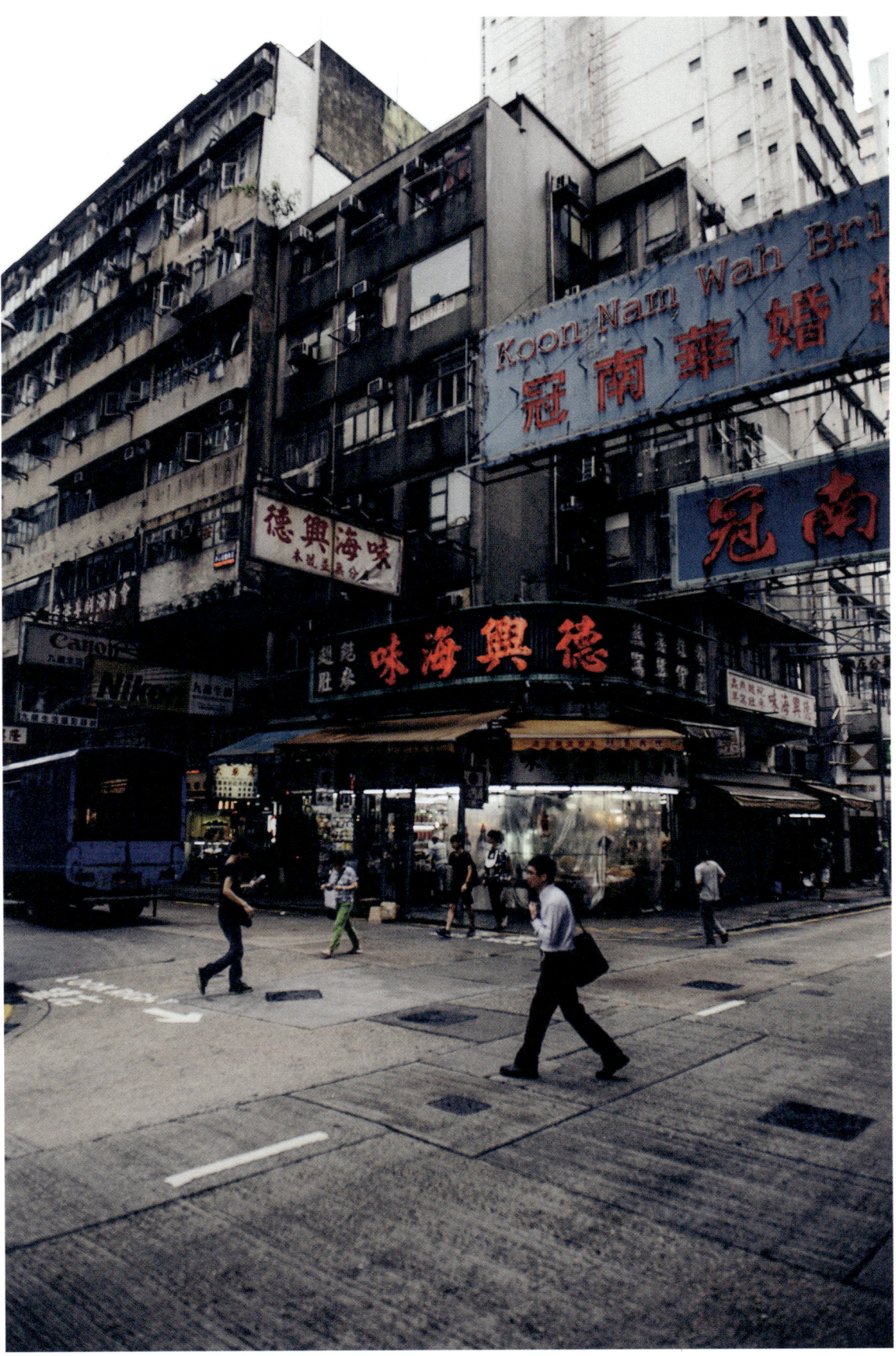

Everybody going about their business in Hong Kong. Loved observing the hustle and bustle of this street.

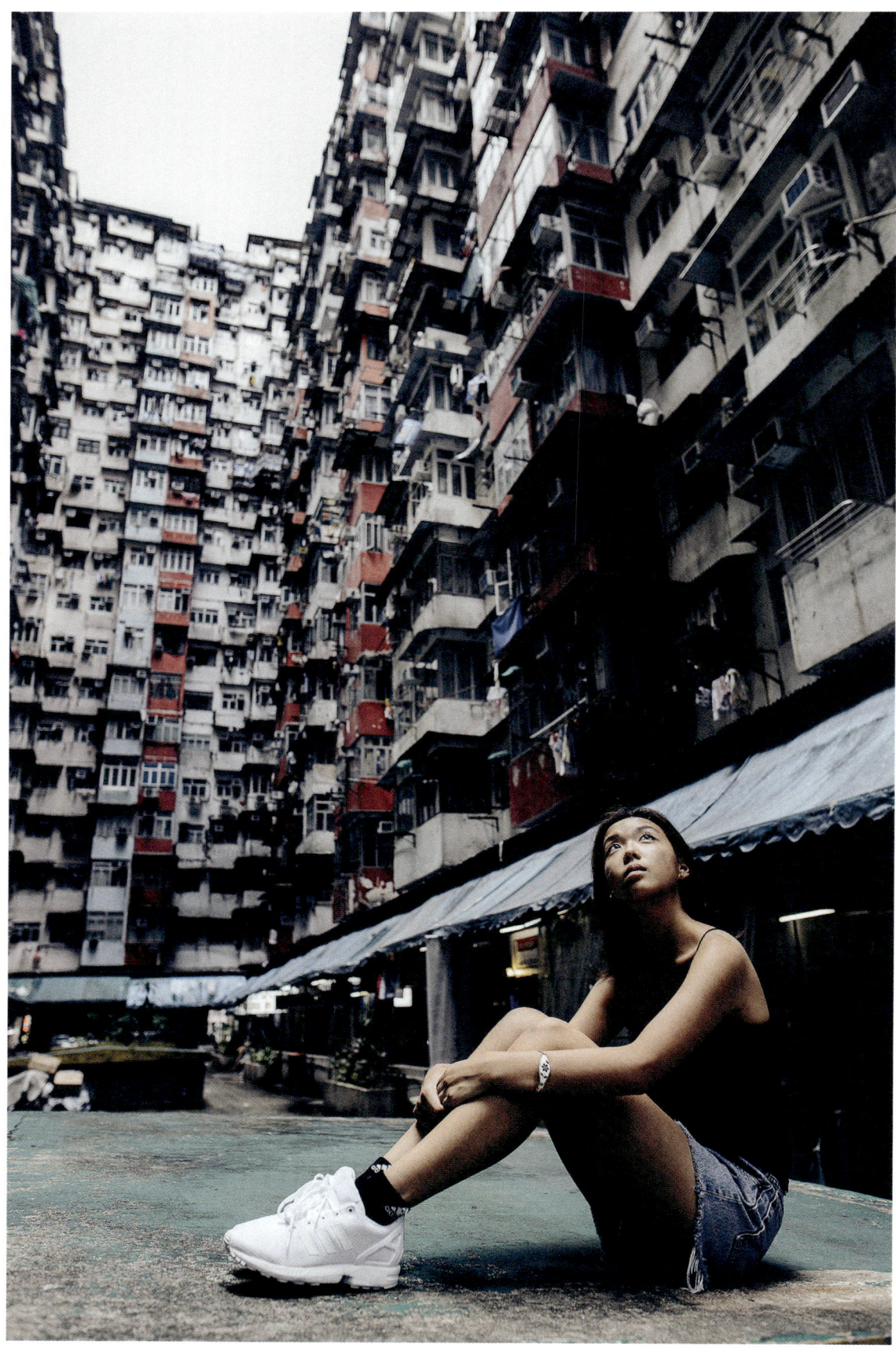

I have such an appreciation for the architecture of Hong Kong, the symmetry of it. Everything is just on top of each other, but in each window, there's a different story.

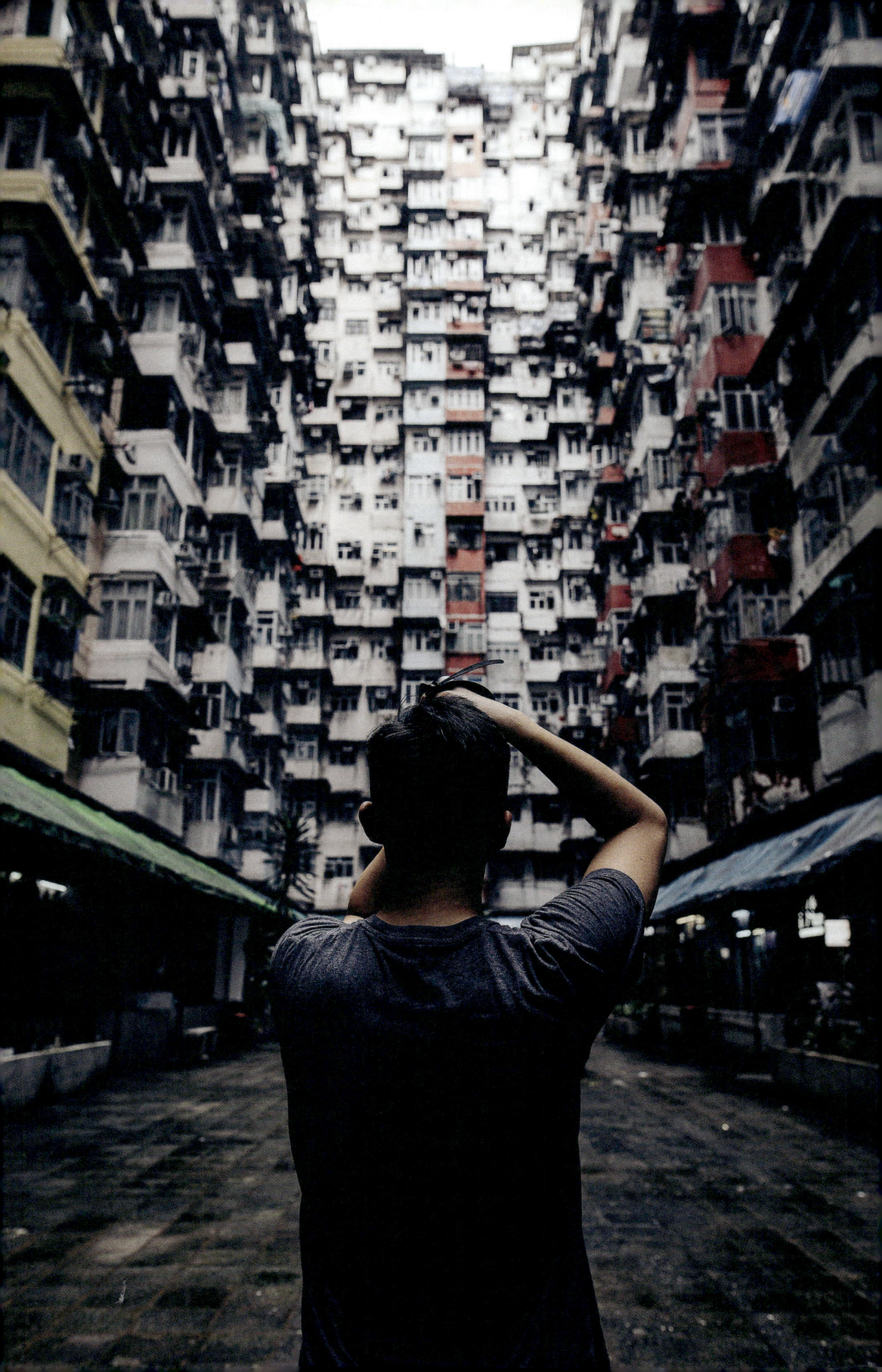

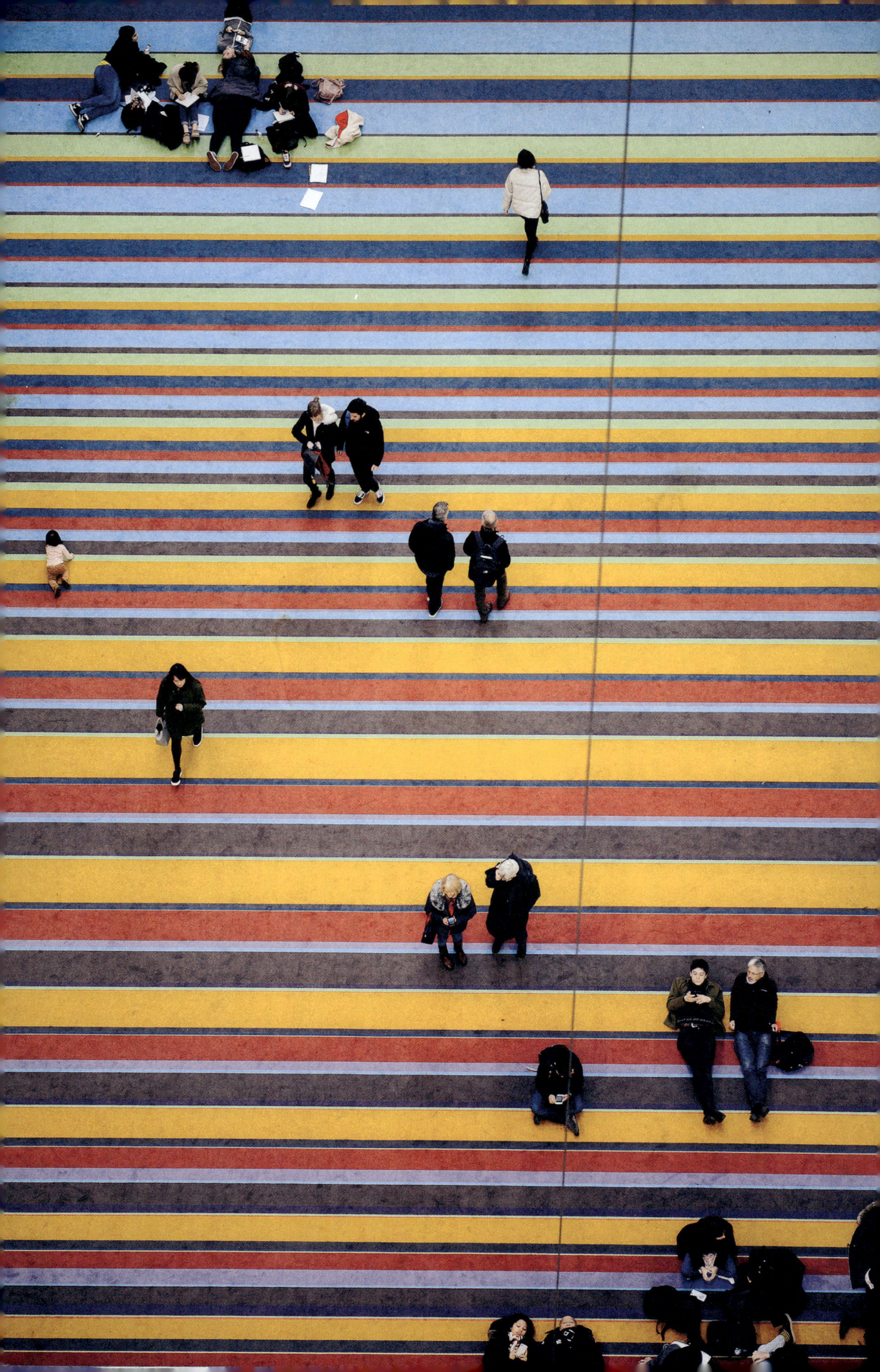

THERE'S
NO TIME
TO BE BORED
IN A WORLD AS
BEAUTIFUL
AS THIS

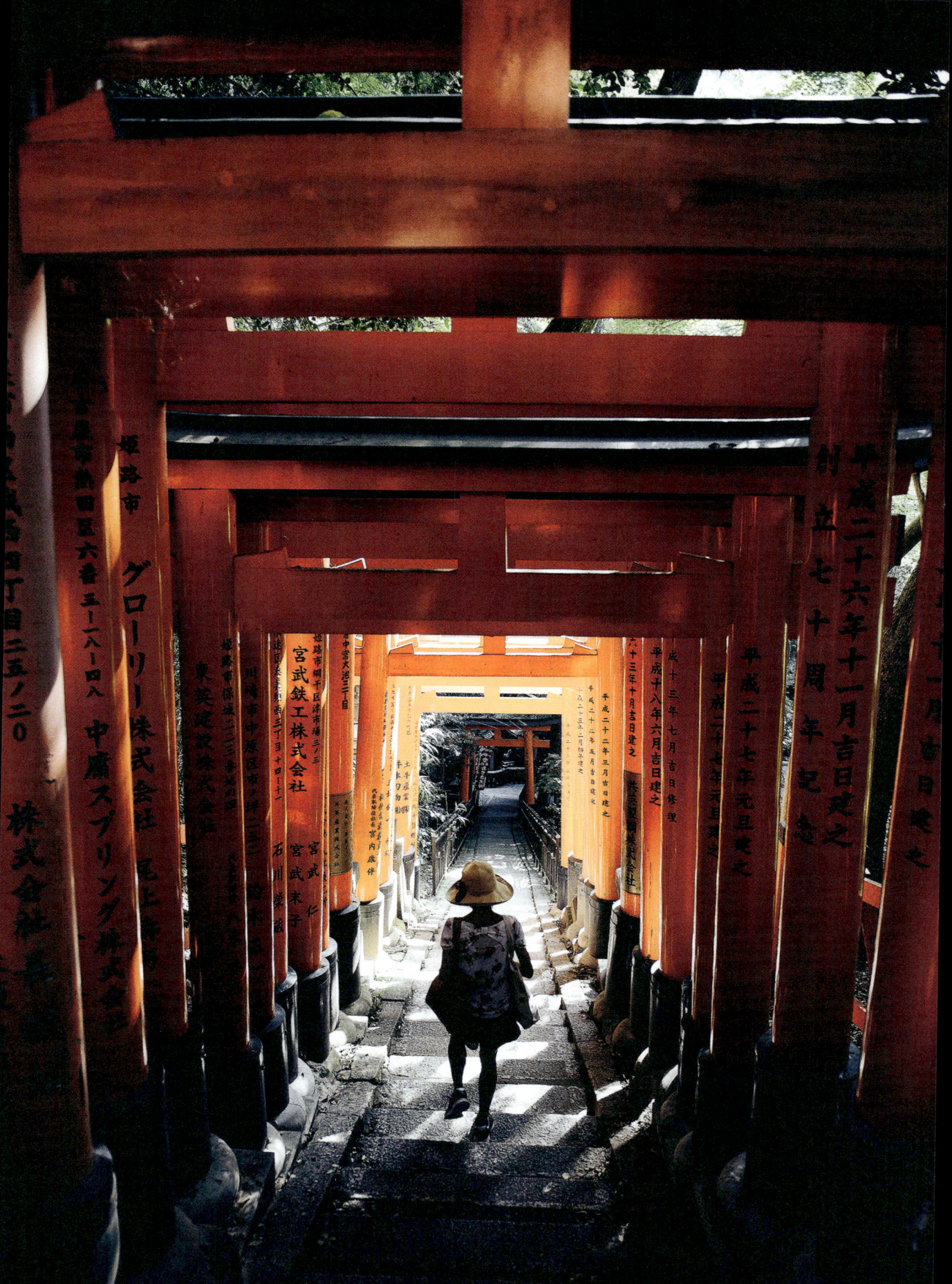

NEVER STOP WANDERING

Being able to travel whilst doing what I love is such a blessing, one I'll never take for granted. I feel as a photographer, you must seize every opportunity you can to travel because it opens your eyes to so much this world has to offer. You can meet and experience so many different people, cultures, landscapes, foods and traditions. Not to mention, it keeps you fully motivated to explore more and more.

I can't speak for everyone else, but I find if I stay put for too long, I start losing motivation to explore and shoot on a regular basis, but the moment I'm in a totally new environment... BAM! Without fail I'm out every day from morning to night, wanting to photograph anything and everything. Then I come back home and it's like I feed off of that desire and thirst to create more content. I strongly feel it's a cycle I'll always aim to continue. The adventure in it is worthwhile!

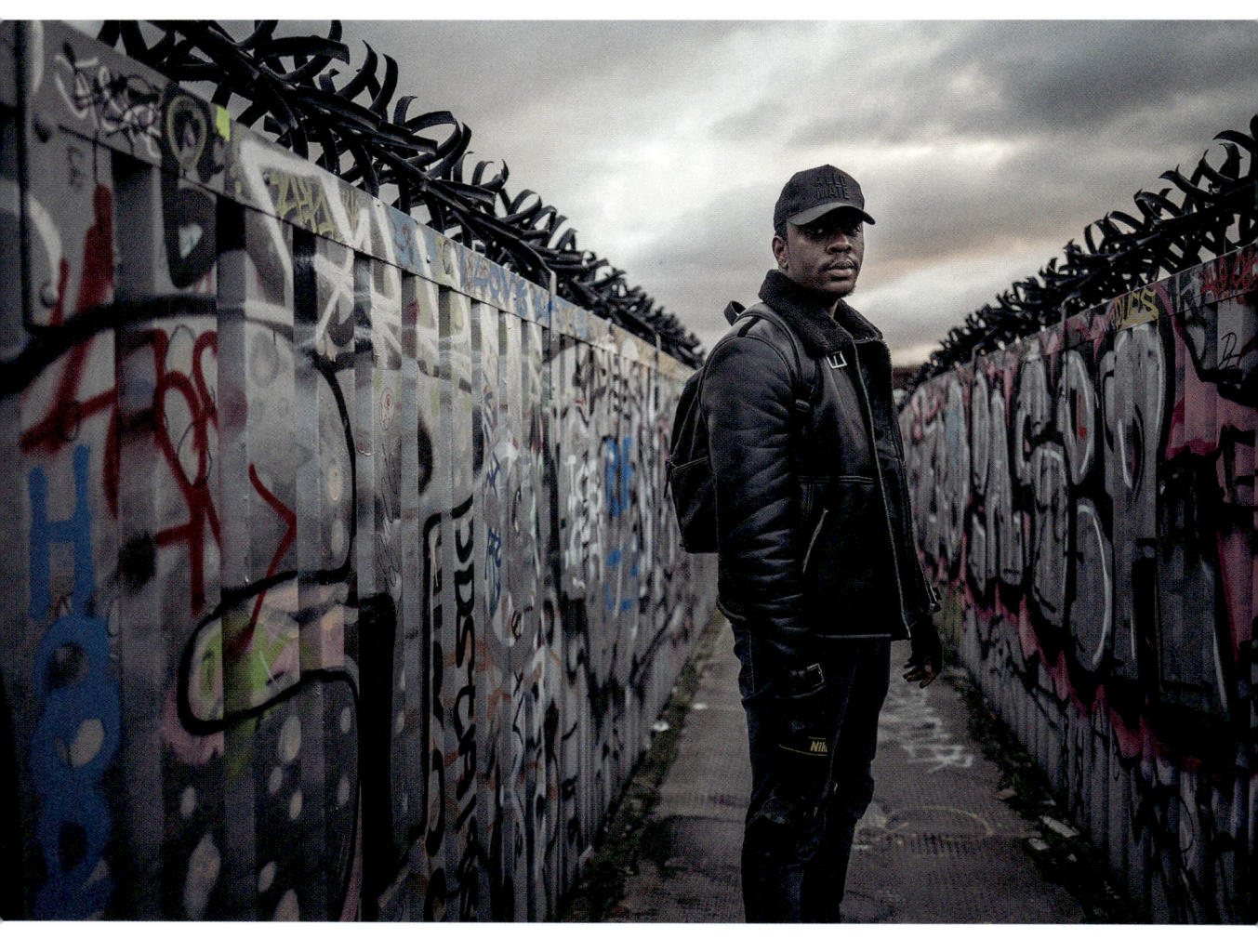

OPE ODUEYUNGBO

I had a keen interest in art as a youngster growing up in South East London (New Cross). In secondary school, I developed a love for graphic design and digital art. I went off to Christ the King College with that path in mind, going on to study at Ravensbourne University.

I'd begun experimenting with photography at 16, but my interest in it really took off by the age of 18. It was a gradual shift; through my first year, I'd started to realize that my design work just wasn't to the standard I needed it and wanted it to be. After one particularly candid portfolio critique confirmed my suspicions, I pivoted wholeheartedly to the brand-new Digital Photography course, and have never looked back.

Instagram launched in 2010 when I was a university student, and I signed up not long after. It started out as a lark, just a mess-around thing, but it was also a place to get feedback, something I could use to get better. I was going out nearly every single day shooting, and trying to shoot with other people as much as possible.

My first freelance job came whilst still at university. It was a bit of a shock; the company contacted me through Instagram, and I'd never imagined that my postings could turn into actual income. But from that point on I committed to trying my best, and seeing where it led. Eventually I saw Instagram not just as a place to show my work, but to build relationships with brands and clients. Once I saw people liking what I did, it motivated me to do a lot more, and it really grew from there.

At first I wanted to be a photojournalist, working for PR agencies, maybe newspapers. My main focus was capturing moments and people on the street. I still love to do that; travelling the world and connecting with people really feeds my work both personally and professionally. But as I started getting more social media-based jobs, I realised how much I enjoyed what I was doing. It's really exciting when brands come to me and say 'we'd love you to shoot this for us' because they want my specific style.

These last few years as a full-time freelancer have been incredible. I've worked with so many amazing brands: Adidas, Audi, Timberland, BMW, Puma, Huawei are just a few. And of course, getting to work with (my beloved) Arsenal Football Club, there's no topping that! @greatarsenal

Portrait by Tom Maday

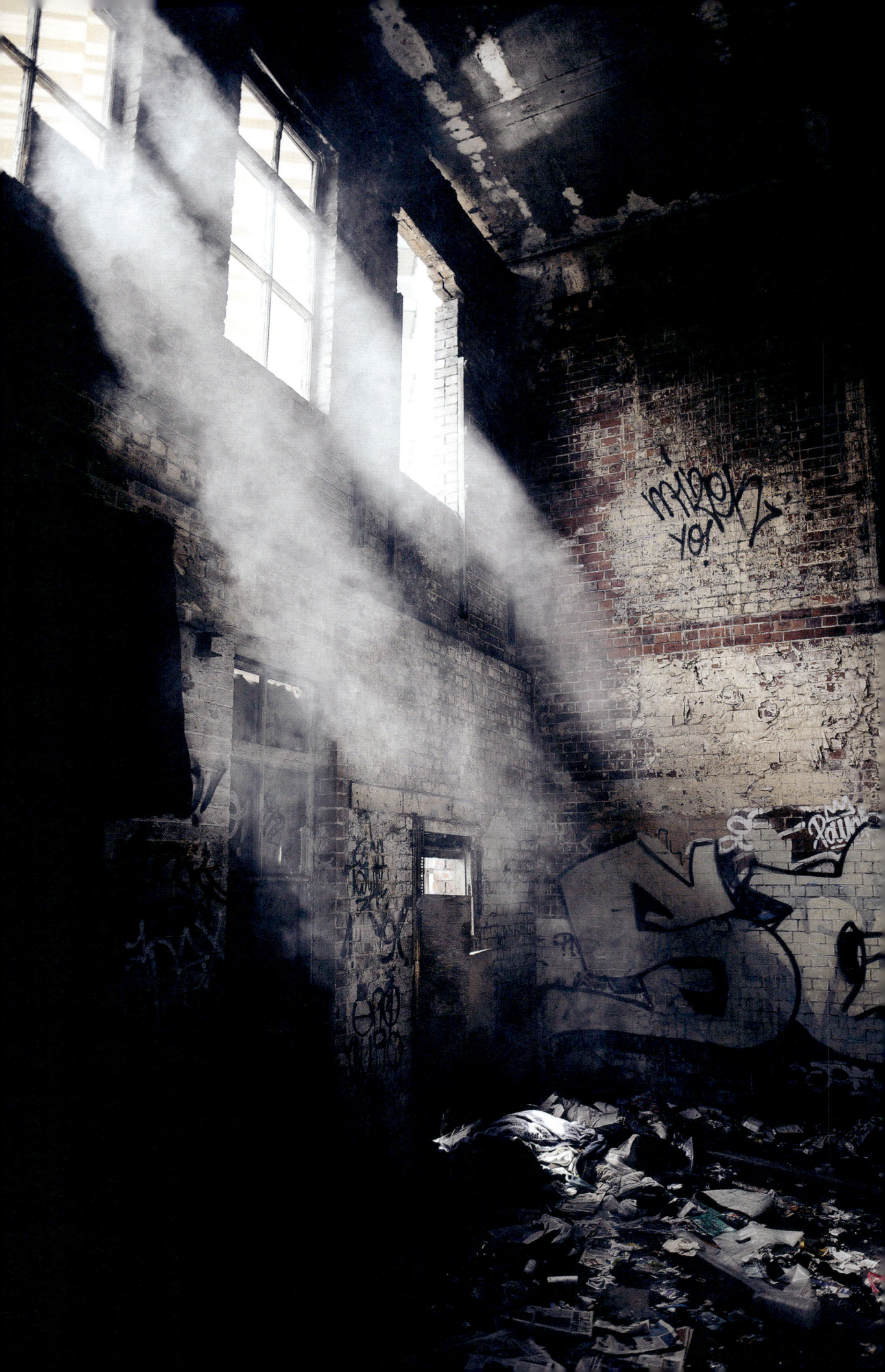

ACKNOWLEDGEMENTS

I want to thank God most of all, because without Him, none of this would be possible

- My parents Ronke Odueyungbo & Gbenga Odueyungbo, for allowing me to follow my creative passions and supporting me every step of the way

- All my family and friends who have motivated and encouraged me over the years

- My partner Grace Inyang for her ever-present love, acceptance and support

- My university tutor, Julian Hawkins, for understanding and believing the vision

- My photography inspirations:
  Henri Cartier-Bresson, Andreas Gursky, Boogie, Jamel Shabazz, Eric Kim and many more

- All the brands and creative agencies I've worked with over the years

- Maday Productions, for the time and effort they've put into showcasing me and my craft

- Everyone who appears in this book or allowed me to photograph them

- Last but not least, Sam Landers and everybody at Trope Publishing for giving me this amazing opportunity

© 2019 Trope Industries LLC.
This book and any portion thereof may
not be reproduced or used in any manner
whatsoever without the express written
permission of the publisher. All rights
reserved.

© 2019 Photographs and text
by Ope Odueyungbo

LCCN: 2019937884
ISBN: 978-1-7320618-9-7

Printed and bound in Latvia
First printing, 2019

Trope Publishing Co.

+ INFORMATION:
For additional information on
the Trope Edition Series, visit
www.trope.com

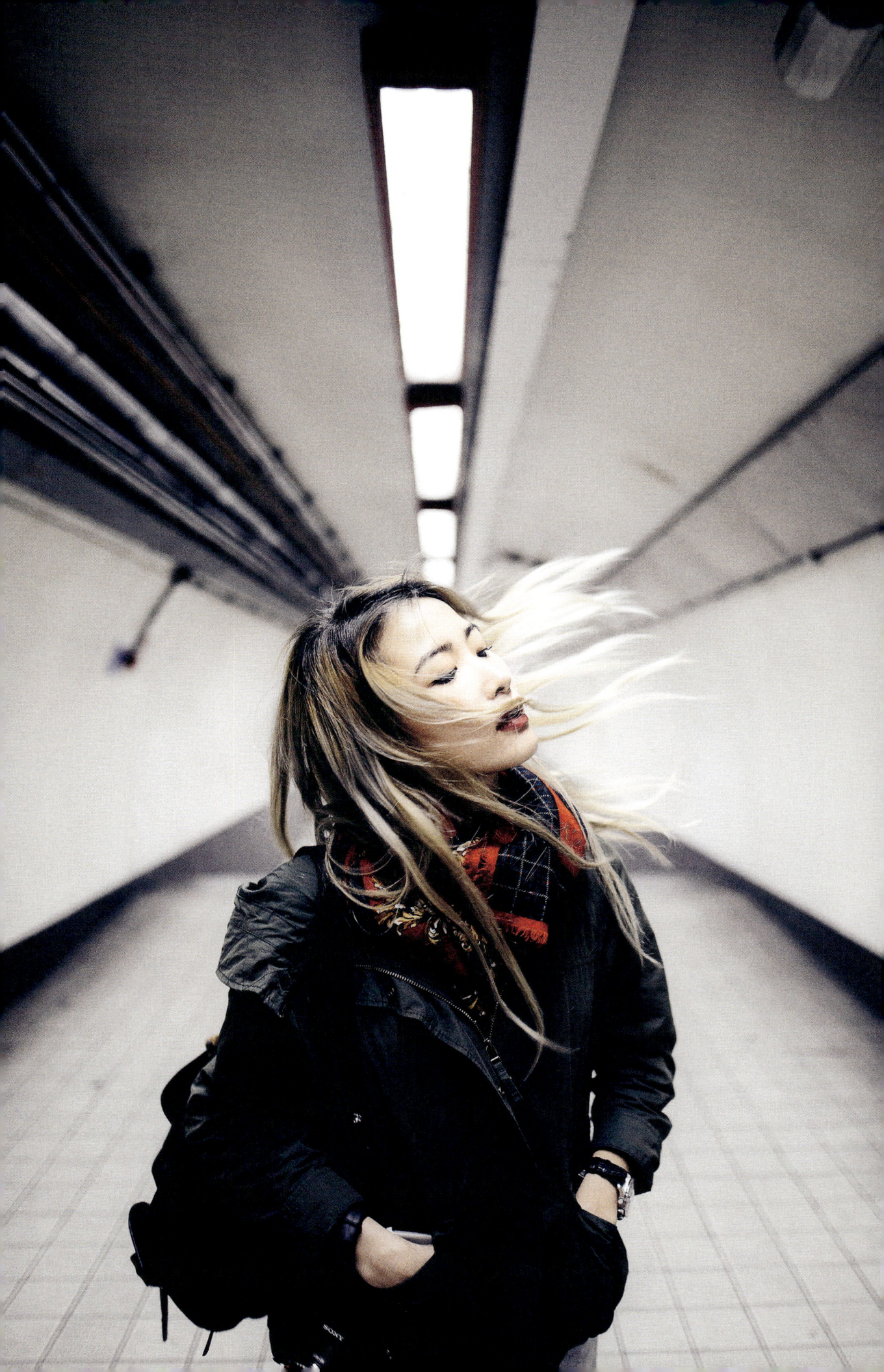

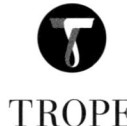

TROPE

TROPE EDITION

VOLUME II